table of contents

introduction

Introduction

Characters

Enemies

Weapons and
Ammunition

Key Items
and Treasures

Game System
and Strategies

Walkthrough

Secrets and
Bonuses

BradyGames' *Resident Evil 4 Official Strategy Guide* aims to be the most complete resource on *Resident Evil 4*, quite possibly one of the best games released in the last few years. Contained in this guide are plenty of useful tips for surviving encounters with enemies as well as the locations of necessary items, valuable treasures and powerful weapons. The book is written for both the first-time player enjoying their first video game, as well as for the expert gamer seeking hidden items and secrets.

This guide was designed to explore the entire game on a room-by-room basis. When starting out, first read the **Game System and Strategies** chapter to understand how to control the character, fire weapons, and interact with the environment. The tactics and strategies outlined in that chapter are actions that a player must repeat in virtually every portion of the game. The **Enemies** chapter contains specific tips for eliminating the enemies encountered frequently in most areas of the game. Monsters that appear only once during the game - and are much harder to kill than the others (called "boss" enemies) - are examined thoroughly in the walkthrough chapters. It calls for a small amount of page flipping on your part, but it prevents the guide from becoming repetitive and hard to read.

The walkthrough that describes the progression of the game step-by-step is broken up according to the in-game chapters and chapter portions, for easier reference. The game starts in Chapter 1-1. Each chapter description is broken down on an area-by-area basis. The area description starts with a map displaying the locations of all known items. Below that is an extensive and in-depth exploration of the environment's interactive features. There are often references to "triggers" that may cause additional enemies to appear in an area. Some areas are so wide open and the possibilities for action are variable. In such instances we have tried to provide all the strategies that the game allows, but you'll probably need to perform only some of the actions listed in order to handle all of the combat in the area.

Additionally, please remember that *Resident Evil 4* features a random-item system. Some items can definitely be found in an area every time you play the game. But most areas contain several randomly determined items. When smashing a barrel or crate, you might reveal money, ammunition, recovery items or grenades. Or, it could be empty. In such instances, we've attempted to point out the locations where random items might be found, and we've included the total number of random items possible in each area.

Now stop reading about *how* to use the guide, and *use* it! One of the best experiences in video game history awaits, and this book helps you explore every nook and cranny and squeeze every moment of fun out of it!

leon s. kennedy

Arriving in Raccoon City for his first day of work as a police officer, Leon Scott Kennedy found a community in chaos. Forced to flee from hordes of dead citizens brought back to life by an insidious virus manufactured by the Umbrella Corporation, Leon worked his way through the tunnels and sewers of the city to safety. He watched in overwhelming sadness as the government handled the outbreak situation in Raccoon City with an overwhelmingly final solution - nuclear annihilation. With the downfall and dissolution of Umbrella, Leon felt slightly relieved and convinced himself, like everyone else, that the horror could never happen again…

That was six years ago.

Determined to protect the people, Leon is now a government agent. Having worked his way up from agency to agency to the top ranks of national security, Leon has now completed the training necessary to join the secret security service of President Graham himself. There's just one hitch. The President's daughter has been kidnapped.

Leon's first assignment is to rescue and return the President's daughter. Searching the world for clues to the whereabouts of Ashley Graham and the group that kidnapped her, Leon eventually travels to a tiny European community. The local police scoff at his requests for assistance, but agree to drive him to the village regardless. Leon is not surprised to be receiving resistance from foreign agencies, but the resistance he will face in the village is nothing like he has ever experienced before… except for that time, six years ago, when death was all around and the amount of time you could survive was measured by the number of bullets left in your gun. Is there a possible link between the events of six years ago and the violent actions of the villagers?

ashley graham

Ashley is the teenage daughter of the President of
the United States. On the day she was abducted,
Leon S. Kennedy was assigned to track down her
abductors, rescue her from them, and return her
to the States. Ashley is a sweet young girl with
no knowledge of combat or self-defense, and
she's depending completely on Leon to protect
her and guide her to safety. But what Ashley
does not realize is that her captors have
insidious plans for her that involve returning
her to her father. What good could it possibly
do the bad guys to kidnap her and then
return her?

Introduction

Characters

Enemies

Weapons and
Ammunition

Key Items
and Treasures

Game System
and Strategies

Walkthrough

Secrets and
Bonuses

luis sera

While searching for the President's daughter
in the village, Leon finds a document that
indicates she is being held in an abandoned
farmhouse. When he arrives at the location,
he finds Luis Sera instead. Bound and
gagged, Luis is a local citizen who seems
to know a great deal more than he is
willing to admit. Leon questions Luis'
true part in the events playing out, and
wonders what his connection is to 'Los
Illuminados'.

JACK KRAUSER

jack krauser

During his tours in various agencies, Leon has seen a lot of good operatives come and go, and he has also seen some die. Leon thought Krauser died years ago in a helicopter accident, but unfortunately he is wrong. Krauser appears to be alive and well, and working for the wrong side in the current situation. Although Krauser is aiding 'Los Illuminados', he does not appear to be controlled by a parasite. Still, his abilities seem to be augmented to superhuman levels. Krauser's military training and combat prowess already made him more than a match for Leon, so it seems that the traitorous commando may prove more than the would-be rescuer can handle. Who is Krauser truly working for, and what is his role in the abduction of the First Daughter?

Introduction

Characters

Enemies

Weapons and
Ammunition

Key Items
and Treasures

Game System
and Strategies

Walkthrough

Secrets and
Bonuses

bitores mendez

BITORES MENDE

The village chief is an
abnormally tall and menacing
figure with multi-colored eyes
that leads the other villagers in
their attacks on Leon. Unlike
other villagers, Mendez seems
intelligent and educated, and
leaves several written agendas
and notes lying around. In their
first meeting, Leon experiences
the savage strength of the village
chief firsthand. What is Mendez's
agenda, and what is the secret of his
false eye?

ada wong

Years ago there was a woman who died to save her man. The rookie officer named Leon Kennedy wanted to protect her, but failed. Her death has haunted him for years. Leon met Ada as she was searching Raccoon City for her boyfriend - a researcher named John. But Ada was looking for much more than that. She was a secret agent of an unknown company, a competitor of Umbrella's, and she wanted to obtain a sample of William Birkin's G-virus. In the end, she chose life over money, and gave her life to protect Leon's…

Or so he thought.

Introduction

Characters

Enemies

Weapons and
Ammunition

Key Items
and Treasures

Game System
and Strategies

Walkthrough

Secrets and
Bonuses

ingrid hunnigan

Ingrid is a long-time communications officer and field contact for undercover agents working for the federal government. During Leon's mission, she provides him with intelligence, advice and mission objectives as needed.

osmund saddler

The leader of the strange cult called 'Los Illuminados' is as much of an obscurity as the group he leads. Insidiously intelligent, he tricked castellan Ramon Salazar into releasing Las Plagas from centuries of captivity underground. As the plague swept through the nearby village, Saddler made the locals his slaves and forced them to build a massive facility on a remote island formerly used for research. Leon must penetrate the layers of Saddler's cult and organization in order to find out this megalomaniac's plans for Ashley Graham, and the world.

ramon salazar

Upon entering the massive castle east of the village, Leon and Ashley encounter the devious and insane castellan, Ramon Salazar. He acts with intelligence and cruelty of which only an adult is capable. His childlike appearance is obviously deceiving. Long ago his ancestors recognized the dangers of the horror called 'Las Plagas', and sealed away the parasitic monsters deep underground. Unfortunately, young Ramon fell under the spell of the leader of 'Los Illuminados', a secretive cult lead by Osmund Saddler bent on world domination. Saddler convinced Salazar to atone for the "sin" his ancestors committed, and together they revived Las Plagas. Salazar believes the cult is under his control, but only because Saddler allows him to believe as much.

enemies

LOS GANADOS

The term used by the main villains in the game to refer to common enemies with a humanlike appearance is "Los Ganados," which means "the cattle" and references the plans of the Los Illuminados cult involving taking over the population by parasitic infection.

Los Ganados includes a broad range of enemies with a variety of strengths and a range of different appearances. In the early moments of the game, Los Ganados appear as male and female villagers of various ages that are extremely hostile and violent to Leon for then-unknown reasons. Villagers may be unarmed, or they may carry pitchforks or axes. Villagers armed with axes or sickles may throw their weapons when at long range. Villagers that light and toss dynamite sticks should be targeted immediately, both to prevent Leon from being caught in a blast and to cause the enemy to drop their explosive, killing themselves and others in the resulting explosion radius. Rare villagers carrying chainsaws are quite a bit tougher to kill than the rest, requiring several attacks. Chainsaw maniacs and hags typically drop valuable treasures and gold bars, so killing them is an easy get-rich quick scheme.

At the outset of the game, the best way to eliminate Los Ganados is by shooting them in the head, attempting to score a critical headshot that decapitates the villager completely. Even if the villager is not decapitated, shooting them in the face causes them to scream in pain and stagger, allowing you to run up to them and perform a kick when the action button appears onscreen. Throwing flash grenades blinds villagers, allowing you to move in close to attack or kick them to the ground. By knocking several villagers to the ground, Leon is in less danger of being attacked. Prone villagers can be shot continuously until dead. Shoot approaching villagers in the knees or feet to trip them, then shoot them while they're down. Crowds of oncoming villagers can be eliminated or knocked to the ground instantly with shotgun blasts, hand grenades or incendiaries. Once a crowd has been reduced in size, switch to a handgun or lesser weapon and pick off the remaining enemies individually.

At night, the parasites that control Los Ganados may be revealed if the enemy is decapitated. These monsters, called "Las Plagas" and detailed further in the following description, give a Ganado a second chance to attack Leon. Because emerging Plagas require more ammunition to kill, it becomes necessary to reduce attempts to inflict critical headshots. Shoot enemies in the torsos to reduce the chances of revealing Las Plagas.

In later stages, Los Ganados take the form of Los Illuminados cultists in black or red robes. The religious zealots in red are quite a bit harder to kill and usually reveal their Plaga regardless of where they are shot. Cultists wearing steel masks cannot be eliminated with a critical headshot. Zealots behave more intelligently than villagers, and attack by throwing scythes or by firing flaming arrows from crossbows. The Island stage at the end of the game is inhabited by all new commando enemies, incredibly resistant to damage and well-armed. Soldiers on the island sometimes fire guns or crossbows, or even rocket launchers. Commandos wearing helmets can only be decapitated by shooting them in the face, and then only rarely. Enemies toting massive gattling guns or giants wearing bulletproof armor prove extremely difficult to kill. Aim for the head, and throw grenades to take out tougher enemies.

Los Ganados sometimes drop pesetas, recovery items or ammo when killed. Special Ganados - such as red-robed zealots - may drop important key items or treasures.

LAS PLAGAS

Introduction

Characters

Enemies

Weapons and Ammunition

Key Items and Treasures

Game System and Strategies

Walkthrough

Secrets and Bonuses

Los Ganados
Las Plagas

Garrador
Colmillos

Novistador
Armadura

Regenerator
Iron Maiden

The parasites that control the villagers, and in turn are controlled by Los Illuminados, are referred to as Las Plagas, which means "the plagues." Las Plagas are extremely light-sensitive and do not appear during daylight hours. Once darkness settles, Las Plagas begin revealing themselves. When a Plaga emerges from the neck of a decapitated human, additional ammunition and greater accuracy is required to put the enemy down. Therefore, attempting critical headshots after daylight hours is a tricky business.

Once a Plaga emerges from a person's neck, damage to any other part of the body is reduced to 1/3rd normal. The Plaga itself is the only weak spot. Shoot the Plaga repeatedly with the handgun to make the entire body stagger, so that a kick can be performed. Plagas can be eliminated more quickly with shotgun blasts, or instantly with a sniper rifle. The best way to eliminate multiple Plagas at once is by throwing a flash grenade, which kills the creatures instantly.

Plagas take several forms, gradually becoming stronger and more deadly as the player progresses through the game. The first type of Plaga encountered consists of a gooey and bubbly central mass from which several long tentacles sprout. Some tentacles serve merely as whips, causing staggering and minor damage. One tentacle in particular ends in a razor-sharp bone used to slash victims.

The second form encountered is seen immediately after entering the Castle stage. Las Plagas emerging from many of the cultists in the Castle take the form of centipede-like monsters similar to the ones that emerge from the El Gigante boss. While this creature can attack only at close range, a successful attack proves instantly fatal, decapitating Leon or Ashley. This form is even stronger than the tentacle form, requiring several shotgun blasts or two rifle shots to kill.

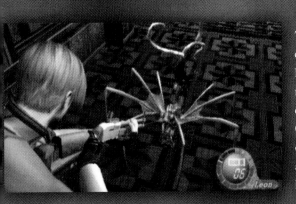

The third form is the largest. Somewhat spider-like, this form is capable of the same fatal decapitation attack. It can also spray Leon and Ashley with a heavily damaging acid from a medium range. When this form of a Plaga's host body is finally eliminated, it detaches itself from the body and quickly crawls up to Leon's feet. One shot kills this form immediately. But, if it's not destroyed soon enough, this creature can seize Leon and soak him in damaging acid. Rotate the thumbstick rapidly to escape from this attack and lessen the damage received.

13

GARRADOR

The term "Garrador" means, "man with claws," and refers to gigantic men in gladiator-like armor with retractable tri-blade claws. Garradors are practically blind, capable of seeing only within a two foot radius in front of itself. They seek out their victims by sound. Therefore, if Leon stays some distance back from a Garrador and walks instead of runs, there is a great chance the creature may not be able to locate him.

The only weak spot on a Garrador is the Plaga visible on his back. To damage a Garrador, navigate around the monster and shoot it from behind. When the opportunity to damage a Garrador arises, use a rifle or shotgun to maximize the damage inflicted. Leon has the opportunity for only one shot before the Garrador starts staggering around in pain, ruining the chances of aiming. After shooting, it is important to move away from the spot where you were previously standing. As soon as the Garrador regains itself, it goes berserk, runs to the spot the gunshot sound emanated from and commences swinging its claws.

Hand grenades are particularly effective when thrown behind a Garrador. Flash grenades are completely ineffective, and detrimental to boot. The flash actually brightens the room enough for a Garrador to see Leon clearly, and the monster quickly attacks. The mine thrower or a rocket launcher are the most effective weapons to use for eliminating a Garrador quickly. Sometimes bells are hung in the vicinity of Garradors. Shoot the bell to make it ring, causing the monster to attack the bell instead of Leon. As the Garrador goes for the bell, it provides an opportunity to run up behind it and blast its Plaga at close range.

COLMILLOS

The locals call the vicious mountain wolves infected by Las Plagas "Colmillos," which means "eyeteeth." They are often used as guard dogs by Las Plagas to prevent outsiders from entering important areas. Colmillos have a shortened range of sight, so that Leon might be able to spot them from a dozen yards away before they spot him. When a Colmillos notices an intruder, it grows and runs forward immediately. A Colmillos' favorite form of attack is to tackle a person to the ground and then try to rip their throat apart with their teeth. This attack can be shortened and the damaged lessened by placing your palm on the thumbstick and rotating it as fast as possible. Colmillos also employ a close range thousand tentacle whip attack, wherein they begin lashing Leon back and forth rapidly with a myriad of tentacles shooting out of an open wound on the wolf's back. Although an escape button is not displayed onscreen, Leon can escape this attack sooner by rotating the thumbstick.

The best way to take out Colmillos packs is with incendiary grenades, which tend to kill them instantly. Individual Colmillos can be taken out with several shotgun blasts.

NOVISTADOR

The sewers and caves beneath Salazar's sadistic palace are inhabited by lurking horrors he calls "Novistadors," insect-like mutants that seemingly have nothing to do with Las Plagas but are deadly nonetheless. The name is a play on Spanish words meaning something like "no see the man." Novistadors are capable of bending the light spectrum around their skin, rendering them virtually invisible. The only way to spot a Novistador before it spots you is to search the areas in which they typically dwell with a sniper rifle. Novistadors create a light ripple in space, and their cold breath and constant drool often give away their positions. Novistadors can also be spotted with thermal imaging, by equipping an infrared scope on a compatible sniper rifle. However, this option is only possible in a replay game, and only if the infrared scope is retained at the end of the previous play through.

Novistadors take up positions on the floor, ceiling and walls. When they close their eyes, they become completely invisible until unsuspecting prey enters their territory. But in order to move or advance on a victim, Novistadors must open their glowing eyes. Their eyes give away their position and proximity, allowing you to shoot them preemptively.

Use powerful weaponry such as a shotgun or grenades to take on Novistadors at close range. Every time a Novistador has been shot, it writhes in a moment of agony, allowing Leon a split second opportunity to kick it and knock it away. Maintaining a safe distance from Novistadors is important, since they are capable of leaping on Leon from some feet away. If ever you lose sight of a Novistador in front of you, it may have leapt onto the ceiling or walls and crawled behind you for a surprise attack. Relocate immediately in order to force the Novistador to pursue you and give away its position again.

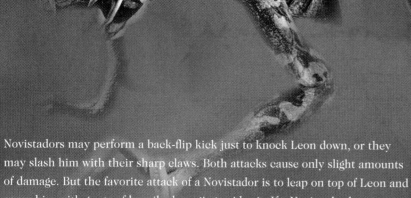

Novistadors may perform a back-flip kick just to knock Leon down, or they may slash him with their sharp claws. Both attacks cause only slight amounts of damage. But the favorite attack of a Novistador is to leap on top of Leon and spray him with gouts of heavily damaging acid spit. If a Novistador leaps onto Leon, place your palm on the thumbstick and rotate it fervently to break free of the grip as soon as possible.

Novistadors encountered in a deep underground cave take flight, and may swoop in to a hovering position over Leon. They're extremely vulnerable when shot out of air, so use a shotgun to try to take advantage of this vulnerability. Flying Novistadors attacked with a sniper rifle while hovering in the air over a chasm or pit are instantly killed. However, it is worthwhile to try and kill Novistadors on land that Leon can access, because they very frequently drop valuable Red Eyes, Green Eyes or rare Blue Eyes. These three types of gems sell for thousands of pesetas on their own, but they can also be inserted into a Blind Butterfly Lamp to add tremendous value to the treasure piece.

ARMADURA

Introduction

Characters

Enemies

Weapons and
Ammunition
Key Items
and Treasures
Game System
and Strategies

Walkthrough

Secrets and
Bonuses

Las Plagas also take up residence inside armored suits within Salazar's gothic castle, and animate them. "Armaduras" positioned like sentinels in richly decorated corridors within the Castle stage may attack at a moment's notice, so when walking past an armored suit be prepared to press the two dodge buttons displayed onscreen or you may suffer massive damage from an axe attack.

There are also times when Armaduras leave their posts and begin lumbering after Ashley or Leon. When an Armadura gets within swinging range, they slowly rear back and then swing their sword or axe. It is important to get out of the way, and to understand that the attack may be a vertical swing or a horizontal cut.

Walking Armaduras can sustain heavy amounts of damage before the Plaga inside the suit shows any signs of pain. Use hand grenades or incendiaries to damage the suit until the helmet is knocked off, revealing the parasite. If grenades are in short supply, blast the helmet repeatedly with a shotgun until the suit is decapitated. Then shoot the exposed Plaga, or toss a flash grenade to eliminate the parasite immediately. When Ashley is pursued by Armaduras, all you can do is run for safety, and try to escape to other rooms.

REGENERATOR

Regenerators are experimental monsters encountered in the Island stage created using Las Plagas that are capable of instantly re-growing dismembered body parts. A Regenerator's arms and head can be blown clean off, and the monster grows a new limb immediately. Even a large gaping hole blown through the monster's torso closes up in a few seconds. The regenerative power of the monster comes from several Plagas attached to the skin of the creature, which emit powerful hormones that regenerate skin tissue. These symbiotic parasites are also capable of bending the light spectrum to become invisible.

The only way the Plagas covering a Regenerator can be detected is by using thermal imaging. The infrared scope must be obtained from the Freezer room of the Island stage, and mounted on a compatible sniper rifle. When aiming at a Regenerator with infrared, the Plagas become visible as small red spots on the creature's skin. Shoot the parasites, and creature soon becomes unstable on the cellular level. After taking a few more steps, it should implode with a sickening sound. If the Regenerator continues advancing even after the Plagas are eliminated, toss a hand grenade or incendiary in its direction or shoot it with a shotgun several times to break it apart.

Regenerators attack only at close range, either by slamming Leon to the ground or by seizing him and attempting to strangle him. As long as Leon maintains a safe distance from an advancing Regenerator and uses an infrared-equipped sniper rifle to attack the monster, he should easily escape from harm.

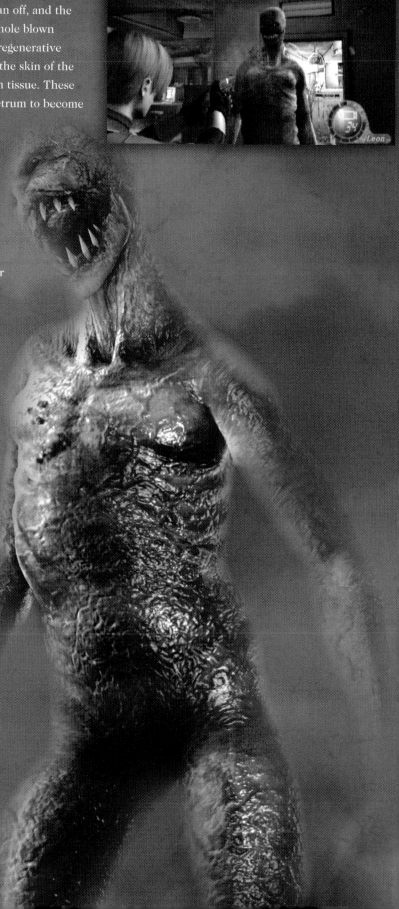

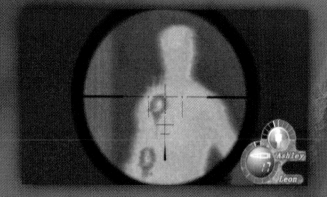

IRON MAIDEN

Regenerators covered with skin piercing spikes are nicknamed "Iron Maidens." Like Regenerators, Iron Maidens are covered with several Plagas that only register in the infrared spectrum. Use a thermally equipped sniper rifle to spot the Plagas on the Iron Maiden, and shoot them. Iron Maidens are considerably stronger than most Regenerators, and may continue to attack even after its Plagas are removed. After shooting all of the parasites off an Iron Maiden's body, throw hand grenades or incendiaries to finish it off, or blast it repeatedly with a shotgun.

Iron Maidens use their spikes to perform a devastating attack, wherein the monster stretches out across a medium distance to seize Leon or Ashley. The creature then pulls the victim inward and impales them on its extended spikes. For this reason, it is important to maintain a greater distance between the heroes and an Iron Maiden at all times.

weapon systems

Top-secret U.S. agent Leon Kennedy, a former Raccoon City police officer and the game's protagonist, begins *Resident Evil 4* with the two weapons he needs to complete his mission: a handgun and a knife. However, if you use nothing but these two weapons during your play-through, the game is sure to be a long and bumpy road. To make the game easier, you can spend the money you find to purchase weapons from merchants appearing in certain locations. Upgrade weapons to improve damage capabilities, increase rate of fire, reduce the time required to reload a magazine, or increase the number of bullets contained in the clip.

Buying and Selling Weapons

Leon encounters the first merchant after he escapes from captivity in the Valley area of the Village stage, or at the very start of Chapter 1-2. While smashing barrels and killing enemies yields plenty of pesetas, it is not enough to pay the merchant's high prices. You can also sell valuable treasures, such as gems and collectibles, to merchants for large sums of money—this is what the "Sell" option is for in the merchant's menu. Also, if Leon's attaché case gets too full, items such as ammunition and recovery items can be sold to simultaneously make room and increase Leon's peseta count.

As you progress further in the game, the merchant sells new weapons that are much more powerful than the guns initially on offer. To make room for new weapons, old ones must be sold off. The merchant pays higher prices for upgraded weapons, and he also considers how many bullets are loaded in them at the time of sale. However, regardless of upgrades and included ammo, the merchant pays only a pittance compared to your initial investment. When you add up the full cost of a weapon with all the upgrades you've purchased, the merchant exacts a heavy depreciation penalty when you sell it. Therefore, don't make a habit of selling weapons too often. It's a good idea to buy all new equipment at the start of the Castle stage, but then try to stick with it.

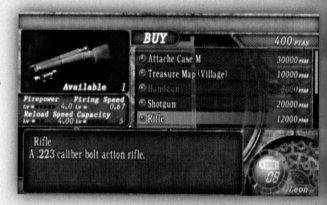

Terminology

The tables in the following weapon descriptions show the weapons available during the game, their cost, the upgrades possible, and the point of advancement at which the merchant makes the weapon or upgrade available. In all of the tables, "Stg.1" refers to the Village, "Stg.2" is the Castle, and "Stg.3" is the Island.

Firepower

The weapon's firepower figure is a damage multiplier. For instance, Leon's initial handgun has a firepower figure of 1.0. All other weapons' firepower is based on the initial damage capability of the default handgun. Therefore, a weapon with a firepower rating of 1.1 inflicts a little more damage than the initial handgun. A weapon with a firepower figure of 4.0 causes four times the damage per shot than the handgun.

Firing Speed

The firing speed of a weapon determines how quickly the next bullet can be fired after the last. Automatic weapons like handguns can be fired continuously, sometimes as fast as you can press the fire button. Weapons like shotguns and magnum handguns have a fixed rate of fire that cannot be improved. This is because of the weapons' powerful kick and the time Leon needs to recover between each blast, or because the gun's chamber has to be reloaded between shots. A smaller firing speed statistic is better. If a weapon's firing speed cannot be decreased, no table is listed under the weapon.

Reload Speed

When a weapon's magazine runs empty, Leon must reload. Reload times are different for each weapon, measured here in the number of frames displayed onscreen. Most television sets display 30 frames per second. If a weapon's reload speed is higher than 30 frames, then Leon takes more than a full second to reload the magazine. Make sure that Leon is a safe distance from enemies when reloading, so that he is not vulnerable to attack. Also, reload between battles even when the coast is clear, and always carry a full weapon into the next area so that you are ready for anything.

Capacity

The capacity of a weapon indicates the number of bullets or cartridges that can be held in the weapon's clip. Leon can fire a gun repeatedly as long as there are bullets remaining in the magazine. Once the magazine runs out, Leon must stop firing and reload. The quicker the reload time, the faster Leon can get back to pumping bullets into a monster's face.

Availability

The first possible room where a weapon becomes available for purchase is listed in each weapon's description. Certain weapons are supplied for free in the game, and notes indicate such instances.

If the player can somehow skip the room, such as the Lake Cave in stage one, then the next merchant encountered will still offer the upgrade. The availability of weapons and upgrades is listed just to give you an idea of where you can find the next merchant inventory update.

Exclusive Upgrades

When all the weapon's levels are tuned-up to the maximum, an "Exclusive" upgrade may become available. The player may have to progress to a farther point in the game before an Exclusive upgrade shows up on the shop list, even though a weapon is at maximum levels. Pay attention to tune-up availability as listed in the weapon tables.

Introduction

Characters

Enemies

Weapons and Ammunition

Key Items and Treasures

Game System and Strategies

Walkthrough

Secrets and Bonuses

Buying and Selling Weapons

Terminology

Handguns

Shotguns

Magnums

Rifles

Special

Accessories

Grenades

Ammunition

HANDGUNS

The handgun category includes all small firearms compatible with 9mm parabellum Handgun Ammo. Handguns fire once each time the fire button is pressed. While handguns are generally the weakest weapons in terms of firepower, they are extremely accurate. Handguns tend to be useful throughout the game for breaking open crates, setting off traps, and shooting switches or levers that are out of reach. Because ammunition for handguns is the most plentiful in the game, always keep a handgun ready in case ammunition for other weapons runs out.

Handgun — Price: 8000 — Available for Purchase: Stg.1 Valley (Leon's initial weapon)

FIREPOWER

Lvl.	Power	Price	Available From
Lv.1	1.0	(default)	Game Start
Lv.2	1.2	7000	Stg.1 Valley
Lv.3	1.4	10,000	Stg.1 Lake Cave
Lv.4	1.6	15,000	Stg.2 Castle Entrance
Lv.5	1.8	18,000	Stg.2 Observation Hall
Lv.6	2.0	20,000	Stg.2 Clock Tower Exterior
*	Critical x4	57,000	Stg.2 Ancient Ruins

*Exclusive: Increases chance of critical headshot by 4 times.

FIRING SPEED (ANIMATION FRAMES)

Lvl.	Frames	Price	Available From
Lv.1	14	(default)	NA
Lv.2	12	5000	Stg.1 Valley
Lv.3	10	12,000	Stg.2 Castle Entrance

RELOAD (ANIMATION FRAMES)

Lvl.	Frames	Price	Available From
Lv.1	52	(default)	NA
Lv.2	44	4000	Stg.1 Valley
Lv.3	26	10,000	Stg.2 Castle Entrance

CAPACITY

Lvl.	Qty.	Price	Available From
Lv.1	10	(default)	NA
Lv.2	13	4000	Stg.1 Valley
Lv.3	16	6000	Stg.1 Lake Cave
Lv.4	19	8000	Stg.2 Castle Entrance
Lv.5	22	10,000	Stg.2 Observation Hall
Lv.6	25	12,000	Stg.2 Clock Tower Exterior

Red9 — Price: 14,000 — Available for Purchase: Stg.1 Tunnel (Night)

FIREPOWER

Lvl.	Power	Price	Available From
Lv.1	1.4	(default)	NA
Lv.2	1.7	15,000	Stg.1 Tunnel (Night)
Lv.3	2.0	20,000	Stg.2 Castle Entrance
Lv.4	2.4	24,000	Stg.2 Observation Hall
Lv.5	2.8	28,000	Stg.2 Clock Tower Exterior
Lv.6	3.5	45,000	Stg.2 Ancient Ruins
*	5.0	80,000	Stg.2 Dock

* Exclusive

FIRING SPEED (ANIMATION FRAMES)

Lvl.	Frames	Price	Available From
Lv.1	16	(default)	NA
Lv.2	14	10,000	Stg.1 Tunnel (Night)
Lv.3	12	15,000	Stg.2 Observation Hall

RELOAD (ANIMATION FRAMES)

Lvl.	Frames	Price	Available From
Lv.1	71	(default)	NA
Lv.2	66	6000	Stg.1 Tunnel (Night)
Lv.3	50	10,000	Stg.2 Observation Hall

CAPACITY

Lvl.	Qty.	Price	Available From
Lv.1	8	(default)	NA
Lv.2	10	6000	Stg.1 Tunnel (Night)
Lv.3	12	8000	Stg.2 Castle Entrance
Lv.4	15	12,000	Stg.2 Observation Hall
Lv.5	18	16,000	Stg.2 Clock Tower Exterior
Lv.6	22	22,000	Stg.2 Tower

Punisher

Price: 20,000 (0 on first purchase)	
Available for Purchase: Complete blue medallion sub-mission. Merchant offers one time for free, charges thereafter.	

FIREPOWER

Lvl.	Power	Price	Available From
Lv.1	0.9	(default)	NA
Lv.2	1.1	10,000	Stg.1 Waterway
Lv.3	1.3	15,000	Stg.1 Tunnel (Night)
Lv.4	1.5	20,000	Stg.2 Observation Hall
Lv.5	1.7	25,000	Stg.2 Clock Tower Exterior
Lv.6	1.9	35,000	Stg.2 Ancient Ruins
*	Up to 5 hit	40,000	Stg.2 Dock

Exclusive* Single shot can penetrate up to 5 targets in a line!

FIRING SPEED (ANIMATION FRAMES)

Lvl.	Frames	Price	Available From
Lv.1	14	(default)	NA
Lv.2	12	10,000	Stg.1 Waterway
Lv.3	10	20,000	Stg.2 Observation Hall

RELOAD (ANIMATION FRAMES)

Lvl.	Frames	Price	Available From
Lv.1	51	(default)	NA
Lv.2	44	8000	Stg.1 Waterway
Lv.3	25	18,000	Stg.2 Observation Hall

CAPACITY

Lvl.	Qty.	Price	Available From
Lv.1	10	(default)	NA
Lv.2	13	8000	Stg.1 Waterway
Lv.3	16	10,000	Stg.1 Tunnel (Night)
Lv.4	20	15,000	Stg.2 Observation Hall
Lv.3	24	18,000	Stg.2 Clock Tower Exterior
Lv.6	28	24,000	Stg.2 Ancient Ruins

Blacktail

Price: 24,000	
Available for Purchase: Stg.2 Castle Entrance	

FIREPOWER

Lvl.	Power	Price	Available From
Lv.1	1.6	(default)	NA
Lv.2	1.8	15,000	Stg.2 Castle Entrance
Lv.3	2.0	18,000	Stg.2 Courtyard & Bedroom
Lv.4	2.3	24,000	Stg.2 Clock Tower Exterior
Lv.5	2.7	30,000	Stg.2 Ancient Ruins
Lv.6	3.0	40,000	Stg.2 Dock
*	3.4	80,000	Stg.2 Dock

* Exclusive

FIRING SPEED (ANIMATION FRAMES)

Lvl.	Frames	Price	Available From
Lv.1	14	(default)	NA
Lv.2	12	10,000	Stg.2 Castle Entrance
Lv.3	8	20,000	Stg.2 Clock Tower Exterior

RELOAD (ANIMATION FRAMES)

Lvl.	Frames	Price	Available From
Lv.1	51	(default)	NA
Lv.2	44	8000	Stg.2 Castle Entrance
Lv.3	25	15,000	Stg.2 Clock Tower Exterior

CAPACITY

Lvl.	Qty.	Price	Available From
Lv.1	15	(default)	NA
Lv.2	18	8000	Stg.2 Castle Entrance
Lv.3	21	10,000	Stg.2 Courtyard & Bedroom
Lv.4	25	15,000	Stg.2 Clock Tower Exterior
Lv.5	30	20,000	Stg.2 Ancient Ruins
Lv.6	35	25,000	Stg.2 Dock

Matilda

Price: 70,000	
Available for Purchase: Replay Game	

FIREPOWER

Lvl.	Power	Price	Available From
Lv.1	1.0	(default)	NA
Lv.2	1.2	15,000	Replay
Lv.3	1.4	17,000	Replay
Lv.4	1.6	20,000	Replay
Lv.5	1.8	25,000	Replay
Lv.6	2.0	35,000	Replay

RELOAD (ANIMATION FRAMES)

Lvl.	Frames	Price	Available From
Lv.1	52	(default)	NA
Lv.2	44	6000	Replay
Lv.3	26	15,000	Replay

CAPACITY

Lvl.	Qty.	Price	Available From
Lv.1	15	(default)	NA
Lv.2	18	7000	Replay
Lv.3	21	10,000	Replay
Lv.4	24	12,000	Replay
Lv.3	27	16,000	Replay
Lv.6	30	20,000	Replay
*	100	35,000	Replay

* Exclusive

SHOTGUNS

Introduction
Characters
Enemies
Weapons and Ammunition
Key Items and Treasures
Game System and Strategies
Walkthrough
Secrets and Bonuses

Shotguns include assault rifles that fire standard 12-gauge Shotgun Ammo. These weapons have much greater power than handguns, and they emit a cone-shaped blast when fired, damaging multiple enemies with a single shot. For this reason, it is easy to fall in love with shotguns because they tend to keep crowds and stronger enemies at bay. However, reserving a shotgun for emergency situations is important. When entering a crowded area, use the shotgun to blast the group. As enemies die and only a few stragglers remain, equip a handgun and pick them off individually. Conserve shotgun ammo, as it is harder to come by in the game.

All shotguns inflict greater damage at closer range. Therefore, it's wise to stand ready with your shotgun aimed, and wait for enemies to cluster up and close in on you. Sometimes a single shotgun blast fired at close range can eliminate several enemies simultaneously.

Shotgun

Price: 20,000

Available for Purchase: Stg.1 Valley (found at Pueblo)

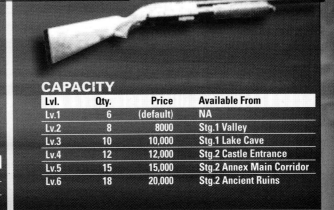

FIREPOWER

Lvl.	Close	Far	Price	Available From
Lv.1	4.0	1.4	(default)	NA
Lv.2	4.5	1.6	15,000	Stg.1 Valley
Lv.3	5.0	1.8	20,000	Stg.1 Lake Cave
Lv.4	6.0	2.2	25,000	Stg.2 Castle Entrance
Lv.5	7.0	2.5	30,000	Stg.2 Annex Main Corridor
Lv.6	8.0	3.0	45,000	Stg.2 Ancient Ruins
*	8.0	6.0	90,000	Stg.2 Dock

* Exclusive

RELOAD (ANIMATION FRAMES)

Lvl.	Frames	Price	Available From
Lv.1	91	(default)	NA
Lv.2	73	7000	Stg.1 Valley
Lv.3	45	15,000	Stg.2 Castle Entrance

CAPACITY

Lvl.	Qty.	Price	Available From
Lv.1	6	(default)	NA
Lv.2	8	8000	Stg.1 Valley
Lv.3	10	10,000	Stg.1 Lake Cave
Lv.4	12	12,000	Stg.2 Castle Entrance
Lv.5	15	15,000	Stg.2 Annex Main Corridor
Lv.6	18	20,000	Stg.2 Ancient Ruins

Riot Gun

Price: 32,000

Available for Purchase: Stg.2 Castle Entrance

FIREPOWER

Lvl.	Close	Far	Price	Available From
Lv.1	5.0	2.0	(default)	NA
Lv.2	5.5	2.3	20,000	Stg.2 Castle Entrance
Lv.3	6.0	2.5	24,000	Stg.2 Castle Entrance
Lv.4	6.5	3.0	28,000	Stg.2 Courtyard & Bedroom
Lv.5	7.0	3.5	32,000	Stg.2 Clock Tower Exterior
Lv.6	8.0	4.0	50,000	Stg.2 Dock
*	10.0	8.0	120,000	Stg.2 Dock

*Exclusive

RELOAD (ANIMATION FRAMES)

Lvl.	Frames	Price	Available From
Lv.1	91	(default)	NA
Lv.2	73	7000	Stg.2 Observation Hall
Lv.3	45	20,000	Stg.2 Dock

CAPACITY

Lvl.	Qty.	Price	Available From
Lv.1	7	(default)	NA
Lv.2	9	10,000	Stg.2 Observation Hall
Lv.3	11	12,000	Stg.2 Courtyard & Bedroom
Lv.4	13	15,000	Stg.2 Clock Tower Exterior
Lv.5	15	20,000	Stg.2 Mine Entrance
Lv.6	17	25,000	Stg.2 Dock

Striker

Price: 43,000

Available for Purchase: Stg.2 Traitor's Pit

FIREPOWER

Lvl.	Close	Far	Price	Available From
Lv.1	6.0	2.0	(default)	NA
Lv.2	7.0	2.4	25,000	Stg.2 Traitor's Pit
Lv.3	8.0	2.7	28,000	Stg.2 Ancient Ruins
Lv.4	9.0	2.9	32,000	Stg.2 Dock
Lv.5	10.0	3.4	40,000	Stg.3 Fortification Cliffs
Lv.6	12.0	4.0	60,000	Stg.3 Armory

RELOAD (ANIMATION FRAMES)

Lvl.	Frames	Price	Available From
Lv.1	90	(default)	NA
Lv.2	72	8000	Stg.2 Traitor's Pit
Lv.3	45	15,000	Stg.2 Dock

CAPACITY

Lvl.	Qty.	Price	Available From
Lv.1	12	(default)	NA
Lv.2	14	10,000	Stg.2 Traitor's Pit
Lv.3	16	12,000	Stg.2 Ancient Ruins
Lv.4	20	16,000	Stg.2 Dock
Lv.5	24	18,000	Stg.3 Fortification Cliffs
Lv.6	28	25,000	Stg.3 Armory
*	100	60,000	Stg.3 Armory

*Exclusive

MAGNUMS

Magnum handguns all fire .45 caliber Magnum Ammo. A single magnum shot is powerful enough to eliminate frequently encountered enemies such as villagers, cultists or commandos. But because Magnum Ammo is found so rarely in the game, it's wasteful to use it on common, less powerful foes. Magnums are best used in boss battles, against powerful creatures that appear only once in the game. Like handguns, magnums are incredibly accurate, so aim each shot carefully. Magnums tend to have smaller magazine capacity due to the large bullet size, and their heavy recoil results in a slow rate of fire. But you're sure to inflict big hurt on whatever you shoot with a magnum!

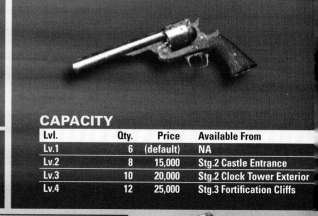

Broken Butterfly	Price: 38,000
	Available for Purchase: Stg.2 Castle Entrance (found in Castle External Wall Area)

FIREPOWER

Lvl.	Power	Price	Available From
Lv.1	13.0	(default)	NA
Lv.2	15.0	25,000	Stg.2 Castle Entrance
Lv.3	17.0	30,000	Stg.2 Courtyard & Bedroom
Lv.4	20.0	35,000	Stg.2 Clock Tower Exterior
Lv.5	24.0	50,000	Stg.2 Ancient Ruins
Lv.6	28.0	70,000	Stg.3 Cave Entrance
Exclusive	50.0	150,000	Stg.3 Campground

RELOAD (ANIMATION FRAMES)

Lvl.	Frames	Price	Available From
Lv.1	110	(default)	NA
Lv.2	90	15,000	Stg.2 Courtyard & Bedroom
Lv.3	60	20,000	Stg.2 Ancient Ruins

CAPACITY

Lvl.	Qty.	Price	Available From
Lv.1	6	(default)	NA
Lv.2	8	15,000	Stg.2 Castle Entrance
Lv.3	10	20,000	Stg.2 Clock Tower Exterior
Lv.4	12	25,000	Stg.3 Fortification Cliffs

Killer7	Price: 77,700
	Available for Purchase: Stg.3 Fortification Cliffs

FIREPOWER

Lvl.	Power	Price	Available From
Lv.1	25	(default)	NA
Lv.2	30	62,000	Stg.3 Armory
Lv.3	35	78,000	Stg.3 Cave Entrance

RELOAD (ANIMATION FRAMES)

Lvl.	Frames	Price	Available From
Lv.1	55	(default)	NA
Lv.2	46	20,000	Stg.3 Armory
Lv.3	28	30,000	Stg.3 Cave Entrance

CAPACITY

Lvl.	Qty.	Price	Available From
Lv.1	7	(default)	NA
Lv.2	10	30,000	Stg.3 Armory
Lv.3	14	40,000	Stg.3 Cave Entrance

RIFLES

In a few areas of the game, Leon enjoys the luxury of a sniper rifle with a scope. In certain parts of the game, using a rifle makes subsequent areas easier to survive. All rifles fire .223 caliber Rifle Ammo, which is only a little less scarce than Magnum Ammo.

When you press **R1**, Leon automatically aims through the rifle's scope. Zoom in or zoom out with the Right Thumbstick. Place the crosshairs over your target, preferably its head, and fire. The merchant offers better scopes for each rifle, sold separately. In the Island stage of the game, Leon must attach an Infrared Scope to the sniper rifle

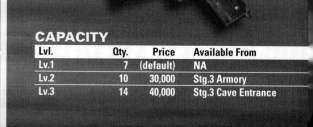

Rifle	Price: 12,000
	Available for Purchase: Stg.1 Valley

FIREPOWER

Lvl.	Power	Price	Available From
Lv.1	4.0	(default)	NA
Lv.2	5.0	10,000	Stg.1 Valley
Lv.3	6.0	12,000	Stg.1 Lake Cave
Lv.4	8.0	20,000	Stg.2 Castle Entrance
Lv.5	10.0	25,000	Stg.2 Observation Hall
Lv.6	12.0	35,000	Stg.2 Annex Main Corridor
*	18.0	80,000	Stg.2 Ancient Ruins

* Exclusive

CAPACITY

Lvl.	Qty.	Price	Available From
Lv.1	5	(default)	NA
Lv.2	7	6000	Stg.1 Valley
Lv.3	9	8000	Stg.1 Lake Cave
Lv.4	12	12,000	Stg.2 Castle Entrance
Lv.5	15	18,000	Stg.2 Observation Hall
Lv.6	18	25,000	Stg.2 Annex Main Corridor

RELOAD (ANIMATION FRAMES)

Lvl.	Frames	Price	Available From
Lv.1	71	(default)	NA
Lv.2	58	8000	Stg.1 Valley
Lv.3	35	18,000	Stg.2 Castle Entrance

Rifle (Semi-Auto)

Price: 35,000

Available for Purchase: Stg.2 Castle Entrance

FIREPOWER

Lvl.	Power	Price	Available From
Lv.1	7.0	(default)	NA
Lv.2	8.0	15,000	Stg.2 Castle Entrance
Lv.3	9.0	18,000	Stg.2 Observation Hall
Lv.4	11.0	24,000	Stg.2 Annex Main Corridor
Lv.5	13.0	30,000	Stg.2 Ancient Ruins
Lv.6	15.0	40,000	Stg.3 Fortification Cliffs

FIRING SPEED (ANIMATION FRAMES)

Lvl.	Frames	Price	Available From
Lv.1	43	(default)	NA
*	12	80,000	Stg.3 Fortification Cliffs

*Exclusive

RELOAD (ANIMATION FRAMES)

Lvl.	Frames	Price	Available From
Lv.1	70	(default)	NA
Lv.2	57	9000	Stg.2 Castle Entrance
Lv.3	34	18,000	Stg.2 Annex Main Corridor

CAPACITY

Lvl.	Qty.	Price	Available From
Lv.1	10	(default)	NA
Lv.2	12	10,000	Stg.2 Castle Entrance
Lv.3	14	12,000	Stg.2 Observation Hall
Lv.4	17	15,000	Stg.2 Annex Main Corridor
Lv.5	20	20,000	Stg.2 Ancient Ruins
Lv.6	24	25,000	Stg.3 Fortification Cliffs

SPECIAL

Certain weapons are not easily categorized. Some of the weapons in this group are available in an initial play-through, while others become available only after beating the game at least once.

TMP

Price: 15,000

Available for Purchase: Stg.1 Valley

The TMP is a modifiable Uzi machine pistol. Because TMP Ammo is so plentiful throughout the game, it is important to purchase this gun so that it becomes an option as soon as bullets are available.

Leon holds the TMP at the hip and fires a continuous stream of bullets until the magazine empties. For easier aiming, purchase the stock from the merchant. With the stock equipped, Leon aims more accurately and steadily.

FIREPOWER

Lvl.	Power	Price	Available From
Lv.1	0.4	(default)	NA
Lv.2	0.5	7000	Stg.1 Tunnel (Noon)
Lv.3	0.6	14,000	Stg.1 Tunnel (Night)
Lv.4	0.8	18,000	Stg.2 Castle Entrance
Lv.5	1.0	24,000	Stg.2 Observation Hall
Lv.6	1.2	35,000	Stg.2 Annex Main Corridor
*	1.8	100,000	Stg.2 Dock

*Exclusive

RELOAD (ANIMATION FRAMES)

Lvl.	Frames	Price	Available From
Lv.1	71	(default)	NA
Lv.2	58	5,000	Stg.1 Tunnel (Noon)
Lv.3	35	15,000	Stg.2 Observation Hall

CAPACITY

Lvl.	Qty.	Price	Available From
Lv.1	30	(default)	NA
Lv.2	50	7000	Stg.1 Tunnel (Noon)
Lv.3	100	15,000	Stg.1 Tunnel (Night)
Lv.4	150	20,000	Stg.2 Annex Main Corridor
Lv.5	200	25,000	Stg.2 Ancient Ruins
Lv.6	250	35,000	Stg.2 Dock

Introduction

Characters

Enemies

Weapons and Ammunition

Key Items and Treasures

Game System and Strategies

Walkthrough

Secrets and Bonuses

Buying and Selling Weapons

Terminology

Handguns

Shotguns

Magnums

Rifles

Special

Accessories

Grenades

Ammunition

Mine Thrower

Price: 28,000
Available for Purchase: Stg.2 Castle Entrance

The mine thrower is an experimental device that Umbrella's weapon technicians attempted to develop a few years back, such as the kind previously seen in *Resident Evil 3 Nemesis*. When fired, the mine thrower launches a small, grappling-cap mine that punctures the target's skin and attaches itself. The mine emits a series of beeping signals that intensify just before it detonates. When the mine triggers, it creates a small explosion of intensely damaging power. The target and any other creatures in the area feel the effects. Therefore, Leon and Ashley should be at a safe distance before you use this baby.

The mine thrower can be equipped with a scope for long range sniping. Upgrading the firepower of the mine thrower extends the exposion's damage radius. The Exclusive upgrade adds homing features to the mines, so that once an enemy has been targeted it cannot dodge the attack. This weapon's worst characteristic is that the only way to obtain more ammunition is to pay for a capacity modification.

FIREPOWER

Lvl.	Power	Price	Available From
Lv.1	2.0	(default)	NA
Lv.2	4.0	25,000	Stg.2 Courtyard & Bedroom
Lv.3	6.0	45,000	Stg.2 Mine Entrance
*	6.0 + Homing	30,000	Stg.3 Fortification Cliffs

*Exclusive: Mines pursue targets even when they move out of view!

RELOAD (ANIMATION FRAMES)

Lvl.	Frames	Price	Available From
Lv.1	104	(default)	NA
Lv.2	87	18,000	Stg.2 Clock Tower Exterior
Lv.3	77	*	Stg.3 Fortification Cliffs

* Upgrade occurs simultaneously when Exclusive upgrade is purchased.

CAPACITY

Lvl.	Qty.	Price	Available From
Lv.1	5	(default)	NA
Lv.2	7	25,000	Stg.2 Castle Entrance
Lv.3	10	40,000	Stg.2 Dock

Handcannon

Price: 0
Available for Purchase: Replay Game

The Handcannon is a .50 caliber magnum revolver of the type cherished by one Barry Burton. Speaking of Barry, how could he be missing out on a weapons bonanza like the one in this game? While the initial price is a bargain, the upgrades will empty your pockets. Raising each level of the weapon costs a ton of pesetas. Until you can afford the Exclusive upgrade to infinite ammo, this non-reloading weapon mainly takes up space in your inventory. However, if you have beaucoup bucks to spend, this is the kind of present to yourself that just keeps on giving.

FIREPOWER

Lvl.	Power	Price	Available From
Lv.1	30	(default)	NA
Lv.2	35	40,000	Replay Game
Lv.3	40	50,000	Replay Game
Lv.4	45	70,000	Replay Game
Lv.5	50	90,000	Replay Game
Lv.6	60	120,000	Replay Game
*	[Inf]	200,000	Replay Game

* Exclusive: Infinite ammo, 99.9 firepower

RELOAD (ANIMATION FRAMES)

Lvl.	Frames	Price	Available From
Lv.1	110	(default)	NA
Lv.2	86	25,000	Replay Game
Lv.3	55	50,000	Replay Game

CAPACITY

Lvl.	Qty.	Price	Available From
Lv.1	3	(default)	NA
Lv.2	4	15,000	Replay Game
Lv.3	5	20,000	Replay Game
Lv.4	6	25,000	Replay Game
Lv.5	7	35,000	Replay Game
Lv.6	10	50,000	Replay Game

Rocket Launcher

Price: 30,000
Available for Purchase: Stg.1 Valley (found in Stg.2 Exhibition Room and provided during the Saddler boss fight)

The usually unattainable rocket launcher, so highly sought after in previous *Resident Evil* games, is available as soon as Leon finds the first merchant. The rocket launcher is an expensive, one-use weapon that inflicts 9999 points of damage to the target it strikes. This sucker takes up major space in Leon's attaché case. However, with the rocket launcher handy, you can slay even boss monsters with a single shot. All you have to do is make the boss reveal its weak spot (if there is one), and then aim and fire. Enemies closely surrounding the target also suffer major damage. The rocket launcher is equipped with a scope for highly acc When you hold R1, Leon raises the launcher and peers through the scope. Zoom in or out using the Right Thumbstick. The Rocket la provided twice in the game, including one with a special rocket designed to kill the Los Illuminados' leader.

Infinite Launcher

Price: 1,000,000
Available for Purchase: Replay Game

The infinite rocket launcher is identical to the normal rocket launcher, except it can be reloaded and fire an unlimited number of times. Blast your way through large crowds in seconds. Just be sure to fire at targets from long range, or Leon could suffer in the blast.

Chicago Typewriter

Price: 1,000,000	
Available for Purchase: Clear Assignment Ada	

You can purchase this infinite ammo, .45 caliber classic World War II era machinegun from the merchant for a measly one million pesetas after you complete the main game and then complete a short mini-game staring Ada Wong, titled "Assignment Ada." Without need to reload or stop firing, subsequent play-throughs are a cinch. The weapon is so powerful that short bursts down single enemies. Even boss monsters wrath when Leon sprays them with this Thompson machinegun.

ACCESSORIES

Items in this category attach to specific weapons for improved performance.

Stock (Red9)
Price: 4000

The Red9 is a heavy handgun, and Leon has trouble aiming steadily with it. Attaching this stock to the Red9 allows Leon to aim more accurately with greater speed, and it allows him to maintain aim even while firing several shots in a row.

Stock (TMP)
Price: 4000

When attached to the TMP, this stock allows Leon to aim more precisely from the shoulder instead of the hip. It also allows Leon to maintain relatively accurate aim while firing continuously.

Scope (Rifle)
Price: 7000

A custom scope for the bolt-action .223 caliber rifle. To attach this scope, either set it on top of the rifle in the case or select it and combine it with the rifle. The scope changes the rifle's crosshair and allows Leon to zoom in roughly fifty feet closer than the rifle's default scope.

Scope (Semi-Auto Rifle)
Price: 10000

A custom scope for the semi-auto .223 caliber rifle. To attach this scope, either set it on top of the semi-auto rifle in the case or select it and combine it with the semi-auto rifle. The scope changes the crosshair of the rifle and allows Leon to zoom in approximately fifty feet closer than the semi-auto rifle's default scope.

Infrared Scope
Price: 4000

The infrared scope displays the heat signatures of all objects. When attached to a rifle, the infrared scope shows everything in thermal imaging. Using this scope is the only way to identify and target the rejuvenating parasites that cover the bodies of Regenerators and Iron Maidens. Only after the parasites are eliminated can these monsters be killed. The infrared scope is found in the Freezer room of the Island Stage.

Scope (Mine Thrower)
Price: 8000

A custom scope for the Mine Thrower. Enables long-range sniping and accurate aiming with the Mine Thrower. Zoom in and out with the C Stick. You may find the scope is not practical in close-range situations, such as boss fights.

GRENADES

Hand-tossed explosives and flash devices can be extremely helpful to Leon in crowd control situations. When a grenade is equipped, press **R1** to raise the bomb and press ✖ to toss it. Without aiming adjustments, Leon tosses the bomb at just the right arc so that when it detonates, he is out of the blast radius. However, if the aim is tilted up or down, Leon may throw it a little farther or a little shorter. Use caution when throwing grenades.

Each grenade takes up two blocks in the attaché case, which means that grenades can consume a lot of space. Remember to use grenades to break up crowds of enemies or when fighting particularly tough opponents, such as those that carry chainsaws or Gatling guns.

Hand Grenades

Hand grenades are small fragmentation explosives that burst into hundreds of metal shards, spreading out and piercing all targets in a small radius. Enemies on the edge of the range suffer reasonable damage and are knocked to the ground.

Flash Grenades

Flash grenades emanate a bright light in a wide radius that blinds all enemies in range. When used successfully, enemies are stunned, and can be safely approached and kicked to the ground. The blinding effect wears off momentarily, so move quickly to take advantage. Shooting or slashing enemies causes the effect to subside instantly. Flash grenades are fatal to Las Plagas. Whenever Plagas are exposed from the necks of Los Ganados, or when they detach and crawl across the ground, throw a flash grenade to take out one or more Plagas instantly.

Incendiary Grenades

Incendiary grenades create an instant wall of fire at the spot they are thrown. Enemies caught in the small blast range are instantly engulfed, and any enemies that charge into the flames are set ablaze as well.

AMMUNITION

Handgun Ammo

These 9mm parabellum rounds are compatible with all types of handguns. Leon can hold up to 50 handgun bullets within a 2 x 1 block in his attaché case.

Shotgun Shells

These 12-gauge shotgun shells are compatible with all types of shotguns. Leon can hold 15 shells in a 2 x 1 block in his attaché case.

Rifle Ammo

.223 caliber bullets that load into the rifle and the semi-auto rifle are a bit harder to acquire, and even harder to tote around. Leon can hold 10 bullets in a 2 x 1 block in his attaché case.

TMP Ammo

Ammunition for the TMP is surprisingly plentiful in the game. Leon can hold 100 machine pistol bullets within a 2 x 1 block in his case.

Magnum Ammo

The most rare type of ammunition found in the game, these .45 caliber revolver rounds should be conserved strictly for boss fights and for dealing with stronger than average enemies. Leon can hold 10 magnum rounds within a 2 x 1 block in the case.

Key Items

Key items include all the items that Leon must find in order to unlock a door that prevents him from proceeding farther in the game. Sometimes pieces must be combined before they can be used.

CAMP KEY

DEFEAT: The chainsaw-swinging hag who wears this key around her neck to obtain it.

USE: Unlocks the door marked with an insignia in the pit where the chainsaw woman first appeared.

CASTLE GATE KEY

LOCATION: western room of the Castle Gate area.

USE: Unlocks the front gate of the Castle, located in the same area.

DYNAMITE

LOCATION: Coal Mine Area beneath the Castle.

USE: Blasts the giant boulder blocking the path to the exit of the same area.

EMBLEM (RIGHT HALF)

LOCATION: Valley area of the Village.

USE: Combine this with the other half to form the seal that unlocks the northeast exit from the area.

EMBLEM (LEFT HALF)

LOCATION: Valley area of the Village.

USE: Combine this with the other half to form the seal that unlocks the northeast exit from the area.

FALSE EYE

The red false eye of village chief Bitores Mendez.

DEFEAT: Mendez at the Torture Shed to obtain the eye.

USE: Activates the retinal scanner on the east door in the Gondola area go escape from the Village stage.

FREEZER CARD KEY

LOCATION: Autopsy Room on the Island.

USE: Unlocks the door leading to the freezer room in the Stairwell Corridor area.

GALLERY KEY

LOCATION: Gallery Area of the Castle worn around the neck by a red-robed enemy. Kill the enemy to obtain the key.

USE: Unlocks the exit door of the first room in the area.

GOAT ORNAMENT

LOCATION: Final room of the Gallery Area in the Castle.

USE: One of three plaque pieces required to lower the raised wall blocking access to the north portion of the Audience Hall.

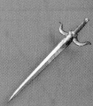

GOLDEN SWORD

LOCATION: Barracks of the Castle.

USE: Remove it from the platinum plate and insert it into the gold plate to open the exit door on the upper level.

INSIGNIA KEY

LOCATION: Inside the Village Chief's House in the Village stage.

USE: Unlocks the door marked with a similar insignia in the Pueblo area.

JET-SKI KEY

LOCATION: Obtained by defeating the final boss o' the game.

USE: Starts up the jet-ski parked in the underground escape tunnel.

KEY TO THE MINE

Location: Underground Ruins Entrance in the room guarded by two chainsaw-swinging maniacs.

Use: Unlocks the door in the Underground Ruins Entrance of the Castle.

KING'S GRAIL

Location: Armor Suit Room of the Castle annex.

Use: Place in the hands of the queen bust at the north end of the Annex Main Corridor to unlock the north exit.

LION ORNAMENT

LOCATION: The Dragon Room area in the Castle.

USE: One of three plaque pieces required to lower the raised wall blocking access to the north portion of the Audience Hall.

MOONSTONE (LEFT HALF)

LOCATION: Found in the same area within the hedge maze.

USE: Half of the Blue Moonstone, a seal that unlocks the bedroom door in the Courtyard & Bedroom area of the Castle.

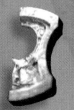

MOONSTONE (RIGHT HALF)

LOCATION: Courtyard & Bedroom area of the Castle within the hedge maze.

USE: Half of the Blue Moonstone, a seal that unlocks the bedroom door in the Courtyard & Bedroom area.

OLD KEY

LOCATION: Inside the second cabin in the second section of the Other Passage area in the Village.

USE: Unlocks the exit door of the area.

PIECE OF THE HOLY BEAST, EAGLE

LOCATION: Atop the tower in the center of the Fortress Ruins area on the Island.

USE: One of three plaque pieces required to assemble the Holy Beast on the fresco to the northwest, revealing the exit from the area.

PIECE OF THE HOLY BEAST, PANTHER

LOCATION: Northeastern section of the Fortress Ruins area on the Island.

USE: One of three plaque pieces required to assemble the Holy Beast on the fresco to the northwest, revealing the exit from the area.

PIECE OF THE HOLY BEAST, SERPENT

DEFEAT: Krauser in the Fortress Ruins area on the Island.

USE: One of three plaque pieces required to assemble the Holy Beast on the fresco to the northwest, revealing the exit from the area.

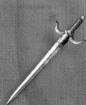

PLATINUM SWORD

LOCATION: The Barracks of the Castle.

USE: Remove it from the gold plate on the downstairs level and insert it into the platinum plate to open the exit door on the upper level.

EMERGENCY LOCK CARD KEY

LOCATION: The Double-Secured Yard of the Island. (It was stolen by an enemy.)

USE: Required to activate the two lock consoles that must be operated to unlock the north exit door of the area.

PRISON KEY

LOCATION: Hanging on the portrait in the easternmost corridor of the Audience Hall area.

USE: Unlocks the door to the submerged prison in the same area.

QUEEN'S GRAIL

LOCATION: The Weapon Exhibition Room of the Castle annex.

USE: Place in the hands of the queen bust at the north end of the Annex Main Corridor to unlock the north exit.

ROUND INSIGNIA

LOCATION: The Waterfall area of the Village.

USE: Unlocks the front doors of the Church in the Graveyard.

SALAZAR FAMILY INSIGNIA

LOCATION: The Servant Quarters 2 area of the Castle.

USE: Reveal the secret passage exit in the Servant Quarters 1 area of the Castle.

SERPENT ORNAMENT

LOCATION: The Servant Quarters 2 area in the Castle.

USE: One of three plaque pieces required to lower the raised wall blocking access to the north portion of the Audience Hall.

STONE OF SACRIFICE

LOCATION: The Mine Cart Room beneath the Castle.

USE: Unlocks the eastern exit door in the Ancient Ruins area of the Castle stage.

STONE TABLET

LOCATION: The first room in the Servant Quarters 2 area.

USE: Required to solve the sliding-tile puzzle in th area.

STORAGE ROOM CARD KEY

LOCATION: The Research Laboratory of the Island

USE: Unlocks the storage room where Ashley is being held captive in the Administration Corridor.

WASTE DISPOSAL CARD KEY

USE: Obtained by rewriting the data on the Freeze Card Key using the computer in the Freezer room on the Island.

Treasures

Treasures are items that sell to a merchant for a high value. Typically they're hidden throughout stages in hard-to-spot places that you might not think to look. Fortunately the merchant sells treasure maps that reveal the location of every valuable treasure. Unfortunately this costs you 10,000 of your hard-earned pesetas. Instead, use the maps in the walkthrough chapters to determine the locations of treasures and spend the money more wisely. Before selling treasures to the merchant, keep in mind that certain pieces and gems can be combined to acquire an item of even greater value than the individual parts.

AMBER RING

VALUE: 10,000
LOCATION: Stg.1 Waterfall
A ring with a red jewel.

ANTIQUE PIPE

VALUE: 10,000
LOCATION: Stg.1 Swamp
A pipe of fine craftsmanship.

BEERSTEIN

VALUE: 3000
LOCATION: Stg.1 Farm
A beer stein with three indentations where gems can be set, increasing the value of the whole tremendously.

Combination	Value
Beerstein w/G	10,000
Beerstein w/R	10,000
Beerstein w/Y	10,000
Beerstein w/G & R	15,000
Beerstein w/R & Y	15,000
Beerstein w/Y & G	15,000
Beerstein w/G, R & Y	20,000

BUTTERFLY LAMP

VALUE: 4500
LOCATION: Stg.2 Prison Area, Stg.2 Ballroom

A lamp with three notches where Green Eye, Red Eye and Blue Eye gems can be set (one of each only), increasing the value of the combined piece greatly.

Combination	Value
Butterfly Lamp w/G	6500
Butterfly Lamp w/R	7000
Butterfly Lamp w/B	8500
Butterfly Lamp w/G & R	11,000
Butterfly Lamp w/G & B	13,000
Butterfly Lamp w/R & B	15,000
Butterfly Lamp w/G, R & B	32,000

BLUE EYE

VALUE: 3000
LOCATION: Defeat a Novistador in Stg.2

A small gem dropped by defeated Novistador enemies as well as the Novistador hive in the Castle's Ballroom. It can be inserted into a Blind Butterfly Lamp to increase the value.

BLUE STONE OF TREASON

VALUE: 3500

LOCATION: Stg.3 Campground

A catseye gem that can be fit into the Golden Lynx statue for greater value.

BRASS POCKET WATCH

VALUE: 10,000

LOCATION: Stg.1 Village Chief's House, Stg. 3 Stairwell Corridor

An antique worth some value.

CROWN JEWEL

VALUE: 11,000

LOCATION: Stg.2 Abandoned Irrigation Station

A jewel removed from a crown. Can be returned to the crown to add greater value.

CROWN

VALUE: 9000

LOCATION: Stg.2 Traitor's Pit

A crown with two portions missing. When the two pieces are fitted back into the crown, the object is restored to its former glory and value.

Combination	Value
Crown w/Jewel	25,000
Crown w/Insignia	27,000
Salazar Family Crown	48,000

DIRTY BRASS POCKET WATCH

VALUE: 1000

LOCATION: Stg.1 Village Chief's House

A Brass Pocket Watch that fell into filthy water—virtually worthless.

DIRTY PEARL PENDANT

VALUE: 1000

LOCATION: Stg.1 Farm

A Pearl Pendant that has been dropped into filthy water—practically worthless.

ELEGANT CHESSBOARD

VALUE: 13,000

LOCATION: Stg.2 Weapon Exhibition Room

A chessboard suitable for a king's game.

ELEGANT HEADDRESS

VALUE: 10,000

LOCATION: Stg.1 Tunnel, Stg.3 Throne Room

A beautiful adornment for women's hair.

ELEGANT MASK

VALUE: 3000

LOCATION: Stg.1 Stronghold, Stg.2 Observation Hall

A mask with three divots where gems can be set, increasing the value of the whole.

Combination	Value
Elegant Mask w/G	10,000
Elegant Mask w/R	10,000
Elegant Mask w/P	10,000
Elegant Mask w/G & R	15,000
Elegant Mask w/G & P	15,000
Elegant Mask w/R & P	15,000
Elegant Mask w/R, G & P	20,000

ELEGANT PERFUME BOTTLE

VALUE: 10,000

LOCATION: Stg.2 External Wall Area

A perfume bottle fit for a queen.

EMERALD

VALUE: 3000

A small gem of great value. Found frequently on the Island.

GOLD BANGLE

VALUE: 8500

LOCATION: Stg.2 Battlement Area, Stg.2 Hall of Water, Stg.2 Servant Quarters 2, Stg.2 External Wall Area, Stg.2 Clock Tower Exterior (enemy)

A bracelet that can be sold for substantial gain. Found in several locations in the Castle.

Introduction

Characters

Enemies

Weapons and Ammunition

Key Items and Treasures

Game System and Strategies

Walkthrough

Secrets and Bonuses

Key Items

Treasures

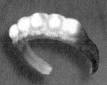

GOLD BANGLE WITH PEARLS

VALUE: 10,000

LOCATION: Stg.1 Lake

A gold armlet fitted with pearls.

GOLDEN LYNX

VALUE: 15,000

LOCATION: Stg.3 Fortification Cliffs

A golden cat idol with three indentations in the face where gems can be set, increasing the value of both the idol and the gems.

Combination	Value
Golden Lynx w/G	20,000
Golden Lynx w/R	20,000
Golden Lynx w/B	20,000
Golden Lynx w/G & R	25,000
Golden Lynx w/G & B	25,000
Golden Lynx w/R & B	25,000
Golden Lynx w/G, R & B	35,000

GREEN CATSEYE

VALUE: 3000

LOCATION: Stg.1 Graveyard

Can be fitted into the Beerstein to increase the value.

GREEN EYE

VALUE: 1000

LOCATION: Defeat a Novistador in Stg.2

A small gem dropped by defeated Novistador enemies as well as the Novistador hive in the Castle's Ballroom. Can be inserted into a Blind Butterfly Lamp to increase the value.

GREEN GEM

VALUE: 3000

LOCATION: Stg.1 Lake Cave, Stg.2 Audience Hall

A gem that fits into the Elegant Mask, raising the value of the whole piece.

GREEN STONE OF JUDGEMENT

VALUE: 3500

LOCATION: Stg.3 Mess Hall

A catseye gem that can be fit into the Golden Lynx statue for greater value.

HOURGLASS WITH GOLD DECOR

VALUE: 12,000

LOCATION: Stg.2 Last Supper Corridor

An hourglass of fine craftsmanship.

ILLUMINADOS PENDANT

VALUE: 12,000

LOCATION: Stg.2 Observation Hall (enemy), Stg.2 Dragon Room

A grotesque symbol of an evil cult. Said to corrupt those who hold it.

MIRROR WITH PEARLS & RUBIES

VALUE: 12,000

LOCATION: Stg.2 Courtyard & Bedroom

A mirror set with pearls and rubies.

PEARL PENDANT

VALUE: 10,000

LOCATION: Stg.1 Farm, Stg.3 Temple Catacombs

A necklace of some worth.

PURPLE GEM

VALUE: 3000

LOCATION: Stg.1 Other Passage, Stg.2 Annex Main Corridor

A gem that fits into the Elegant Mask, raising the value of the whole piece.

RED CATSEYE

VALUE: 3000

LOCATION: Stg.1 Homestead Ruins

Can be fitted into the Beerstein to increase the value.

RED EYE

VALUE: 1500

LOCATION: Defeat a Novistador in Stg.2

A small gem dropped by defeated Novistador enemies as well as the Novistador hive in the Castle's Ballroom. Can be inserted into a Blind Butterfly Lamp to increase the value.

RED GEM

VALUE: 3000

LOCATION: Stg.1 Barrier Station, Stg. 2 Courtyard & Bedroom

A gem that fits into the Elegant Mask, raising the value of the whole piece.

RED STONE OF FAITH

VALUE: 3500

LOCATION: Stg.3 Monitor Station

A catseye gem that can be fit into the Golden Lynx statue for greater value.

ROYAL INSIGNIA

VALUE: 13,000

LOCATION: Stg.2 Abyss

A crest removed from a crown. Can be returned to the crown to add greater value.

RUBY

VALUE: 10,000

Dropped by certain chainsaw-wielding villagers.

SPINEL

VALUE: 2000

A small ore of value. Found frequently in all stages.

STAFF OF ROYALTY

VALUE: 20,000

LOCATION: Stg.2 Underground Ruins Entrance

A staff once held by a king.

VELVET BLUE

VALUE: 2500

A small crystal of some value. Found frequently in the Castle.

YELLOW CATSEYE

VALUE: 3000

LOCATION: Stg.1 Gondola

Can be fitted into the Beerstein to increase the value.

game system and strategies

This chapter contains a wealth of instructions, information, tips, tricks and strategies that are to be considered "common knowledge" in the walkthrough sections of this book. In other words, you must understand everything that is described in this chapter while attempting the game, or failure is imminent.

BASICS

Controller Setup

Left Analog Stick	Move/Turn/Highlight Menu Choice
✖	Action Button
◉	Run/Cancel/Exit Menu
R2	Ashley Commands
START	Weapons Recovery Screen
△	Quick Map
R1	Aim Firearm
L1	Prepare Knife
SELECT	Options Menu/Skip Cinematic
Right Analog Stick	Look/Zoom Scope

Menu Navigation

When navigating all menus, use the Left Analog Stick or D-Pad to highlight choices or move a cursor. Press ✖ to select a choice, or press ◉ to return to previous screen or exit the menu.

Weapons Recovery Screen

Press START to open the Weapons Recovery Screen, displaying Leon's attaché case and his entire inventory. Items collected in the case include weapons, ammunition, and recovery items. Items can continue to be collected as long as there are empty blocks remaining in the attaché case. Be sure to combine herbs, use recovery items when low on health and reload weapons with ammunition in order to clear more room in the case. Larger attaché cases can be purchased from the merchant, one new one in each stage.

While viewing the Weapons Recovery Screen, move the cursor to the top row and select one of the headers to view a different menu.

Arranging Items

To move an item within the case, use the Left Analog Stick or D-Pad to select the item, then press R2 to lift it from its spot. Rotate the item clockwise with R1 or counterclockwise with L1. Move the item over a space big enough in which to set the item, with the Left Analog Stick or D-Pad, then press again to place the item in its new spot.

While rearranging items in the attaché case, the secondary item space to the right can be used to temporarily store items until enough blocks are cleared to set the item back in the case. Exiting the Weapons Recovery Screen discards all items in the secondary space. If this is not your intention, choose "No" when the discard prompt appears onscreen.

Item Menu

Select an item with ✕ to raise a pop-up menu. Select from the choices on this pop-up to use the item, examine the item in detail, combine the item with another or discard the item from the attaché case.

Combining items can also be accomplished by moving one item on top of another item. This provides a quicker way to combine herb or mount weapons with scopes, stocks or silencers.

Key Items and Treasures Screen

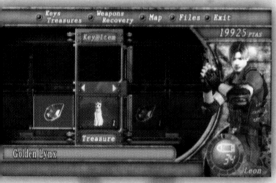

While viewing the Weapons Recovery Screen, press L1 to enter the Key Items and Treasures Screen. Key items that unlock doors or provide access to new areas are stored in the upper row, and valuable treasures that can be sold for profit are stored in the lower menu. While in the Key Items/Treasures Screen, press R1 to return to the Weapon Recovery Screen.

Select an item with ✕ to examine it, discard it, use it or combine it with another item. Sometimes key items must be assembled before they fit into the place they belong. Certain treasure pieces can be combined to create a new piece of greater value that the individual parts.

FILES

Documents and notes left behind by agents, cultists and co-conspirators provide useful clues as to how to proceed. These documents are collected in the Files menu. To review documents and also a communication log of the most recent radio transmission, press START to open the Weapon Recovery Screen, move the cursor to the headers along the top row and select the Files option.

Files are divided into three categories depending in which stage the document was found. To change stages, move to the top row of the file listing and move the cursor left or right to switch stages.

Map

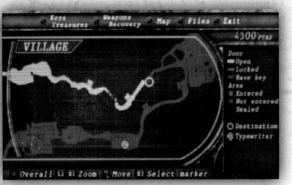

While exploring areas, press ▲ to quickly bring up the map menu. Various icons on the map indicate Leon's and Ashley's positions (when Ashley is following Leon), typewriter save points, merchant positions, open doors, locked doors, and doors that can be unlocked because you currently possess the right key. As you progress and learn new mission objectives, flashing destination markers appear at the location you should head to next.

Press ✕ to switch to overall view to see the entire stage at once. Hold L1 or R1 to zoom in and out of the map. Press R2 to view a list of markers and turn them off or on. Merchant and typewriter locations can be shown or cleared from the map. Other markers might indicate the locations of sub-mission objects such as the blue medallions in the Village stage or shooting galleries in the Castle and Island stages. If a Treasure Map item is purchased from the merchant for the stage, white markers denote the locations of all valuable treasures.

Movement

When controlling Leon, move the Left Analog Stick or D-Pad upward to move forward, left or right to turn in either direction, and downward to step backwards. Stepping away from enemies is strategically advantageous, especially when dealing with El Gigante boss monsters and Villagers. When moving, hold ● to run.

Instant Turn

When controlling Leon, hold the Left Analog Stick or D-Pad down and then press ●. Leon spins around to face the exact opposite direction he was previously facing. Instant turns are extremely useful when surrounded by enemies or surprised from behind. Whenever enemy sounds seem to be coming from behind, perform an instant turn before the monsters have a chance to attack.

Reloading

Whenever Leon's weapon runs out of ammo, he reloads the next time the action button is pressed. To reload the weapon on the fly, hold R1 and press ● to reload. Watch the magazine count displayed in the Leon's status window carefully and avoid emptying your clip entirely during a battle. Reload your weapon after dealing with enemies or while they recover between your attacks. Always keep a single bullet in the chamber in case your enemies pop back up to surprise you.

Action Button Functions

❌ is a kind of context-sensitive accept-all command. When navigating a menu, press ❌ to make a choice or confirm an option. When aiming a weapon or the knife, press ❌ to attack.

As you explore the environment, an ❌ icon might appear onscreen, along with words such as "TAKE," "JUMP OUT," "KNOCK DOWN," "OPERATE," etc. Press ❌ while these words appear onscreen to collect items or interact somehow with the environment.

Opening Doors

Move toward a door until the "OPEN" command appears onscreen, then press ❌ to open the door and proceed into the next room. Leon's default method of opening a door is quiet, with less chance of alerting the enemy to your presence. However, Leon can also kick the door open loudly and dramatically. To kick open a door, press ❌ twice when opening a door. Kicking open a door can be useful, especially when the door is padlocked. Also, enemies standing on the other side of the door might take damage or be knocked aside if Leon kicks it open.

Jumping Through Windows

When near a large enough window, the option to "JUMP OUT" or "JUMP IN" may appear onscreen. Press ❌ while this indicator is onscreen to make an evasive leap through the window.

Knowing that you can do this, look for windows to jump out of in situations where enemies are attempting to surround Leon. Run for the window and leap through it to escape to, what you hope is, a relatively safer spot.

Ladders

To pursue Leon into higher areas, such as the second story of a building, enemies often raise ladders. Knocking out windows with the ladder's end, enemies then climb the ladder and crawl through the window. While the enemies are climbing the ladder, move to the window and knock over the ladder by pressing ❌ when the option appears onscreen. Enemies climbing the ladder may take falling damage as a result, weakening or even killing them.

Introduction

Characters

Enemies

Weapons and Ammunition

Key Items and Treasures

Game System and Strategies

Walkthrough

Secrets and Bonuses

Items

Files

Combat Strategy

Recovery Items

Merchants

The Merchant's List

Target Practic

If a ladder is at a windowsill, Leon cannot jump out of the window without first knocking down the ladder. If Leon needs to climb a ladder and one is lying on the ground, stand over the ladder and press ✖ to raise it back up when the option appears.

Look for raised areas or platforms that can only be reached by utilizing a ladder. If Leon is being pursued by a large mob, climb the ladder and then knock it down to prevent enemies from following. Keep in mind that this will not prevent enemies from throwing weapons or firing projectiles at Leon. While the enemies are busy trying to re-raise the ladder, you can drop grenades on them or pick them off individually with a gun.

Commanding Ashley

Leon's main objective is to rescue the President's daughter, Ashley Graham. In certain portions of the game, Leon must safely lead Ashley through enemy lairs. Whenever Ashley is accompanying Leon, press R2 to commanded her "wait" in a certain spot, and then press it again to make her "follow" Leon further.

When a group of enemies is directly ahead, it is sometimes a good idea to keep Ashley out of the fighting by commanding her to wait in a safe spot while you rush forward and meet the enemies head-on. However, avoid leaving Ashley too far behind in a large area, or an enemy might materialize out of nowhere and kidnap her!

Ashley Icons

Ashley's status is indicated by the various icons that appear in the circular gauge directly above Leon's on the display.

Following	**Waiting**	**Warning**	**Captured**

Ashley is following Leon.	Ashley is waiting for Leon to come back.	Ashley is in danger of being attacked by an enemy and needs Leon's help.	An enemy has picked up Ashley and is attempting carry her to the nearest If the enemy carries Ash out of the area, the game ends immediately.

Hiding Ashley

Ashley can hide in certain containers to avoid being attacked by large groups of enemies, or to protect her from abduction. When you see a human-sized open container, approach it while Ashley is following and press R2 to command her to hide inside. When the coast is clear, press R2 again to whistle for Ashley.

Cooperation

Working together, sometimes Ashley and Leon can open a door or overcome an obstacle that one person cannot bypass alone. Certain doors are locked from the other side, and one person cannot climb over without help. When Ashley is with Leon at a tall door or a high ledge and the "PIGGYBACK" option appears onscreen, press ⊗ to lift Ashley over the obstacle.

Sometimes Ashley can operate a lever or turn a crank while Leon contends with enemies in the area. Whenever an option to allow Ashley to operate something becomes available, always let Ashley perform the action. Sometimes Ashley takes a little longer to complete a task, but at least you can protect her while she is working.

Camera Angle

While walking or running through areas, move the Right Analog Stick to adjust the camera angle for a better view of whatever is above, below or to the side. In some areas, you might spot a bird's nest in a tree or a shiny treasure embedded in a cave ceiling by holding the Right Analog Stick up while moving.

Zoom Scope

While aiming a sniper rifle, Leon automatically looks through the scope to aim. Move the Right Analog Stick upward to zoom in for a closer look, or move the Right Analog Stick down to zoom out. Place the center of the crosshairs on the target and press ⊗ to fire.

When the scope is zoomed in, movement speed of the scope reduces. Therefore, if you wish to adjust your aim more quickly or if you need to follow a moving target, zoom out.

Items

Finding and collecting various items is the key to surviving the game and defeating enemies. Items can be found by moving near shelves until the "TAKE" option appears onscreen. Items are also hidden inside cabinets or lockers. Use your knife or gun to break open crates and barrels to find items.

Defeated enemies sometimes drop items as well. When an enemy drops an extra item, it remains on the map only a short period of time. You must pick it up before it disappears, or the opportunity is lost. Unfortunately other enemies still active in the area might prevent you from reaching items before they disappear. Items dropped by enemies are highlighted with columns of light, colored to indicate the type of item. A green light indicates a recovery item, a red light indicates ammunition, and a blue light indicates pesetas, or money.

Random Items

Some areas may contain randomly determined items. Random items are contained in crates and barrels that must be broken to obtain the item. When a crate that contains a random item is smashed open, you might find ammunition, recovery items, pesetas, or nothing at all. If you smash a crate or barrel where a random item is sometimes located and you do not like the results, press START/PAUSE to open the Option Menu and choose the "retry" option to play the game over again from the last continue point. Continue points are typically established every time Leon enters a room, defeats a powerful enemy, survives some kind of deathtrap, or after story events. When you retry from a continue point, random item results may differ from the previous attempt, and you might get a better item.

Pesetas

Boxes of pesetas, the local currency, are located all over the maps. They may appear randomly when crates or barrels are broken open. Defeated enemies or crows may drop additional boxes. Special enemies and boss monsters drop gold bars worth large amounts of pesetas when they die. Pesetas are used to purchase and tune-up weapons at merchant shops, so garner all the money you can! The pesetas Leon has accumulated is displayed in the Weapons Recovery Screen as well as the merchant's shop menu.

Using Items

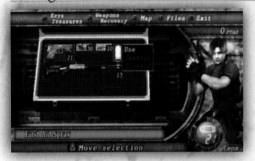

To make use of items, press START to open the Weapon Recovery Screen. Move the cursor to an item in Leon's attaché case and press ✪ to bring up the item pop-up menu. If the item is a recovery aid, select the "Use" command to consume the item and regain lost health. When Ashley accompanies Leon, recovery items in the attaché case can be used to cure her as well.

Equipping Weapons

Weapons and weapon accessories can be equipped by pressing START to open the Weapon Recovery Screen. Highlight the weapon you want to equip in the attaché case, then press ✪ to bring up the pop-up menu. Choose the "Equip" option.

Combining Items

Combine items such as herbs and separate quantities of ammunition to make room in the attaché case or to increase the power of recovery items. To combine two items, select one item in the attaché case, choose the "Combine" option, and then move the blue cursor to a compatible item. Or, pressR2 to lift one item from the space it inhabits, move it on top of a combinable item, and press R2 again to combine the two.

accessories such as stocks and scopes can be purchased from a merchant and mounted on weapons for better aiming or increased firing stability. To combine a weapon and its accessory, press ✖ to select the item and choose "Combine" from the pop-up menu. Move the blue secondary cursor to the weapon it can be mounted upon, and press ✖ again to fit the weapon with the part. Or, press R2 to lift the accessory from the attaché case, move it over the weapon it can be mounted on and press R2 to equip the two simultaneously. The accessory continues to be equipped every time the weapon it is attached to is equipped until the accessory is removed from the weapon. To remove an accessory from a weapon, select it in the attaché case and choose the "Remove" command.

Wildlife

Crows and snakes in outdoor areas drop items when shot. When shooting crows, try not to drive off the flock while shooting a single bird. By approaching too closely or firing your weapon from too short a range, the other birds take flight and the opportunity to shoot them for an item is missed. Avoid wasting time trying to shoot crows flying above. Leave the area and reenter to reset the crows to their initial positions.

The villagers love to set traps for Leon by placing live snakes inside crates. When Leon breaks open the box, the snake attacks him and causes small amounts of damage. In the opening portion of the game, it's all right to break open crates and barrels with the knife. But as the game progresses, use the gun to break open crates so that you can quickly shoot a snake that may be waiting inside the box. If you shoot a snake before it attacks Leon or slithers away, it drops some type of Chicken Egg.

Hens in the Pueblo and farm areas might lay Chicken Eggs, Brown Chicken Eggs or rare Gold Chicken Eggs if left alone for long enough. If Leon walks toward the hen and makes them run away, they will not lay an egg for quite some time. Look for green light columns where hens and roosters roam to find eggs.

Dodge Buttons

During certain life or death situations that arise during Leon's mission, the player must press two buttons displayed onscreen immediately in order to dodge out of harm's way. Such instances include rolling boulders, certain attacks of boss enemies, and even attacks performed during cinematic sequences where characters are having conversations. There is no time to let your guard down in this game! The dodge buttons are typically L1 + R1 or ✖ + ⬤. Press both buttons simultaneously when they are displayed onscreen to avert death or disaster.

DODGE

In some cases, the ✖ or ⬤ buttons must be tapped rapidly in order to push away an enemy or climb up from hanging off the side of a ledge. The game basically counts the number of times and the frequency at which the button is pressed, decides if you are really trying or not, and determines the outcome appropriately. Sometimes you must start by tapping one button, and then switch to the other button when the onscreen display changes. Stay on your toes!

SPRINT

Introduction

Characters

Enemies

Weapons and Ammunition

Key Items and Treasures

Game System and Strategies

Walkthrough

Secrets and Bonuses

Typewriters

Opportunities to save arise whenever a chapter of the game ends. You may also save your progress to a memory card by approaching a typewriter and using it to save. Sometimes saving at a typewriter is a wise idea, especially if you are about to purchase things from a merchant and tend to experience buyer's remorse. Also, if a boss battle is imminent, save your game at a typewriter before heading into the war zone.

COMBAT STRATEGY

STRATEGY

Aiming Weapons

Press and hold R1 to aim the firearm equipped in Leon's right hand. While aiming, move the Left Analog Stick or D-Pad to adjust Leon's aim. Leon must remain stationary in order to shoot. If an attack is imminent, release R1 and try to escape.

Leon aims most of his weapons with a laser sight. Move the Left Analog Stick or D-Pad to adjust Leon's aim until the laser connects with a valid target, forming a tiny "ball" at the end. When Leon has targeted an enemy, press ✕ to fire. Due to weapon recoil and Leon's own natural amount of human trembling, aim becomes unsteady between shots. If you fire repeatedly and start missing, stop firing and reaffirm your aim with the laser sight.

Rifles are aimed by looking through the scope. While holding R1, move the crosshairs over your target, move the C-Stick up or down to zoom in or out respectively, and press ✕ to fire.

Using the Knife

Press and hold L1 to raise Leon's knife, and press ✕ to slash horizontally in front of Leon. The knife does not have to be equipped like the other weapons, and Leon does not have to make room for it in the attaché case. The knife is always at the ready. It does not require ammunition and never needs to be reloaded. Use the knife to defend yourself against enemies that are too close for comfort and to smash crates and barrels to conserve ammo in the early stages of the game.

Limb Targeting

By targeting and shooting enemies in the limbs, you can disable them in certain ways. For instance, by shooting an enemy in the arm, you can make him drop the weapon he/she holds. Shoot enemies in the knees to stop them from moving, or shoot them in the lower leg while they are running forward to "trip" them. Once you have "tripped" an enemy, shoot them continuously on the ground to make sure they do not get back up. If a shot to the lower leg causes an enemy to drop to one knee, shoot them in the torso to knock them over.

Kicking Enemies

When an enemy is shot in the head or forced to their knees, Leon can kick them if he is in range. If he is not in range, run forward until the "KICK" option appears onscreen. Press ✗ to kick them. Kicking enemies causes a small amount of damage, and knocks the enemy to the ground. It's then easier to continue shooting the enemy while they are down and cannot hurt Leon.

When a crowd is approaching, it's possible to knock the whole group down with a single kick. Shoot the closest enemy in the face to make them stagger in pain. Then run forward and perform a kick. Leon's roundhouse nails the enemy as well as any other foes in range of the kick. The whole group is flattened! However, this is a finesse move, so be sure to practice kicking single enemies a few times before moving on to this complex maneuver.

Projectile Deflection

When enemies throw weapons or fire arrows at Leon, a quick and reflexive shot can knock the projectile right out of the air. The chances a shot will deflect a projectile increase as the object gets closer to Leon. If your eyes are quick enough that you can watch the weapon fly through the air toward Leon, wait to fire until the last minute and you'll knock axes, sickles and arrows out of the air left and right.

Certain enemies light the fuses of dynamite sticks and then hurl them toward Leon. If you can shoot the explosive in the enemy's hand, or immediately after he tosses it, the bomb detonates right in the midst of enemies, taking them all out. Also, once an enemy lights the fuse on a dynamite stick, shoot him to death. As soon as he falls to the ground, the dynamite explodes, killing everything in a medium blast radius.

Projectiles like rocket launcher missiles and machinegun bullets cannot be blocked by a deflective shot, so do not attempt it!

Weak Spots

Many of the enemies in the game have a "weak spot", a limb or area on their body where you can shoot them to inflict greater damage than if you shoot them anywhere else. Los Ganados of all types are weak when shot in the head. However, at night a headshot might reveal the Plaga inside the Ganado, making the enemy even stronger and requiring greater firing accuracy in order to hit the exposed parasite.

The giant, claw-armed Garradors' only weak spot is the parasite attached to their backs. Somehow, you must get behind them in order to blast the parasite. Colmillos, or wolfhound enemies with tentacles, are weak against fire. One incendiary grenade takes out whole packs of these animals.

Read the **Enemies** chapter to learn the weak spots of all enemies, and exploit these weaknesses to shorten battle time, reduce damage taken and conserve ammunition for battles where it is needed the most.

Introduction
Characters
Enemies
Weapons and Ammunition
Key Items and Treasures
Game System and Strategies
Walkthrough
Secrets and Bonuses

Basics
Files
Combat Strategy
Recovery Items
Merchants
The Merchant's List
Target Practice

Crowd Control

Over and over again the game throws hordes of enemies at Leon. When faced with a "crowd," exerting crowd control becomes important. Use more powerful weapons to deal with crowds, and use lesser weapons to deal with individual enemies. For instance, when a crowd of villagers come at Leon with pitchforks in hand, toss some type of grenade into the mob to decimate their numbers or stun them all so that an escape can be made.

Or, equip the shotgun, let the group move in closer and blast all of them simultaneously with the weapon's cone-shaped emission. Once a few members of the crowd have died off and only one or two are left behind, equip a handgun to take on the individuals. The more powerful the weapon, the less it can be used. Conserve ammunition by using it only when needed, and avoid exerting "overkill" on individual enemies.

Funneling Enemies

Enemies are programmed to invade Leon's area, surround him, and come at him from all sides. Avoid this enemy tactic by moving into narrow passages or beyond doorways in dead-end corridors, and then wait for enemies to funnel into the room in pursuit. As foes come through narrow doorways or windows, they cluster up and become easy to eliminate en masse with a single grenade or shotgun blast.

This strategy of funneling enemies into narrow spaces is a tactic you can use repeatedly to survive encounters and conserve ammo all the way up until the last stage of the game. Enemies in the Island stage, however, are programmed not to pursue Leon so readily through narrow doorways. They sometimes attempt to bait you into an open area where they can surround you. Smart monsters!

Boss Enemies

Unique enemies in the game have exceptional abilities and limited weakness. Known as boss enemies, these amazing foes require special strategies to defeat. Turn to the appropriate section of the walkthrough chapters to read a detailed, blow by blow method of overcoming the most powerful of enemies while avoiding damage and death from their attacks.

RECOVERY ITEMS

As enemies inflict attacks on the characters, their remaining life diminishes. The character's condition suffers when the health gauge becomes yellow or red, and he or she begins to hold their side and limp when walking. Administer recovery items to regain lost health. Recovery items must be carried in the attaché case along with Leon's weapons and ammunition. When picking up a recovery item, Leon may have the option to use it immediately, rather than store it in the case. When Ashley accompanies Leon, recovery items can be used to restore her health.

Green Herb

An indigenous plant that restores a small amount of health. Two or three Green Herbs can be combined to create compounds that restore more health.

MIXED HERB CHART

Combined Herbs	Effect
Green + Green	Medium recovery.
Green + Green + Green	Close to full recovery.
Green + Red	Full recovery.
Green + Yellow	Small recovery, increases maximum health.
Green + Red + Yellow	Full recovery, increases maximum health.

Red Herb

A mysterious plant that has no effect alone. But when combined with a Green Herb, it forms a compound that restores maximum health.

Yellow Herb

A strange plant not found anywhere else in the world. It has no use by itself, but when combined with a Green Herb it forms a compound that restores a small amount of health and raises the maximum amount of life of the character. It can also be combined with a Red Herb, or with a Red-Green mixed herb compound to form a new substance that raises the maximum life limit and completely restores health.

First Aid Spray

Completely restores the character's health. Leon carries one of these along in his mission. Because they are found so rarely, it is wise to reserve their use for emergency situations when Leon is about to die. First Aid Sprays can be purchased from merchants for 10,000 pesetas.

Black Bass

A small fish that swims in lakes and reservoirs. When shot, the fish floats to the surface and can be collected just like other recovery items. A Black Bass can be eaten to restore half of the character's life. However, each Black Bass takes up three blocks in the attaché case, making them burdensome to carry.

Black Bass (L)

A large fish that swims in lakes and reservoirs. When shot the Black Bass floats to the surface and can be taken just like other recovery items. A large Black Bass replenishes all life. However, this huge fish takes quite a few spaces in the attaché case, making them difficult to carry. It is best to fish for them and consume them only when in great need.

Chicken Egg

A white egg sometimes laid by hens, or left behind by snakes when shot. Restores a tiny amount of health. Takes up only one space in the attaché case.

Brown Chicken Egg

A brownish egg sometimes lain by hens, or left behind by snakes when shot. Restores a medium portion of health. Takes up only one space in the attaché case.

Gold Chicken Egg

A rare golden egg that completely restores health. Lain by hens or dropped by snakes when shot. Takes up only one space in the attaché case, so be sure to hold onto these for emergency purposes.

MERCHANTS

Roughly thirty minutes into the game (depending on how you play), Leon encounters a masked villager who seems more interested in personal wealth than the almighty cause of Los Illuminados. These merchants offer to sell Leon powerful weapons and weapon upgrades in exchange for pesetas. Merchants also buy extra items and valuable treasures from Leon, so that he can afford better weapons and tune-ups. The prices are high, so look for opportunities to collect extra cash by defeating high-dollar enemies.

Don't Shoot the Shop Clerk!

Be careful with the violence around merchants. Even the slightest damage kills them. If a merchant happens to be standing in the vicinity of enemies, which happens two or three times in the game, try to lead foes away from the merchant's location so that he is not accidentally killed in the process. Once a merchant dies, he never reappears in that location!

THE MERCHANT'S LIST

The complete price list of the merchant is below. Larger Attaché Cases become available in each new stage, i.e., one in the Village, one in the Castle, and one in the Island. Treasure Maps marking the locations of valuables on the map become available for sale if an item in the previous stage was overlooked. The Treasure Map of the Village is always available. As for weapon availability, please refer to the **Weapons and Ammunition** chapter to determine when you can purchase that mega-gun you have your eye on.

Item	Price
Attaché Case M	30,000
Attaché Case L	40,000
Attaché Case XL	73,000
Tactical Vest	60,000
Treasure Map (Island)	10,000
Treasure Map (Castle)	10,000
Treasure Map (Village)	10,000
Handgun	8000
Red9	14,000
Punisher	0 (20,000)*

Item	Price
Blacktail	24,000
Broken Butterfly	38,000
Killer7	77,700
Matilda	70,000
Handcannon	0
Shotgun	20,000
Riot Gun	32,000
Striker	43,000
Rifle	12,000
Rifle (semi-auto)	35,000

Item	Price
TMP	15,000
Mine Thrower	28,000
Chicago Typewriter	1,000,000
Rocket Launcher	30,000
Infinite Launcher	1,000,000
Stock (Red9)	4000
Stock (TMP)	4000
Scope (Rifle)	7000
Scope (semi-auto rifle)	10,000
Scope (Mine Thrower)	8000
First Aid Spray	10,000

* Becomes available for free when the blue medallion sub-mission is completed in the Village stage. If sold back to the merchant, the price changes to 20,000.

TARGET PRACTICE

In the Observation Hall of the Castle, Leon finds a blue door with golden gun engravings. Beyond this door is a shooting gallery, where Leon can sign up to shoot stationary and moving targets. This fun mini-game is a great way to make the extra money required to upgrade weapons. Read the **Target Practice** document, available on the counter, to learn the rules of the game and how you can win awards. To review your highest score, examine the postings on the wall to the right of the counter.

Speak to the clerk behind the desk to try your skill in the shooting range. Take the Rapid-fire weapon set or the sniping weapon set, and then head through the double doors into the next room and ring the bell to begin. Shoot the targets to score points. For every five targets hit, the backdrop opens and a tiny Salazar target moves across the back. Shoot annoying little Salazar to score big! If you shoot four targets and miss the fifth, Salazar can be heard laughing at you.

When the castle is the backdrop, firing into the ceiling causes a strange reaction. The sky and the castle begin to glow and sparkle, and then an explosion occurs. If timed right, this might take out several targets simultaneously. If timed wrong, it might damage an Ashley target and deduct 1000 points from your score. Scoring headshots continuously causes fireworks to commence in the background. Little Salazar will do anything to distract you!

SCORING

Hit Target	50pts.
Male Villager Headshot	100pts.
Female Villager Headshot	200pts.
Salazar	500pts.
Ashley	-1000pts.

Bottle Caps

Score more than 3000 points in one game to receive bottle caps. Rare bottle caps are awarded for certain feats, such as shooting all twenty-five targets (except Ashley targets), or scoring over 4000 points. The sniping weapon set is good for scoring high, and the rapid-fire set is good for shooting all the targets to win the rare bottle cap.

Each new shooting range you enter has six new bottle caps available to win. If you have not won all of the bottle caps from the previous range yet, then choose Game Type A to win bottle caps on the bottom row, Game Type B to win bottle caps on the second row, etc. View the bottle caps you won by selecting their panorama in the Key Items/Treasures Screen.

Changing Features

Winning the Ashley Graham bottle cap changes the targets that appear, so that Ashley Graham targets begin popping up right in your way. Run to the left or right to shoot around her and hit other targets. Hitting an Ashley target deducts 1000 points from your score.

After playing a certain game type repeatedly, the pattern of target appearance changes entirely. The backdrop stays open for the entire game. The targets appear so far away from Leon's position that only the sniper rifle is a practical choice.

Try to score big in the shooting gallery during a replay game. Just try it! The difficulty increases to the point of near-impossibility. Attempt to win all the bottle caps before clearing the game.

GAME TYPE A (BOTTOM ROW)

No.	Bottle Cap
1	Leon w/handgun
2	Leon w/shotgun
3	Ashley Graham
4	Luis Sera
5	Leon w/rocket launcher
Rare	Ada Wong (hit all targets)

GAME TYPE C (THIRD ROW)

No.	Bottle Cap
1	Merchant
2	Leader zealot
3	Zealot w/scythe
4	Zealot w/shield
5	Zealot w/bowgun
Rare	Don Pedro

GAME TYPE B (SECOND ROW)

No.	Bottle Cap
1	Don Jose
2	Don Esteban
3	Don Manuel
4	Don Diego
5	Dr. Salvador
Rare	Bella Sisters

GAME TYPE D (TOP ROW)

No.	Bottle Cap
1	Soldier w/bat
2	Soldier w/stun-rod
3	Soldier w/hammer
4	Isabel
5	Maria
Rare	J.J

TARGET PRACTICE AWARDS (PESETAS)

No.	Bottle Cap
All bottom row bottle caps	15,000
All second row bottle caps	25,000
All third row bottle caps	35,000
All fourth row bottle caps	50,000

Introduction

Characters

Enemies

Weapons and Ammunition

Key Items and Treasures

Game System and Strategies

Walkthrough

Secrets and Bonuses

Basics

Files

Combat Strategy

Recovery Items

Merchants

The Merchant's List

Target Practic

chapter one

The walkthrough portion of the guide is divided into chapters and sub-chapters, just like the game itself. This should make this volume easier to reference while playing through **Resident Evil 4**.

The game is explored in these sections area by area. Examine the maps to determine the possible locations of items. Keep in mind that every area has a certain number of randomly determined items, and that there is also a chance that breaking certain crates and barrels may not yield any item at all.

Therefore, the number of Random items listed in the **Items Found** table for each area lists a number of chances for a random item, rather than a total. Should you check all five random item locations and find little or nothing, consider opening the Options menu and retrying the area.

CHAPTER 1-1

FOREST

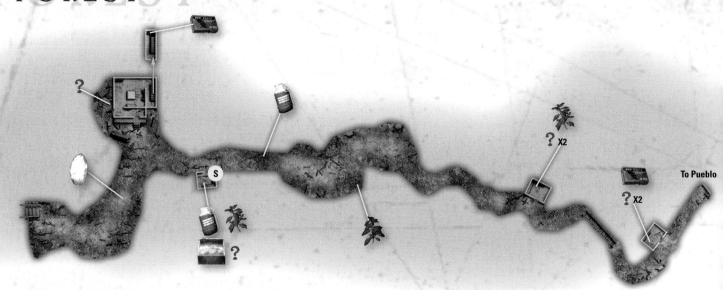

ITEMS FOUND

Item	Occurrence	Remark
Handgun Ammo	3	
Hand Grenade	1	Crow
Green Herb	2	
Red Herb	1	Bush
Pesetas (Box)	2	
Random	5	
Spinel	1	Crow

Let the Chase Begin...

The surly local police drop Leon off at the edge of a forest just outside the village where the President's daughter, Ashley Graham, was last seen. Return to the car and speak to both officers to hear them deride Leon a little more.

Wildlife Hunting

Move a few steps up the path until you spot three crows perched around a tree. Shoot the crows for a chance to possibly obtain money and a **Spinel**. Fire from a distance to avoid driving them off with the gunshot noise.

Un-Welcoming Party

A large truck blocks the path leading east, so head north to the nearby house. Be sure to smash the box on the cart west of the house for a chance to get another item.

Enter the house to question the inhabitant. After a violent greeting, kill the occupant. Other villagers suddenly appear and attack the police officers parked nearby. They block the front door shut, but won't enter for the time being. Head to the back of the house and go upstairs to find **Handgun Ammo**. Then go downstairs and jump through the window near the front of the house to get outside.

Allow the hostile villagers to approach, and then shoot the closest enemy in the head to make him stagger. When he holds his face in pain, move in close until the "KICK" command appears onscreen. Press ✗ to boot the staggering man, knocking down all the other villagers as well. Jump over the woodpile to put a barrier between you and the villagers if needed. Also consider retreating inside the house. From this location, you can shoot the villagers as they attempt to enter via the door or windows (with less chance of being surrounded).

Once the uprising is suppressed, collect any items dropped by enemies and head back to the cliff's edge. Look over the cliff to see the junked police car in the stream below.

Continuing Toward the Pueblo

Follow the path beyond where the truck was parked to find a small shed full of items. Collect the **Handgun Ammo** on the counter, and smash the three crates to collect various randomly determined items. Use the typewriter to save your game.

Sniping More Crow

Two more crows are perched near a strange signpost. Shoot them both from a distance to obtain pesetas and a **Hand Grenade.**

Bear Traps

Continue east until you spot a wolf caught in a bear trap. Release the wolf from the trap by approaching and pressing ✗. Freeing the wolf from the trap proves extremely beneficial to Leon in future events. Note that the areas off the sides of the path are lined with more bear traps. Shoot them with the handgun to set them off, making the area safe to cross. However, sticking to the path ensures that you'll avoid them entirely.

Tripwires

Reaching the signpost that points the way to the "Pueblo," explore the area to the right to find a **Red Herb** among the bushes near the fence. Proceed into the next section cautiously, and notice the trip wires strung between the trees. That's not all. Two bear traps are set on the ground between the trees.

Use the handgun to set off the bear traps, then move toward them until a villager gardening along the path nearby cries out. As he approaches Leon, back away from the tripwires a few steps, then turn and aim at the claymore attached to one of the trees. When the villager moves between the trees, shoot the claymore to set off the bombs, killing the villager. Whenever possible, use exploding barrels and bombs to kill one or more enemies more efficiently and with less ammo.

What Do the Gory Signposts Mean?

The signposts with skulls are the villagers' way of indicating that there are booby traps ahead. Upon entering an area marked by this signpost, start searching the ground and trees for traps.

Cabins Along the Path

A small cabin farther along Leon's route contains a gruesome sight, as well as two item crates and a **Green Herb**.

Herbs: Green and Red Combination

Combine Green Herbs and Red Herbs whenever possible to create fully restorative compounds.

Kill two villagers on your way to the next cabin. Approach the structure cautiously, because an enemy lies in ambush. Grab the **Handgun Ammo** and other items from inside the cabin and continue through the gate bearing a strange symbol.

PUEBLO

ITEMS FOUND

Item	Occurrence	Remark
Shotgun	1	
Handgun Ammo	5	
Shotgun Shells	2	
Hand Grenade	1	
Flash Grenade	1	
Incendiary Grenade	1	
Green Herb	2	
Red Herb	2	
Yellow Herb	1	
Pesetas (Box)	3	
Gold Bars	1	Chainsaw Man
Ruby	1	Chainsaw Man
Random	6	
Spinel	1	On Roof

Ruby (Chainsaw)

To Farm

Alert Order

To Tunnel

To Forest

To Village
Chief's House

Hub of Anarchy

Move forward until the "LOOK" command appears onscreen. Press ✖ to use Leon's binoculars to spy on the villagers. While looking through the scope, use the Left Thumbstick to adjust your view and move the Right Thumbstick up or down to zoom in or out. Although the villagers appear to be going on with their everyday lives, a grizzly reminder that something is terribly wrong burns in the central pyre.

You must kill 14 enemies to continue past the Pueblo area. Each five enemies killed causes five more to appear, and this happens twice through brief interludes. When the fourteenth enemy dies, a bell sounds from a nearby church and all the villagers leave the area. Until then, you must avoid being overwhelmed by their numbers.

here are two ways to initiate the fight. Either run into the center of town or try to sneak behind the buildings via the path ading west from Leon's spy point by the tree. As soon as the first villager spots Leon, they emit a cry that warns all the others.

scape from the Pueblo is nearly impossible. Running toward any of the exits adds five more enemies to the mix. Heading ward the north exit causes a chainsaw-wielding maniac to appear. Without appropriate weaponry, this enemy can kill Leon a single attack. However, he drops a valuable **Ruby** when defeated.

ighting the Crowd

he Pueblo presents the first of several instances during the ame where Leon must take on a large crowd of enemies efore he can continue the mission. Remaining outdoors is uicide. In the open, Leon can easily be attacked from any de at any time. To survive long enough to kill 14 villagers, uck inside buildings with your back in a corner. Blast the illagers as they attempt to enter through doors or windows. /hen the situation gets too hot, toss a grenade into the rowd and escape through the nearest window or door.

ecause the Pueblo is such an open area with so many good spots for action, specifying exactly how to fight the enemies ould be both wrong and impossible. Instead, we shall simply go over some features of the village and let you decide how to andle the situation.

Avoid the Tower!

The tower at the north end of the area may seem like the highest and safest place to go, but nothing could be further from the truth. If Leon climbs into the tower, the villagers suddenly equip molotov cocktails and toss them into the loft! The only way out is to drop down into a horde of violent peasants or die a fiery death in the tower. Find someplace else to hold up.

he Two-Story House

ntering the two-story house in he village triggers an additional cene where the villagers edouble their efforts as Leon arricades the door. *Be aware hat entering this structure mmediately adds eleven more enemies to the area.* Additionally, the chainsaw maniac appears and goes after Leon via he fastest route possible. Ladders are placed all over the building, giving villagers access to many points of the roof. Avoid ntering the two-story structure until the villagers leave to keep the battle fairly easy, or enter the building to increase the attle intensity.

Once inside the house, move to the bookcase on the west wall and push it in front of the boarded window to slow the ingression. Grab the **Handgun Ammo** on the rear cupboard and smash the barrels under the stairs to possibly obtain pesetas. Then head upstairs and

take the **Shotgun** off the wall. Use the knife to smash the glass cabinet and claim a **Hand Grenade**, take the nearby **1000 Pesetas** and pick up the extra **Shotgun Shells** on the bed.

By this point, enemies should be climbing the ladder as well as banging on the nearby window. Push the ladder down to prevent enemies from climbing in and blast the

enemies trying to come through the window. The best course of action is to get out of this building by leaping through the upstairs window near the bed. Barricading yourself in the more fortified house across the street would be a wise idea.

Kill That Chainsaw-Brandishing Psycho!

The chainsaw-wielding maniac is the toughest villager on the block, capable of withstanding several shotgun blasts and any number of handgun shots. But if you can bring him down permanently, he drops **Gold Bars** worth 10,000 pesetas!

The Southern House

Most of the doors on structures in the village are made of flimsy wood. However, the door to the back bedroom in the southern house is made of metal. A metal door cannot be sawed through and the villagers cannot beat it open so quickly. Therefore, the southern house is a great place to make your last stand against the onslaught.

Kick open the front door and move immediately to the left. Get behind the bureau and push it in front of the door. Blast a barrel to the left of the stove to hopefully obtain some type of ammo, and then head for the back room. The metal door is sealed shut by a padlock. Either blast the padlock off with the shotgun or kick the door repeatedly, positioned to strike the padlock with his foot. Three direct kicks on the padlock should be enough to break the lock and open the door.

Grab the **Pesetas** off the bed, and smash the nearby crate and barrel for additional items as well. Use these scant precious seconds to recover from injuries and reload weapons. When the villagers begin banging on the metal door, prepare for breach. Either toss a grenade or fire the shotgun when the door bangs open, to buffer the crowd attempting to get inside.

Keep an Eye on the Hens!

Avoid shooting chickens in this area and the next. If a chicken is allowed to remain in one spot long enough, it might lay an egg. Eggs can be eaten to recover lost health. There is also a slight possibility of obtaining the extremely rare Gold Egg!

As the Bell Tolls...

When the villagers abandon the Pueblo, collect the remaining items in the area. Walk to the top of the arched rooftop on the two-story house to find a **Spinel**. In the tiny shack near the northeastern exit, the **Alert Order** file hangs on the wall. It seems someone has been following Leon's movements since long before he came here... When finished exploring and gathering, continue through the northeastern exit.

FARM

ITEMS FOUND

Item	Occurrence	Remark
Handgun Ammo	2	
Incendiary Grenade	1	
Pesetas (Box)	2	
Random	6	
Spinel	2	
Pearl Pendant	1	Hung over Well
Beerstein	1	

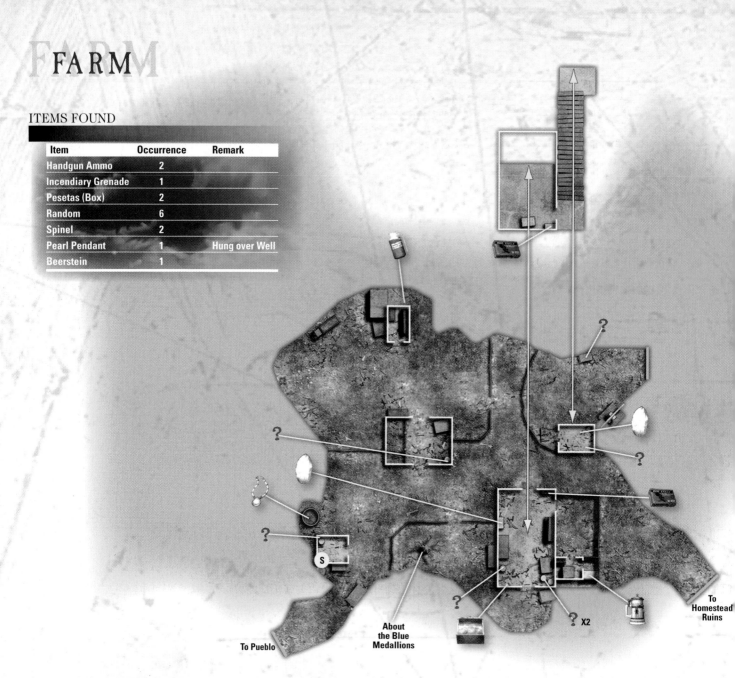

To Pueblo

About the Blue Medallions

To Homestead Ruins

The Blue Medallions

While dealing with the relatively few enemies present in this area, take the **Blue Parchment** off the tree to read a note concerning a sub-mission available during Chapters 1 and 2 of the game. By spotting and shooting the fifteen blue medallions in this area and the graveyard, the weapon merchant makes a bonus weapon available later in the game. Taking the parchment from the tree causes the in-game map to display the locations of all fifteen medallions. Seven of them appear in the farm area, and they are marked on the maps provided above.

Tactical Advantage

Once enemies at the Farm spot Leon and begin to close in, enter the larger barn and wait for the enemy in the loft to drop to the floor. Climb the ladder to the loft, and knock the ladder down. Defend yourself from sickles and axes they might throw, and keep tipping the ladder until all five enemies are gathered below. Toss a hand grenade down to the level below to take them all out!

Treasures at the Farm

The **Pearl Pendant** hangs over the well behind the shack in the western edge of the area. Shoot the pendant to drop it within Leon's reach. However, allowing the Pearl Pendant to drop into the mucky well tarnishes the item and lowers the value from 10,000 pesetas to a measly 1000. First, shoot the rod holding up the well's lid, and then shoot the pendant to drop it safely onto the covering. This way, the Pearl Pendant can later be sold for full value.

The Beerstein's location can only be reached by navigating through the upper level of the barn. Climb up the ladder into the loft of the larger barn in the area. Then jump through the eastern open windowsill onto a covering that spans over to the building next door. Move directly across the covering from the window and drop into the fenced-in area and smash the crate to obtain the **Beerstein**. While this item can be sold for relatively little value on its own, the Beerstein greatly increases in value when fitted with three jewels, found elsewhere.

Tucked Around the Farm

Be sure to collect the **Spinel** from the cabinet inside the large barn, as well another one in the crate inside the connected shed. Do not miss the barrel behind the shed near the northeast corner of the area, which breaks apart to reveal an **Incendiary Grenade**.

To Farm

Red Catseye (bird nest)

ITEMS FOUND

Item	Occurrence	Remark
Handgun Ammo	3	
Hand Grenade	1	
Green Herb	1	
Pesetas (Box)	2	
Random	3	
Spinel	3	
Red Catseye	1	Bird Nest

The Old Boulder Dash Trap

As the familiar signpost near the entrance indicates, the area ahead is full of traps. Proceed down the slope a few feet until villagers push a boulder off a cliff behind Leon. Rapidly tap the button displayed onscreen to sprint ahead of the boulder. Be ready to press either **L1 + R1** or ◉ + ✖ simultaneously to dodge out from in front of the boulder at the last second.

SPRINT

Time for a Little Payback

After surviving the rolling boulder trap, two villagers appear on the bridge above the path area. Move back up the slope, turn and fire at their heads to try and make them drop to the ground below. If you can avoid the weapons they throw, there is a very good chance of causing these villagers to drop pesetas or ammunition.

Sparkling in the Dark

Use the handgun to shoot the sparkling objects in the tunnel roof to obtain two **Spinels**. The bats in the cave should prove harmless, but attempting to slash them out of the air with Leon's knife can be a bit of fun.

Mad Bombers

Proceed just past the end of the tunnel to the edge of a fence. Use the handgun to shoot a villager standing directly ahead. Once you have a bead on him, shoot him repeatedly to prevent him from tossing dynamite sticks in Leon's direction. If you can shoot him often enough to prevent him from throwing the live bomb in his hand, he blows himself up!

Another bomb-thrower inside the house can be best dealt with by firing the shotgun at the bomb in his hand. If you fire at the right time, just after the bomb is thrown, the shotgun blast should detonate the bomb right in the thrower's face, killing him.

Move inward until you spot another bomber between the house and the shed on the left. Hit him with shotgun blasts to knock him toward the claymores to his side, if possible. Then shoot the claymores to blow him up.

Circle the house on the south side, avoiding the multiple bear traps set on the ground near the building's corner. Move behind the house and quickly blast another man as he attempts to run past the window into the back room. Shoot the two men in the back room of the bombed-out house, then smash the barrels to obtain items and collect the **Hand Grenade** in the back room.

More Traps in the Shed

The dilapidated shed northeast of the bomber's house is booby-trapped with a bear trap and a tripwire. Be sure to check the shed carefully before entering, just in case the bombs were not already tripped while fighting other enemies in this area.

Up a Tree

Approach the house at the back of the area, and use the C-Stick to angle the camera upward. Shoot the bird's nest in the tree outside the house to cause a **Red Catseye** to fall to the ground. The gem alone is fairly valuable when sold. But, when combined with the Beerstein, the two together become worth much more than when sold individually.

House of Confinement

Pick the padlock on the door repeatedly to break it off, and enter carefully. Collect the **Handgun Ammo** on the table and Pesetas in the cabinet, and then use the nearby typewriter to save if needed. Step into the corridor and look to the right to spot a tripwire strung between the walls. Another tripwire stretches across the next room. Be sure to detonate both bombs from a distance before proceeding.

Introduction
Characters
Enemies
Weapons and Ammunition
Key Items and Treasures
Game System and Strategies
Walkthrough
Secrets and Bonuses

Take the **1000 Pesetas** on the table and the
Green Herb in the cabinet, then push the
bookcase aside to uncover the entrance to
the adjoining room. Examine the armoire
at the back of the room to meet Luis Sera,
and the frightening village chief shortly
thereafter…

CHAPTER 1-2

VALLEY

ITEMS FOUND

Item	Occurrence	Remark
Handgun Ammo	3	
Shotgun Shells	1	
Rifle Ammo	1	
Flash Grenade	1	
Green Herb	1	
Red Herb	1	
Yellow Herb	1	
Pesetas (Box)	1	
Random	6	
Emblem (Right Half)	1	
Emblem (Left Half)	1	

Don't Reload!

Avoid reloading your weapons before
you upgrade them, as they will
automatically be reloaded for you!

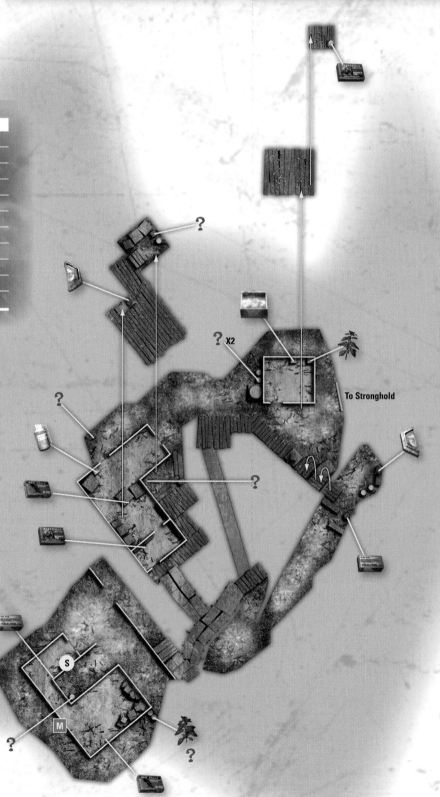

Breaking Confinement

There is no relaxing during scenes. Just as Leon and Luis are getting acquainted, a gruesome executioner staggers into the room with an axe to dispatch them. Be prepared to press a certain combination of buttons the instant they appear onscreen, or the men suffer a gruesome end.

If successful, Leon manages to break free. Collect the **Handgun Ammo** on the shelf and the **Rifle Ammo** next to the typewriter in the hallway. Then exit the building and follow the mysterious figure to the alley behind the building.

Mysterious Merchant

Not everyone in the village is hell-bent on chopping Leon to pieces. Some villagers still value the almighty dollar over mayhem and murder, and these persons gladly offer to sell items, weapons and weapon upgrades in exchange for the pesetas Leon collects throughout his mission. Merchants also buy valuable treasures from Leon, such as Spinels or the Pearl Pendant. Avoid selling combinable treasures such as the Beerstein and the Catseye jewels before combining all the pieces to make the most valuable treasure possible. Refer to the **Key Items and Treasures** chapter before selling incomplete valuables for less money than you could get later.

A complete list of items for sale by the merchant is contained in the **Game System and Strategies** chapter. For now, it is extremely important to purchase the rifle. After that, feel free to purchase the treasure map of the Village and any weapon upgrades you can afford. The Scope for the rifle allows for greater zooming while sniping, giving more accurate aiming at distant targets.

Holster It, Junior!

When a merchant is in the vicinity, take extra care in aiming your shots. Merchants can be shot and killed just like other villagers, except there is no benefit in doing so. Once a merchant is shot, he never reappears in that location for the rest of the game. Essentially you shot yourself in the foot and cannot shop in this location anymore!

Sniper Strike

Quietly smash the barrels around the house to try and garner other items, and then move toward the partially-broken section of wall to the right of the gates. Aim the rifle through the two large gaps in the wall and snipe the

villagers on all levels of the platforms beyond the confinement building. Zoom in on enemies, and zoom out to move the scope sight more quickly. Be sure to hit all enemies in the head, and take out the persons patrolling on the uppermost levels farthest from your position.

Sell Back the Rifle

The rifle is not necessary again until Stage 2 of the game, or Chapter 4. At that point, a better rifle goes on sale anyhow. If you like, sell the rifle back to the merchant behind the confinement building. A small amount of money is lost, but at least you cleared the area!

Blasting Through the Valley

While sniping the villagers positioned on the platforms surrounding the valley, there's a strong possibility that a villager standing near your position might hear the shots and attack. If this occurs, then simply allow the villagers to come through the gate and take them down as they approach. Otherwise, once you assassinate every villager visible beyond the wall, stepping through the gates triggers the appearance of the next set of foes. Many of the initial enemies toss dynamite sticks, so try to detonate the explosives in their hands with the shotgun.

The best tactical position in the valley is the raised middle bridge in the area. While standing on the bridge, one shot with the handgun knocks an enemy over the edge for an instant death.

Be aware that going for the **Emblem (Left Half)** located on the raised ledge to the south triggers the appearance of another enemy group. Use the exploding barrel to decimate their numbers and escape with the Emblem portion by jumping over the side of the cliff.

Rooftop Advantage

The building nearest the exit makes a good standoff position, since you can knock down the ladder and lob hand grenades over the side of the roof to take out crowds below.

Combining the Emblem Portions

Once the coast appears to be clear and the threatening music subsides, approach the building where the Emblem (Right Half) is located. This building is really hard to fight in, and so it is better to wait until all the enemies are drawn out and dispatched. Otherwise, look through a window and toss in a grenade if you spot any enemies. Then climb the ladder in the main room of the building to the roof, and open the red chest to obtain the **Emblem (Right Half)**.

…fter collecting the supplies and ammo in the area, consider returning to the …erchant to make any additional sales or purchases. Open the menu, press …1 to switch to the Keys and Treasures menu and combine the two halves of …e Emblem. Move to the northeastern exit and use the Emblem to unlock …e doors.

…e Yellow Herb

…en the lockers in the building near …e exit to find a Yellow Herb. Alone …is item has no use, but when combined …th a Green Herb or a Mixed Herb …mpound, the substance raises Leon's …aximum amount of health!

STRONGHOLD

To Valley

To Village Chief's House

ITEMS FOUND

Item	Occurrence	Remark
Handgun Ammo	3	
Flash Grenade	1	
Green Herb	1	
Pesetas (Box)	1	
Random	7	
Spinel	1	Oven
Elegant Mask	1	Enclosed Area

Too Quiet...

Search the outdoor areas for items, then proceed through the double doors and the next door. After gaining the attention of the villagers in the twisting corridor, allow them to come through the doorway single file to make them easier to pick off.

Battle Lines

Continue through the winding corridors until you reach a dead-end with two windows. Leap through the window on the left, which should cause Leon to roll to a position behind a metal dumpster directly across from a fortified enemy line with dynamite-tossing enemies. Press ✕ to crouch behind the dumpster to avoid bomb blasts, then raise up to shoot at foes.

When enemies stop entering the room, search the ground for bear traps and shoot them with the handgun to set them off. Open the oven doors to find **Handgun Ammo** and a **Spinel**. Smash the barrels in the back corner to find additional items. Watch out for the bear traps set behind the enemy sandbag pile as you make your way to the door.

Chamber of the Mask

Inside the room where water puddles, use the knife to slash away the boards covering the window. Jump through the opening to an enclosed room and take the **Elegant Mask** from the wall. The Mask can be combined with three jewels found elsewhere in the stage to increase its overall value.

Rudimentary Fishing

ck open the door at the back of the watery room, descend the slope and shoot the enemy on the lower level. This should d the crisis situation in the area. Drop over the side of the platform into the water below to find **Handgun Ammo**, a **Flash enade** and **1000 Pesetas**. Additionally, the ack Bass and **Black Bass (L)** swimming in the ater can be shot and collected to restore great nounts of health. While the larger fish is easy net with the handgun, the smaller fish under e wavy water surface are easier to hunt with e shotgun or a well-placed hand grenade.

VILLAGE CHIEF'S HOUSE

EMS FOUND

Item	Occurrence	Remark
Handgun Ammo	5	
TMP Bullets	1	Bird Nest
Incendiary Grenade	1	
Green Herb	1	
Red Herb	1	
Pesetas (Box)	2	
Random	1	
Insignia Key	1	
Spinel	1	Bird Nest
Ruby	1	Chainsaw Man
Brass Pocket Watch	1	Hung over Well

Chief's Note

To Pueblo

(nest)

(nest)

(Chainsaw)

To Stronghold

(Crow)

S

aps and Trinkets

ree crows peck at food on the path ahead. Slip to a sition behind the well opening and snipe the closest d with the handgun. The other two are positioned knowingly under a tripwire bomb, so shoot the vice to blow them both up simultaneously. When proaching to claim the rewards dropped by the ws, watch out for the bear traps on the path.

Introduction

Characters

Enemies

Weapons and Ammunition

Key Items and Treasures

Game System and Strategies

Walkthrough

Secrets and Bonuses

Nearby is another smelly open well with a piece of jewelry dangling above it. Shoot the rod to drop the well cover, then shoot the hanging piece to obtain the **Brass Pocket Watch**. Check for possible items inside the shack, and then make your way carefully up the path to the double-story house.

House of the Big Cheese

Ascend the back stairs into the house and examine the door. Move the green insignia up and then left to open the door.

Search the bedroom and take the **Note from the Chief** message from the bed. Open the armoire to obtain **1000 Pesetas**, and open the desk drawer to collect **Handgun Ammo**. The box on the nearby dresser contains the **Insignia Key**. Open the door to the corridor to experience another nasty run in with the chief.

CHAPTER 1-3

VILLAGE CHIEF'S HOUSE

ITEMS FOUND

Item	Occurrence	Remark
Handgun Ammo	5	
TMP Ammo	1	Bird Nest
Incendiary Grenade	1	
Brown Chicken Egg	1	Oven
Green Herb	1	
Red Herb	1	
Insignia Key	1	
Pesetas (Box)	2	
Random	1	
Spinel	1	Bird Nest
Ruby	1	Chainsaw Man
Brass Pocket Watch	1	Hung over Well

Chief's Note

To Pue

(nest)

(nest)

To Stronghold

(Crow)

S

(Chainsaw)

Quick Replay

If you reenter the chief's bedroom, an additional scene plays. A mysterious woman saves Leon from another serious pounding by the village chief. Afterwards, examine the windowsill and then go back through the bedroom door again. Open the cabinet at the south end of the hallway to obtain a **Green Herb**.

The Chief's Supplies

Head downstairs and check the portraits for revealing clues. Use the typewriter if desired, and smash the glass cabinet in the back room to obtain an **Incendiary Grenade**. **1000 Pesetas** wait in the nearby hutch. Open the oven door in the kitchen near the front of the house to obtain a **Brown Chicken Egg**.

Occupado!

Avoid entering the bathroom on the lower level under the stairs, because a villager who had to use the facilities won't be pleased by your interruption.

No One Here Gets Out Alive

Exiting the house draws the attention of a small group of villagers, including a chainsaw-swinging psycho. Lead this tough enemy back inside the house along with the others, into the narrow confines of the stairs and the second floor corridor, so that

you may blast the foes without getting surrounded. The chainsaw man drops a valuable **Ruby** upon dying.

Returning to the Pueblo

Fight the villagers along the path leading back to the Pueblo. There are two bird nests in the trees along the path. Shoot them both to obtain a **Spinel** and **TMP Ammo**. Check in the cabin for an item, and unbar the door at the end to reenter the Pueblo.

The Pueblo has no new items, so make your way through as quickly as possible to conserve ammo and recovery items. If you prefer to make a stand instead, move into the house to the left of the entrance and blast groups of enemies as they enter. Otherwise head straight for the door marked with the insignia on the building on the east side of the Pueblo. Unlock the door with the Insignia Key and enter.

You unlocked it.

TUNNEL

ITEMS FOUND

Item	Occurrence	Remark
Handgun Ammo	1	
TMP Bullets	1	
Random	2	
Spinel	3	Lamp, Cave Ceiling
Elegant Headdress	1	Cave Ceiling

The Hatch in the Back Room

Collect the **Handgun Ammo** on the sideboard and use the typewriter to save the game if desired. Smash the barrel in the back room to obtain **TMP Ammo** and shoot the lamp overhead to obtain a **Spinel** that drops to the floor. Be advised that the lamp explodes into flames when shot, so be sure to stand back.

The Merchant's Tunnel

Open the floor hatch and drop into the tunnel below. Shoot the lamp hanging over the watery pool to darken the area, revealing two more **Spinels** and the **Elegant Headdress**, a very valuable piece. Continue into the next cave to encounter another merchant. Purchasing the TMP machinegun pistol might be a good idea, since new tune-ups are already available for it.

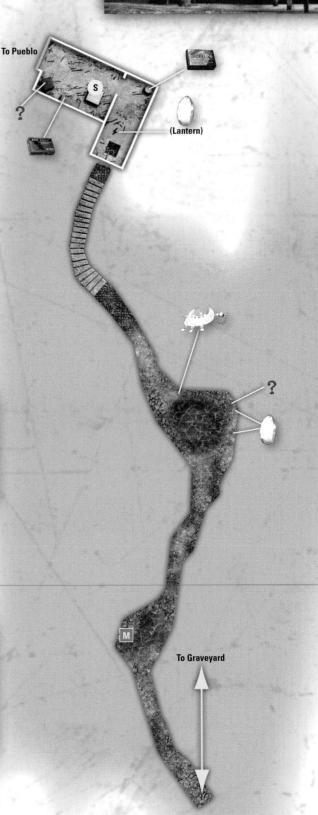

To Pueblo

(Lantern)

?

?

M

To Graveyard

GRAVEYARD

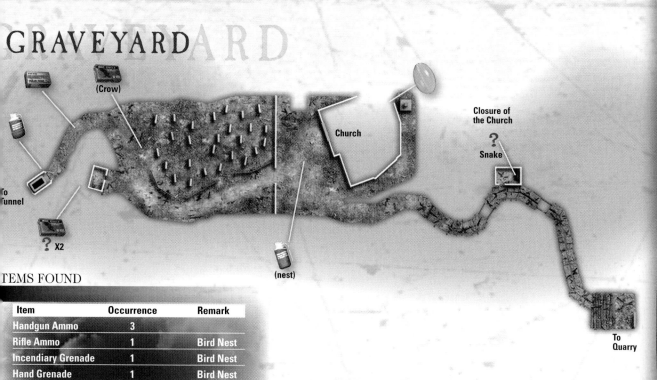

(Crow)

To Tunnel

?X2

Church

Closure of the Church

?

Snake

To Quarry

TEMS FOUND

Item	Occurrence	Remark
Handgun Ammo	3	
Rifle Ammo	1	Bird Nest
Incendiary Grenade	1	Bird Nest
Hand Grenade	1	Bird Nest
Random	3	
Green Catseye	1	Puzzle

(nest)

What a Crow Garners

ook for two bird nests in the trees along the path leading into the cemetery, and shoot them to obtain **Rifle Ammo** and a **and Grenade**. Three crows are perched on tombstones on the edge of the cemetery, and they too can be shot to obtain oney and items. To take them out quietly, shoot them from a few steps back down the path. Use the Handgun and be darn uick about it. If you drive one r more of the birds to flight by cident, you can always reset em at their ground positions by aving and reentering the area.

he Headstone Caretakers

epping through the wooden doorframe or shooting a weapon near the east end of the path leading into the graveyard draws e attention of a woman villager standing nearby. Take out the two villagers that hang out in the east part of the cemetery, then search the shack in the corner of the area to obtain **Handgun Ammo** and other randomly-determined items.

Introduction
Characters
Enemies
Weapons and Ammunition
Key Items and Treasures
Game System and Strategies
Walkthrough
Secrets and Bonuses

Proceed up the road to the side of the gravestones until spotted by the trio hanging out in front of the church. Use the handgun to shoot the two that run ahead until the one that throws dynamite catches up. Then use the shotgun to shoot the dynamite in his hand, and blow up all three at once.

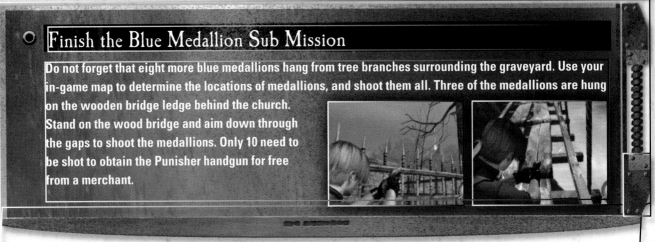

Finish the Blue Medallion Sub Mission

Do not forget that eight more blue medallions hang from tree branches surrounding the graveyard. Use your in-game map to determine the locations of medallions, and shoot them all. Three of the medallions are hung on the wooden bridge ledge behind the church. Stand on the wood bridge and aim down through the gaps to shoot the medallions. Only 10 need to be shot to obtain the Punisher handgun for free from a merchant.

Symbols on the Dial

Check the three double-grave tombstones in the cemetery, marking the burial places of twins. Each monument bears a unique symbol. Keep these three symbols in mind, and move along the east alley behind the church. Take down the villagers guarding the back area by shooting the one who tosses dynamite, and examine the raised pedestal.

The **Green Catseye** is locked within the pedestal. To unlock it, rotate the dial and cause three of the symbols to glow. The three symbols resemble the symbols of the twins' tombstones in the cemetery. However, the dial can only be rotated three or four spaces, making it difficult to activate the three twins' symbols without activating other symbols on the dial. There is no one way to solve this puzzle. You can keep turning the dial until only the three symbols are lit. One sure method to describe how to light the correct three symbols is detailed below:

Turn the dial repeatedly in three space increments until every symbol on the face is lit.

Then turn the dial in four space increments until only two of the twins symbols are lit.

Now turn the dial three spaces to light the final twins' symbol. The pedestal should unlock and let you take the stone.

The Green Catseye is the second gem that fits into the Beerstein, increasing the value of the whole. Just one more gem to go before Stage One is finished, and then the Beerstein can be sold for mucho pesetas!

Two Transmissions

Attempting to open the front doors of the church triggers a radio chat between Leon and Hannigan, but heading past the church and down the southeast path triggers an even funnier conversation. Be sure to head southeast before checking the church doors to see both communications.

Leon, did I mention not to take the scenic route?

Nest Blaster!

Shoot a bird nest in the tree to the right of the church entrance to obtain an Incendiary Grenade.

Around the Wooden Ledge

With no means of ingress into the church, follow the southeast path to a wooden ledge that continues into the next area. Villager enemies can be shot and kicked off the edge to die in the waters below, but this reduces the chances of obtaining items from them.

One of the crates in the shack standing on the wooden ledge contains a snake, which leaps out and attacks Leon if he is too close. Hereafter, it's safer to start shooting barrels and crates from a distance with a handgun than to use the knife to break them. Snakes drop the various types of Chicken Eggs upon death, so be sure to shoot them.

Read the **Closure of the Church** document on the table to determine how to get inside the parish. Then continue along the wooden suspension ledge to the next area.

QUARRY

ITEMS FOUND

Item	Occurrence	Remark
Handgun Ammo	2	
Flash Grenade	1	Crow
Random	3	
Spinel	2	

To Swamp

To Graveyard

?

To Waterway

Blast the Flock

Walk through the doorframe into the wider area to spy a flock of crows feeding in the quarry. Toss a hand grenade or fire a shotgun blast to take out many at once and rake in the pesetas and items. If any birds escape, leave the area and return to reset them to their initial positions. Then you can pick off more and claim more rewards.

Shiny Ores

Search the small shacks to **Handgun Ammo** and other items. A **Spinel** lies on the cart parked near the northwest wall, and another can be found inside one of the buildings. The roaring from behind the massive double doors cannot foretell of anything good.

Before continuing east, be sure to visit the merchant behind the blue doors down the stairs to the south of the exit.

WATERWAY

To Quarry

ITEMS FOUND

Item	Occurrence	Remark
Handgun Ammo	2	
Random	1	

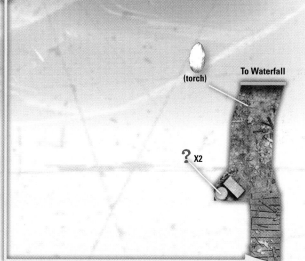

(torch)

To Waterfall

? X2

The Merchant's Dock

Walk forward and drop into the lower room. Take the **Handgun Ammo** from the corner, then continue inward and look for the barrel on the right. Smash the barrel to obtain an item, and then continue eastward to find the merchant shop. In the small area behind the shop is a barrel that can be smashed to obtain more **Handgun Ammo**.

⊙ Earning a Weapon

If you eliminated more than 10 blue medallions by this point, the merchant offers the Punisher handgun for free. While weaker than Leon's normal weapon, it fires bullets through multiple targets at once and its Firepower can be upgraded sufficiently in a single tune-up. Trading in Leon's default weapon isn't a bad idea at all. If you're not interested in the Punisher, then at least take it from the merchant and sell it right back to him at a profit!

SWAMP

To Lake

To Quarry

Snake

Snake

?

(nest)

ITEMS FOUND

Item	Occurrence	Remark
Handgun Ammo	2	
Shotgun Shells	1	
TMP Ammo	1	
Incendiary Grenade	1	
Hand Grenade	1	
Random	3	
Spinel	1	Boulder Landing Zone
Antique Pipe	1	Bird Nest

Outrun Another Boulder

Collect the items possible in the cabin on the right, and then continue down the path past the warning sign. Villagers send another boulder rolling after Leon. As before, tap the correct button rapidly to sprint down the hill, and then press the button combination displayed onscreen to dodge out of the boulder's path. Having successfully dodged the boulder, turn around and aim high on the cliff side to spot a **Spinel**, and shoot it loose.

Take Them Out with Tripwires

Proceed east until you spot the start of a wooden platform built over a small swamp and the enemy positioned before a tripwire a dozen yards away. Shoot the tripwire to blow up the enemy. There are also enemies standing near tripwires down in the muck to the left and the right, about twenty yards away.

Triggering Villager Appearances

Moving to the back of the first dock or into the cabin on the right causes a set of enemies to enter the area from the west. Head back down the platform to meet the oncoming group. Shots may cause enemies near the edge of the platform to fall in the water, and you should also try to kick as many enemies as possible over the side yourself. This way, you have only a few enemies on the platform to deal with at a time.

When the first group is dealt with, move back toward the cabin or the east end of the platform to trigger the appearance of the next group. Don't forget to hop down in the water at some point and head back toward the west edge of the swamp area to find a **Hand Grenade** carelessly discarded on the embankment.

Water Moccasins

When the waves of assault from the east are dealt with, enter the cabin and shoot the crates and barrels to obtain items. One of the crates on the shelf contains a snake, so use caution and shoot twice to kill the creature before it causes damage. A few other water snakes swim in the swamp, and these too can be shot to obtain various types of Chicken Eggs.

Swamp Treasure

Drop from the west platform and continue through the murky waters to the east platform. More enemies should spot you as you make your way around to the stairs on the north side. Deal with them in the most efficient manner possible, and then ascend onto the second platform. An **Incendiary Grenade** rests on the bench. Shoot the bird nest out of the nearby tree and then go fishing to find a valuable **Antique Pipe**.

Getting Out of the Swamp

Head east along the second platform until you reach a tripwire bomb. Standing near the bomb, aim for the villager standing by shack a dozen feet away and shoot him to get his attention as well as that of another man inside the building. Back away as the two approach, allowing them to walk directly into the tripwire.

Collect the **Handgun Ammo** in the cabin.

The crate beside the bullets contains a snake, so waste bullets to break it open. Continue toward the exit. If you haven't seen too many snakes in the water, it is because they are clustered near the exit. Shoot them to obtain Chicken Eggs if you are low on recovery items before proceeding.

LAKE

ITEMS FOUND

Item	Occurrence	Remark
Handgun Ammo	1	
Green Herb	1	
Red Herb	1	
Yellow Herb	1	
Random	1	
Gold Bangle w/Pearls	1	Bird Nest

Feeding Time

Ascend the slope, ignoring the path on the right. Continue to the top of the rise until Leon spots two villagers feeding a little live bait to the local mutant marine life. After the scene, turn from the overlooking ledge and search the grass below the tree on the right to find a **Red Herb**.

Board the Boat

Head back down the slope and take the path south. Shoot a bird nest in the first tree on the left to obtain a **Gold Bangle with Pearls**. Check in the first cabin on the right to obtain **Handgun Ammo** and a **Yellow Herb**. Continue to the bottom of the path and check the cabin near the dock to find a **Green Herb** and a much-needed typewriter. Save your game, then go out to the boat dock and board the motorboat. Drive the boat southeast to trigger your first encounter with a horrific boss monster.

MOTORBOAT CONTROLS

Control	Action
Right Analog Stick or D-Pad Up	Accelerate Forward
Right Analog Stick or D-Pad Down	Reverse
Right Analog Stick or D-Pad Left	Turn Left
Right Analog Stick or D-Pad Right	Turn Right
R1 Button	Ready Harpoon
⊗ Button	Throw Harpoon/Embark or Disembark

Tasty Treat

Throw a handful of spears off of the dock before you board to get a not-so-pleasant surprise.

EL LAGO

The motorboat's anchor gets caught within the fins of a giant monster the locals refer to as "the lake-dweller." El Lago drags Leon's boat across the surface of the water toward floating tree trunks and branches. If the motorboat strikes the debris floating in the water, the craft capsizes and Leon is thrown overboard. To get back to the boat, press ⊗ rapidly to swim. At the start of the encounter, Leon should be close enough to the boat that he can get back with no problem. But as El Lago takes more damage, the distance Leon must swim to get back in the boat increases. Therefore, as you inflict more damage to El Lago, be conscious of where it may be dragging the motorboat in the lake. Always steer clear of debris and El Lago itself rather than take a chance. If El Lago catches Leon out of the boat just once, he swallows the incompetent agent whole.

After steering the boat around a few tree trunks, hold R1 to raise the harpoon and toss it into El Lago's back. Keep tossing harpoons until the monster dives under the water. When the monster dives under the water, it then attempts to swim up under the boat and capsize it. Steer the boat left or right, away from the point where El Lago submerged. This should allow you to avoid being capsized more than necessary.

Sometimes El Lago dives under the water and stops dragging the boat. During instances where everything gets quiet suddenly, pick up a harpoon and turn the boat left or right until you spot El Lago approaching. Pay attention to red arrows that appear onscreen to show you El Lago's position and turn the boat to face it. As El Lago swims across the surface with its jaws open, fling enough harpoons into its mouth to make it submerge rather than capsize the boat.

Repeat the above strategy as necessary until El Lago decides to flee. Unfortunately, the anchor rope wraps around Leon's leg. During the escape scene, rapidly press the displayed button, usually ⊗, to make Leon cut himself loose.

chapter two

At night, the villagers sometimes show their true form when their heads are blown off. Avoid trying for too many head shots, or Las Plagas start making the game a real nightmare.

Torches now light most areas in the village. If a torch is shot enough times or damaged, it goes out. Areas can become almost too dark to navigate if too many torches are destroyed, so avoid damaging or shooting light sources if possible.

CHAPTER 2-1

LAKE

ITEMS FOUND

Item	Occurrence	Remark
Handgun Ammo	2	
Flash Grenade	1	
Pesetas (Box)	1	Colmillos
Random	3	

Leon Awakens

Collect the items in the lakeside cabin, including the **Anonymous Letter** file on the bed. Exit the cabin, board the motorboat and pilot the craft toward the blue torches across the lake. A merchant runs a shop inside the Lake Cave, and there are several items to obtain around his stand. Details in the following section describe their locations.

Option to Explore

Do not head back toward the church without an essential key item located at the waterfalls south of the lake. However, if you choose to pilot the boat back to the northwest shore, new items can be obtained in the cabin by the dock.

Proceeding up the path, Leon encounters Colmillos, or dogs with parasitic tentacles. The best way to deal with multiple Colmillos is with and grenades or incendiary grenades. Two appear in front of Leon, and two appear behind.

Night Fishing

Use the harpoon to spear fish that are swimming just off the southeast shoreline near the cabin where Leon wakes up. When their bodies float in the lake and a green light is showing, pilot the boat over them to collect large or regular Black Bass. Shooting them from the dock or shore may be easier. Then you can just hop in the boat and collect their floating bodies.

LAKE CAVE

ITEMS FOUND

Item	Occurrence	Remark
Handgun Ammo	1	
Rifle Ammo	1	
Pesetas (Box)	1	
Random	5	
Spinel	1	Torch
Green Gem	1	

Multiple Items Around the Shop

Move to the right and shoot the barrels. The containers might hold random items, but one definitely contains a snake. Shoot the blazing torch hanging above the east platform to obtain a Spinel.

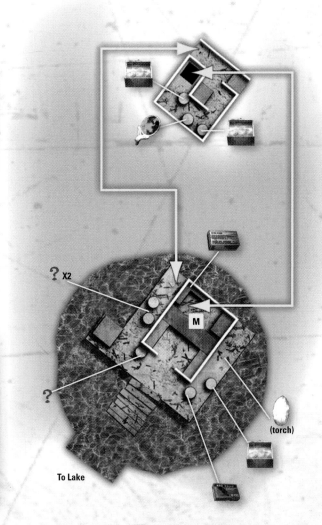

? X2

M

?

(torch)

To Lake

Move to the left of the shop and push the cargo out of the way. Shoot the barrels to clear the path and obtain items. Another one of these barrels contains a snake, so shoot from a distance. Behind the shop, climb the ladder up to the rooftop.

Push the cargo out of the way and shoot the barrels. The second barrel contains the **Green Gem** that combines with the Mask for greater value. Drop through the hole in the roof into the merchant's shop to find **Rifle Ammo**. Speak to the merchant from inside the shop if desired. The merchant offers new tune-ups for the Handgun, Shotgun and Rifle.

SWAMP

ITEMS FOUND

Item	Occurrence	Remark
Handgun Ammo	1	
TMP Ammo	1	
Random	3	

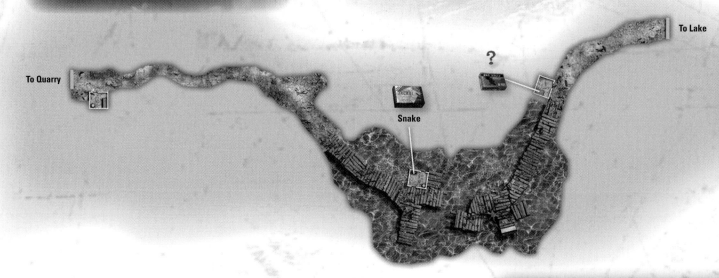

Little Happening at the Swamp

A few enemies are positioned in the actual swamp area, but not many. The majority of foes wait at the top of the slope near the entrance to the quarry. Break the containers inside the cabins surrounding the swamp to obtain ammo and randomly determined items.

WATERFALL

Introduction

Characters

Enemies

Weapons and
Ammunition

Key Items
and Treasures

Game System
and Strategies

Walkthrough

Secrets and
Bonuses

Chapter 1-1

Chapter 1-2

Chapter 1-3

Chapter 2-1

Chapter 2-2

Chapter 2-3

Chapter 3-1

Chapter 3-2

Chapter 3-3

Chapter 3-4

Chapter 4-1

Chapter 4-2

Chapter 4-3

Chapter 4-4

Chapter 5-1

Chapter 5-2

Chapter 5-3

Chapter 5-4

Final Chapter

ITEMS FOUND

Item	Occurrence	Remark
Handgun Ammo	1	
Hand Grenade	1	
Green Herb	1	
Gold Bars	1	Las Plagas
Random	2	
Spinel	1	Cliff Wall
Amber Ring	1	Scaffold

To Lake

Gold Bars
(Plaga Ganado)

(cliff)

To Waterway

Witness the Emerging of Las Plagas

Entering the area, Leon witnesses a villager who reveals Las Plagas.
When a parasite emerges from a villager's head, damage to other parts
of the body is reduced to 1/3 of normal. The best way to damage Las
Plagas is by shooting the emerging parasite. Using a Flash Grenade
kills emerging parasites immediately. If you're out of grenades, use the
shotgun to kill them more efficiently. Avoid trying to inflict too many
head shots to villagers so that Las Plagas do not emerge too often.

Kill the villager
who transforms
during the scene
to obtain **Gold
Bars** worth 5000
pesetas.

Crossing the Flow

Jump across the dam platforms and follow the south bank all the way to the end. Break the barrel to obtain a **Hand Grenade**. Backtrack a few steps and hop across the running water to the north bank.

Climb down the rope and kill the villager standing on the platform. Climb onto his platform to obtain **Handgun Ammo** and shoot the barrel for another item. Shoot the glittering object in the cliff wall to the right of the rope to obtain a **Spinel**.

Creating a Makeshift Bridge

Move to the east end of the bank and shoot the chain suspending the cargo box. With the box floating in the water, Leon can now jump to the center platform.

Move up the central platform to see a cave behind the waterfall. Somehow the water flow must be stopped in order to pass through. Shoot the glittering object off the beam above the falls to obtain the **Amber Ring**. Climb the platform and shoot the barrel to obtain a **Green Herb**. While on the platform, shoot the chains holding the two boxes rotating on posts nearby to drop them into the water. Now the south bank can be reached by hopping across the boxes.

Diverting the Water

On the south bank, shoot the barrel under the mechanism platform to obtain an item. Climb the ladder and pull the lever to stop the water flow. Hop across the boxes to the center to trigger the appearance of villagers. Jump back across the boxes to the south bank and shoot them as they try to hop across in pursuit. One shot, and enemies fall into the water and die. It's too easy!

Move up the center platform into the cave under the waterfall. Take the **Round Insignia** from the wall to reveal a secret passage. Follow this passage to a dock.

WATERWAY

ITEMS FOUND

Item	Occurrence	Remark
Random	2	
Spinel	1	Torch

Convenient Transport

Shoot the torch next to the entrance to obtain **Spinel**, and destroy the barrels next to the boat dock to obtain some randomly determined items. Board the boat for a free ride to the merchant's dock.

QUARRY

ITEMS FOUND

Item	Occurrence	Remark
Handgun Ammo	2	
Shotgun Shells	1	
TMP Ammo	1	
Green Herb	2	
Red Herb	1	
Yellow Herb	1	
Pesetas (Box)	2	
Gold Bars	1	El Gigante
Random	2	
Spinel	2	

Quarry Horror

Smash the barrels near the west entrance to find a **Green Herb** and **Pesetas**. Proceed into the large area to witness the brutal entrance of the monster called "El Gigante."

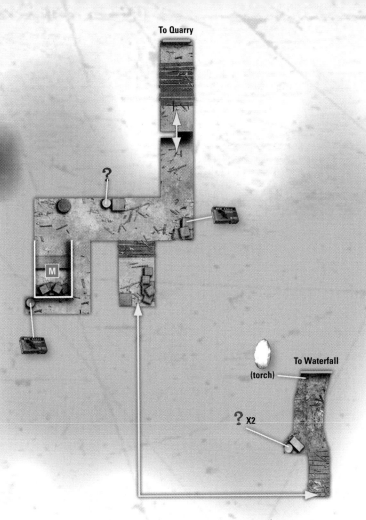

To Quarry

?

M

To Waterfall

(torch)

? X2

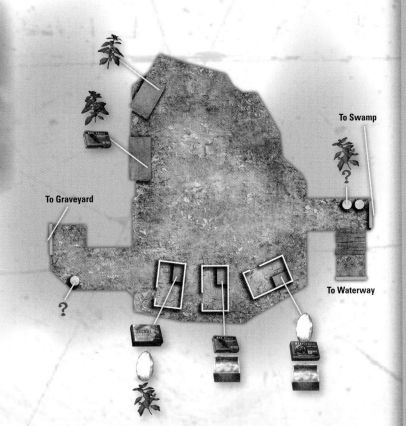

To Swamp

To Graveyard

?

To Waterway

EL GIGANTE

If you saved the wolf in the first area of the game, the faithful friend reappears and barks to distract the monster. Sometimes this works, sometimes not. While El Gigante is going after the wolf, shoot it from the side or behind.

Try to keep the monster from destroying the

shacks in the south part of the area, so that you can enter them safely and obtain items after the battle. If you try to go into the shacks during the battle, El Gigante smashes them, and could cause serious damage to Leon. If the dog leads El Gigante toward a shack and he smashes it before you collect the items, consider opening the Options menu and choosing the "retry" selection.

Use a Flash Grenade to stun El Gigante, then shoot it rapidly with the handgun or TMP. If you're out of Flash Grenades, back away from El Gigante's massive feet as it advances. When it stops to attack, back a few more steps out of harm's way and then shoot the monster as rapidly as possible.

When a certain amount of damage is done to the monster's "outer shell," the creature doubles over in pain and its parasite emerges. Run up to El Gigante and press ✕ to climb onto its back. Rapidly tap the ✕ or ◉ button, whichever is displayed, to slash at the parasite before hoping down. After performing this attack three or four times, El Gigante should go down for the count. The monster drops **Gold Bars** equal to 15,000 pesetas.

Watch out when El Gigante lowers his shoulder and charges, rolls a boulder toward Leon, or rips a tree out of the ground and swings it. Press the dodge buttons displayed onscreen to avoid these attacks. If El Gigante sweeps Leon up in its massive fist, rotate the Left Analog Stick rapidly to get free. To get out of this deathgrip and sustain as little damage as possible, place your palm on the control and rotate it as fast as possible.

GRAVEYARD

(nest)

To
Tunnel

?

Church

? X2

(colmillos)

To Quarry

ITEMS FOUND

Item	Occurrence	Remark
Handgun Ammo	5	
Rifle Ammo	1	Colmillos
Random	3	
Spinel	1	Bird Nest

Guard Dogs at the Gates

Proceed along the wooden ledge, collecting new ammo and other
items from the shack on the side. Proceed up the path and use
grenades to take out the Comillos on guard duty at the end of the
fence. One of the mutts drops **Rifle Ammo**.

Unlocking the Church

Take a moment to gather items from the rest of the cemetery, such as
the Handgun Ammo in the shack at the southwest end of the graveyard.
Shoot the bird nests on the path leading to the tunnel to drop a **Spinel**
and **Handgun Ammo**. When finished procrastinating, use the Round
Insignia to unlock the front doors of the church and enter.

CHURCH

CHURCH

ITEMS FOUND

Item	Occurrence	Remark
Handgun Ammo	4	
Flash Grenade	1	
Incendiary Grenade	1	
Green Herb	1	
Pesetas (Box)	3	
Random	6	

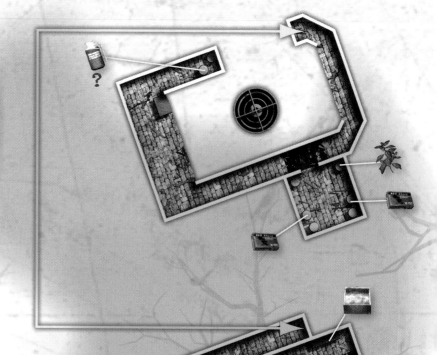

To Graveyard

Wealth of the Parish

Approach the dais and check the altar. On the shelf to the left is a box of **3000 Pesetas**. Narrow passages run along the outside walls of the church. Smash the barrel in the narrow south passage to obtain a **Flash Grenade**. Climb the ladder in the north passage to the balcony above.

Chandelier Swinging

Stand at the center of the upper balcony and jump onto the chandelier. When the fixture swings toward the southwest wall, jump off to the other side. Move around the north side of the upper balcony and smash two barrels to find a random amount of pesetas and an **Incendiary Grenade**.

Introduction

Characters

Enemies

Weapons and
Ammunition

Key Items
and Treasures

Game System
and Strategies

Walkthrough

Secrets and
Bonuses

Uniting the Colors

Examine the panel with three colored lights located on the balcony. The three colored patterns must be adjusted to form the pattern in the center insignia. Rotate the red lens twice, the green lens three times, and the blue lens once. Then choose the "combine" option to mix the colors and form the central insignia. The bars surrounding Ashley Graham's holding cell rise.

Extricating the Subject

Enter the balcony room to meet Ashley, the President's daughter and subject of Leon's search. Hannigan sends Leon **Playing Manual 3** to show him how to lead Ashley to safety and work together.

Shoot the barrels around the room to obtain ammo, money and a **Green Herb,** then exit. Lead Ashley to the ladder on the north side of the balcony and jump down. Stand at the base of the ladder and press ❌ to catch her. Then lead her toward the exit. Unfortunately, Leon and Ashley encounter cult leader Osmund Saddler, and are forced to take a slight detour.

CHAPTER 2-2

CHURCH

Church Sideyard

Shoot the barrel around the area to obtain pesetas and other items. Open the door and exit to the graveyard.

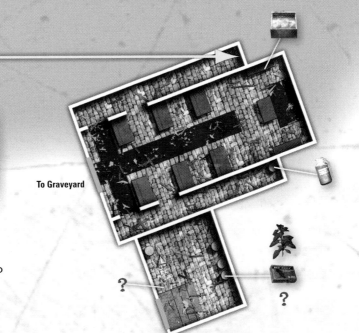

To Graveyard

ITEMS FOUND

Item	Occurrence	Remark
Handgun Ammo	1	
Red Herb	1	
Pesetas (Box)	1	
Random	1	

Pervert!

Ashley won't appreciate it if you angle the camera to look up her dress—and she'll tell you so. Creep.

GRAVEYARD

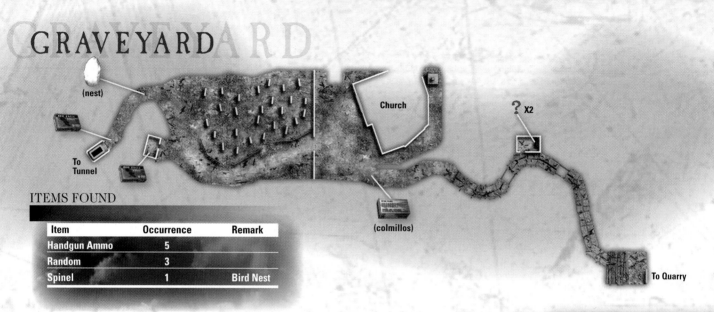

(nest)

To Tunnel

Church

? X2

(colmillos)

To Quarry

ITEMS FOUND

Item	Occurrence	Remark
Handgun Ammo	5	
Random	3	
Spinel	1	Bird Nest

Burn the Wagon

Proceed through the gates until Ashley points out the barrels on the wagon. Shoot the barrels to set them aflame and make the cart roll downhill, exploding on impact and wiping out the crowd of villagers below. At least two boxes of **Handgun Ammo** are dropped in the carnage. Rolling the burning cart should leave just one or two additional villagers standing, so take care of them.

TUNNEL

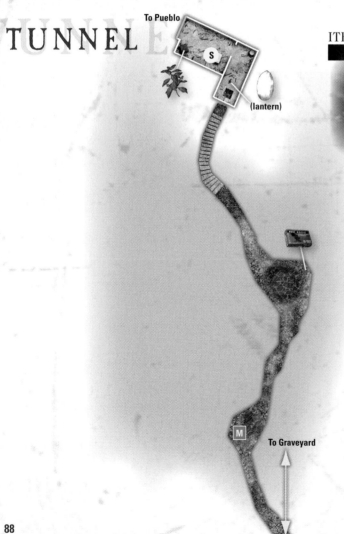

To Pueblo

S

(lantern)

M

To Graveyard

ITEMS FOUND

Item	Occurrence	Remark
Handgun Ammo	1	
Random	2	
Spinel	1	

Merchant Update

The merchant now sells the Red9 and a stock that helps keep this powerful firearm steady between shots. New tune-ups are available for the TMP, the Punisher and the Red9. Before purchasing the Red9, consider that it is 2x8, taking up the most room in Leon's case. While the weapon is powerful, the foreign old-style magazine takes forever to reload.

ETURNING TO EL PUEBLO

ad past the merchant and shoot the crate in the hollow to reveal **Handgun mo**. Climb the ladder into the house. Make sure Ashley's out of harm's y, and then shoot the lantern over the trapdoor again to obtain yet another inel.

UEBLO

EMS FOUND

Item	Occurrence	Remark
Handgun Ammo	2	
Rifle Ammo	1	
TMP Ammo	1	
Pesetas (Box)	2	
Random	9	
Spinel	1	

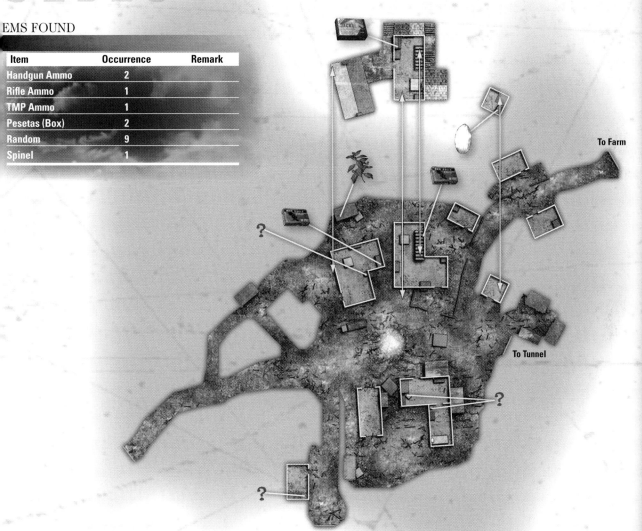

To Farm

To Tunnel

eturn to Scary Town

hile there are extremely few enemies now dwelling in the Pueblo compared previous encounters here, there is a high chance that an enemy's parasite ight emerge if shot. Try to reduce the chances of fighting too many Las agas by aiming for the waist or other parts.

The barricade options are available once again in the two-story building as well as the reinforced one-story to the south. Use the buildings to help protect Ashley and narrow the enemies' path of advance.

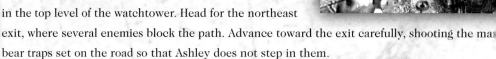

Collect all the new items in the Pueblo, including a **Spinel** in the top level of the watchtower. Head for the northeast exit, where several enemies block the path. Advance toward the exit carefully, shooting the ma[...] bear traps set on the road so that Ashley does not step in them.

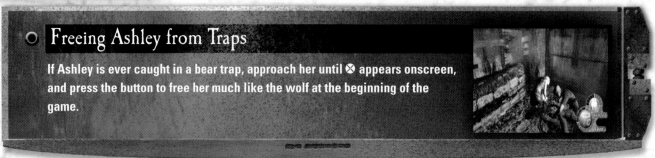

○ Freeing Ashley from Traps

If Ashley is ever caught in a bear trap, approach her until ⊗ appears onscreen, and press the button to free her much like the wolf at the beginning of the game.

FARM

ITEMS FOUND

Item	Occurrence	Remark
Handgun Ammo	2	
Green Herb	1	
Pesetas (Box)	3	
Random	6	

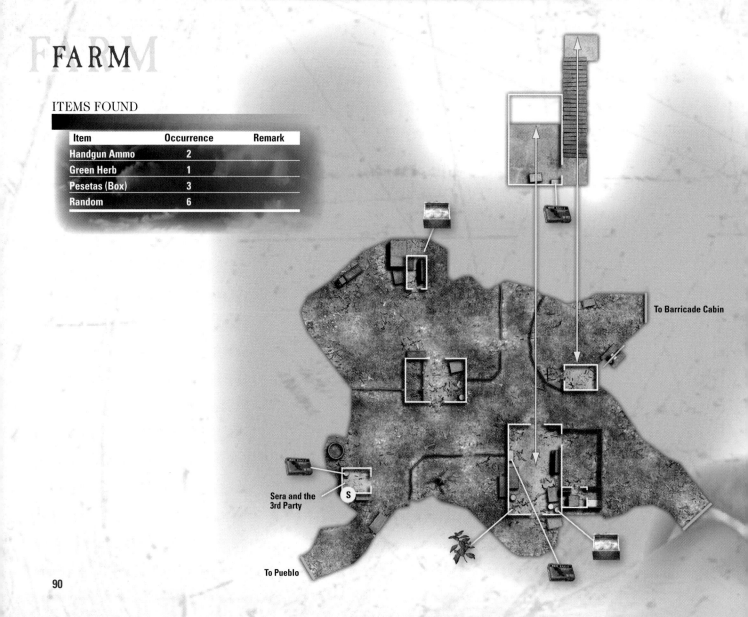

To Barricade Cabin

Sera and the
3rd Party

S

To Pueblo

Clearing the Farm for Ashley

Move up the path to the open red container and press **R2** to make Ashley hide inside. Whenever you want her to exit her hiding spot and continue following Leon, press **R2** to whistle for her. Kill the enemies in the area and spring all the traps before calling for Ashley, so that her health is not in jeopardy.

Inside the small shed where the typewriter is located is a file titled **Luis Sera and the 3rd Party**. Collect the new items at the farm and use the loft in the barn as a strategic point to defeat multiple enemies as they gather below. Just be wary of new enemies positioned in the northeast area, who will climb the ladder by the attached shack and enter the upper level of the barn from the open window in the loft.

Time for a Piggyback Ride

Jump through the southeast window in the upper level of the barn, and cross north to the roof of shed. Shoot the villagers and bear traps positioned near the tall double doors. Drop down and break the crate and barrel inside the shed to try to obtain items.

Call for Ashley to come out of hiding and join you. Approach the northeast gate and perform a "piggyback" to lift Ashley over the barrier. She unlocks the gate from the other side.

BARRICADE CABIN

ITEMS FOUND

Item	Occurrence	Remark
Shotgun Shells	1	
Flash Grenade	1	
Incendiary Grenade	1	
Hand Grenade	1	
Green Herb	1	
Red Herb	1	
Yellow Herb	1	

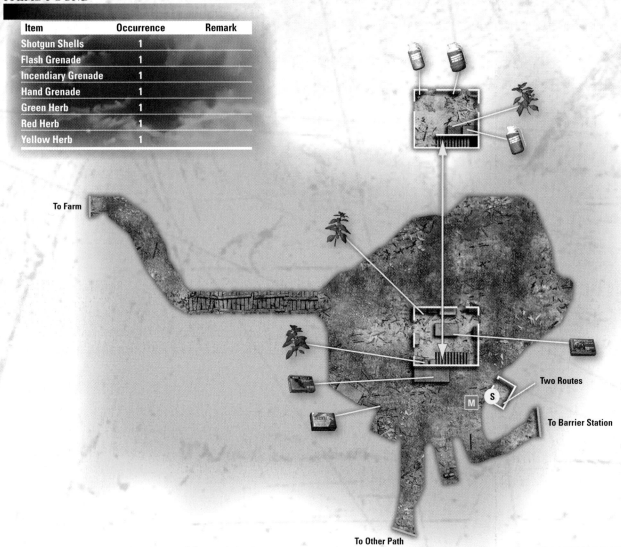

To Farm

Two Routes

M S

To Barrier Station

To Other Path

Prepare for Assault!

Visit the merchant on the path and tune up weapons as much as possible before proceeding. Move along the bridge until Leon receives a call from Hannigan. After the transmission, leave the area and reenter so that you do not have to tune up weapons all over again in case you must restart the game.

Night of the Living Villagers

Cross the bridge. Leon barricades himself and Ashley in a cabin with Luis Sera. However, this won't stop the villagers from trying to break into the cabin and kill everyone inside. Luis helps Leon fight the enemies that break into the cabin with his own Red9. Occasionally Luis tosses out ammo or recovery items, so stay close to him.

...sh three bookcases in front of the three downstairs windows to slow the ingression. ...llect the **Shotgun Shells** on table and the **Red Herb** in corner. A **Yellow Herb** rests ...the shelf left of the fireplace.

When enemies finally break through the window planks and bash through the bookcases, stand at base of stairs and shoot enemies as they pour in through the windows. When the action gets too intense, or when Luis says so, move upstairs and shoot villagers as they come up the steps.

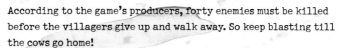

When Does It End?

According to the game's producers, forty enemies must be killed before the villagers give up and walk away. So keep blasting till the cows go home!

...ke it to the Next Level

...e sound of crashing glass upstairs means the horde has erected ...ders to the second level. Run around to the four windows ...ocking down the ladders while Luis pours on the bullets. Stop and ...e a shotgun blast when necessary to knock down enemy groups or ...topple enemies trying to climb through the windows.

If you're fast enough, the enemies trying to climb ladders can be prevented from getting into the second level and overwhelming Leon and Luis. They then resume trying to enter via the first floor, and they come up the steps. Pick up the various grenades on the upper level and use toss them into the clusters attempting to come up the stairs.

Watch Your Aim

Don't shoot at Luis repeatedly or he'll start shooting back, which means automatic Game Over.

Introduction

Characters

Enemies

Weapons and Ammunition

Key Items and Treasures

Game System and Strategies

Walkthrough

Secrets and Bonuses

BARRICADE CABIN

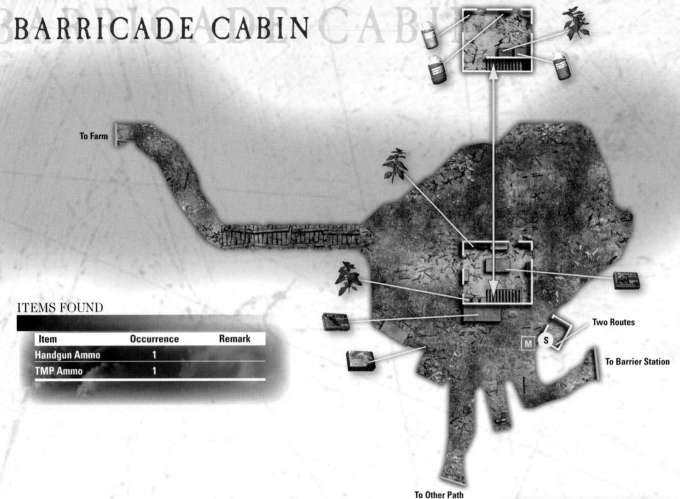

To Farm

BARRICADE CABIN

ITEMS FOUND

Item	Occurrence	Remark
Handgun Ammo	1	
TMP Ammo	1	

Two Routes

M S

To Barrier Station

To Other Path

The Coast is Clear...

Pick up any items remaining inside the cabin and exit. The merchant has moved to a position east of the house. Enter the shack next to the merchant and pick up the document next to the typewriter, entitled **Two Routes.** Check the two woodpiles behind the cabin to find handgun and TMP ammo.

Which Route?

Two routes run east from the cabin. Open the route of your choice by moving the lever of the stockade device. Push the lever left or right. The "left" path goes to the Barrier Station, where Leon faces off against psychopathic chainsaw-loving dames in a gruesome arena. The right path leads to a passage dominated by another El Gigante.

Take Both Paths If You Dare...

Note that valuable treasures as well as many other useful items are located in both areas. After clearing one path, feel free to backtrack to the cabin, switch the stockade lever and clear the other path as well.

BARRIER STATION

STATION

ITEMS FOUND

Item	Occurrence	Remark
Handgun Ammo	6	
Shotgun Shells	1	
TMP Ammo	1	
Flash Grenade	1	
Hand Grenade	1	
Green Herb	1	
Red Herb	1	
Random	5	
Ruby	1	Chainsaw Woman
Red Gem	1	
Camp Key	1	Chainsaw Woman

Cattle in the Corrals

Shoot the wagon loaded with barrels to wipe out the greeting party across from the entrance. Make Ashley hide in the red container on the right, and then head around the corner to deal with the remaining couple of enemies near the entrance. Fight your way to the back of the narrow passage and smash the barrel to obtain **Handgun Ammo**. Make sure the enemy on the level above is dead, and then press **R2** to whistle for Ashley to come along.

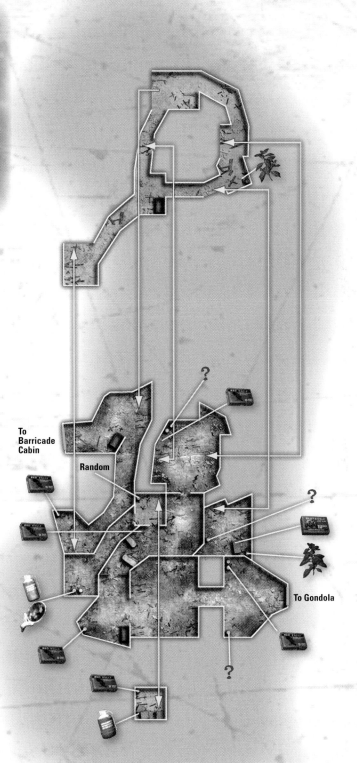

To Barricade Cabin

Random

To Gondola

Climb the ladder and move along the upper level to another red hiding container, and make Ashley hide in it. Kill the three enemies hanging around the upper part of the level. Move east along the upper level and smash the barrel in the corner to obtain a **Green Herb**.

To the right of the Green Herb's location is a ladder. Drop off the south side of the platform into a small area. Smash the barrel to obtain **TMP Ammo** and take the **Shotgun Shells** off the nearby mine cart. Smash the barrel behind the mine cart to obtain a **Red Herb**.

Chainsaw Gladiators

Climb back up the ladder and drop into the circular pit. It's an ambush! Two women with chainsaws and several other villagers drop into the pit as well. One of the chainsaw hags carries the **Camp Key** around her neck, so you must defeat her to get it. The other hag can be killed to obtain a **Ruby**.

The best strategy is to get out of the pit as fast as possible and kick down the ladder behind you. Then take a position on the narrow section of platform west of Ashley's hiding spot. This way the enemies have to funnel toward you from the front, and you can cut them down.

After killing everyone, drop back into the pit and use the Camp Key to unlock the door bearing the insignia. Smash the barrel in the northwest corner of the pit to obtain **Handgun Ammo**. Whistle for Ashley to come along, and then proceed into the next area.

Gathering a Few Items Between Onslaughts

Smash the crate next to the wooden door around the corner to receive **Handgun Ammo**. Enter the small building to the right and drop through the floor hatch to the cellar. Collect a **Hand Grenade** and **Handgun Ammo**, then climb out.

Return to the upper level and smash the boards off the window to the south. Move through the narrow passage and smash the two barrels at the end to receive a **Flash Grenade** and the **Red Gem** for the Mask. Avoid shooting the barrels, or you may attract the attention of the giant mob near the area's exit.

The Last Mob

eturn to the room, command
shley to follow, and move
rough the fortifications to the
nd of the aisle. Hide Ashley in
e red container, and then toss
renades to take out the crowd
villagers. Retreat through
e fortifications and continue

ssing grenades to take out or stun groups of enemies. Switch between
enades and the TMP and mow them down.

hen the coast appears to be clear, head back toward the exit and make sure
ere are no dawdling villagers. Then smash the barrel across from the hiding
ot to obtain **Handgun Ammo**. Lead Ashley toward the exit, unbar the gate
d proceed to the gondola area if you wish. Or, head back to the cabin and
en the right stockade to follow the other route.

OTHER PASSAGE

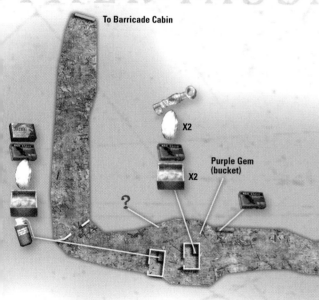

To Barricade Cabin

X2

X2

Purple Gem
(bucket)

?

To Gondola

ITEMS FOUND

Item	Occurrence	Remark
Handgun Ammo	5	
TMP Ammo	1	
Incendiary Grenade	1	
Pesetas (Box)	4	
Gold Bars	1	El Gigante
Random	1	
Spinel	3	
Purple Gem	1	
Old Key	1	

ursued By A Giant

e El Gigante that follows Leon and Ashley into this area
an optional boss. If you do not wish to risk Leon's and
hley's health, then move as quickly as possible through
e area and grab the **Old Key** from the second house in
e second area. Use it to unlock the east door and escape.
herwise, try to fight
e creature without
ting it crush the
uses or kill Ashley.
her way, there is
gh work to do!

Treasure In A Bucket

If the opportunity
affords itself before
you have to flee the
area, shoot the shiny
object out of the
bucket suspended
over the second
shack in the middle
section to obtain
the **Purple Gem**.

Introduction

Characters

Enemies

Weapons and
Ammunition

Key Items
and Treasures

Game System
and Strategies

Walkthrough

Secrets and
Bonuses

Chapter 1-1

Chapter 1-2

Chapter 1-3

Chapter 2-1

Chapter 2-3

Chapter 3-1

Chapter 3-2

Chapter 3-3

Chapter 3-4

Chapter 4-1

Chapter 4-2

Chapter 4-3

Chapter 4-4

Chapter 5-1

Chapter 5-2

Chapter 5-3

Chapter 5-4

Final Chapter

EL GIGANTE

Before even considering taking on another El Gigante, especially in this area with Ashley in tow, make sure you have a few Flash Grenades on hand. Decide beforehand how to fight the battle. If obtaining a plethora of items and money is important, then try to fight the creature in the first section and do not allow it to smash the shacks in the second section of the passage. If the items are not

important, then break through the doors between each area as needed to avoid being grabbed or hit by El Gigante.

Right after the creature enters the area, look where Ashley is pointing. A massive boulder rests on a weak platform. Back up a few steps, behind the boulder's position. When the creature starts to lumber forward, aim upward to the left and shoot the platform out from under the boulder. With the right timing, the giant should walk right under the falling boulder. While the creature recovers, use the opportunity to break through the chained door to the next section, or shoot the creature repeatedly to weaken it.

The three chains locking the doors between each section require six kicks to destroy Blasting the chains off is a faster method. The quickest way to break through the chains is to fire the TMP and cut right upward through all three chains. Then kick th door down and head to the next area.

El Gigante has to stop and smash through the walls dividing the area into sections. Even though it can break down the barrier in a single blow, its motions allow for an opportunity to fill it full of lead and perhaps make it reveal its parasite. Command Ashley to wait before climbing onto the creature and slashing at the parasite. Otherwise, Ashley follows Leon right up to the monster, endangering herself.

Be advised that El Gigante crushes the shacks in the middle section with a single blow. If the shacks are destroyed, the numerous items inside each structure are lost. However, there is another boulder on a platform high above the second section, allowing you another opportunity to damage and slow the monster while you escape or attack.

One rather "sick" strategy that works all too well is to use Ashley as bait. Command Ashley to wait and then back away from El Gigante as it approaches. If the monster comes in contact with Ashley before Leon, it lifts her off the ground and attempts to squeeze the life out of her. But before it does any damage to her, shoot it repeatedly to make it drop her. The creature holds its wrist in pain, allowing you additional opportunities to attack. Repeat this until it bends in agony, revealing its parasite. After cutting the parasite and lopping off the monster, command Ashley to follow you and run behind it. Leave Ashley standing directly behind the monster and back away a few steps. When it picks her up again, repeat the whole process over.

As usual, El Gigante drops **Gold Bars** worth 15,000 pesetas when defeated. When El Gigante wriggles in its death throes, be sure to scramble out of the way. It would be a real shame if Leon died because a dead Gigante fell on him!

GONDOLA

ITEMS FOUND

Item	Occurrence	Remark
Handgun Ammo	4	
Shotgun Shells	1	
Rifle Ammo	1	
TMP Ammo	1	
Flash Grenade	1	
Random	1	
Yellow Catseye	1	

Warning of Things to Come

Whichever door you enter, make your way to the cabin south of the merchant's location. Take the **Handgun Ammo** from the trashcans outside the building and go inside. Use the typewriter if needed, and collect the **Village's Last Defense** document on the overturned locker in back.

Seems the villager chief is cooking up another ambush for Leon. Open the standing locker to obtain **Rifle Ammo**.

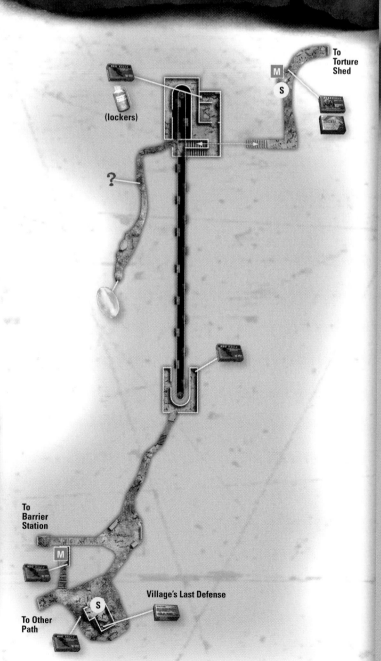

Chasm Crossing

Examine the village's exit. Leon needs Bitores Mendez' left eye to open the gate. Head up the slope to the gondola that conveys travelers to the north side of the great gorge. Before boarding, smash the barrel in the northeast corner to obtain **Handgun Ammo**.

While riding the gondola, weapon-throwing enemies hop onto lifts at the next station. As they approach on the right, shoot them before they can throw their weapons or shoot their weapons out of the air. The TMP works best in this situation, and it also helps to command

Ashley to wait near the back of the gondola. Enemies are positioned at stationary positions along the cliff wall to the left, but they will not attack until your gondola gets within very close range.

Station North

Enter the gondola's control booth, proceed to the back room and open the two lockers to obtain **Handgun Ammo** and a **Flash Grenade**. Exit the booth and descend the first flight of stairs at the cliff's edge. Command Ashley to wait before going into the nearby cave. Have a hand grenade or incendiary grenade ready when entering, and throw it at the villagers guarding the entrance.

Jump over the sandbags and proceed to the back of the cave. Climb the ladder and shoot the villager on the upper level. There's a chest at the back of the sacrificial chamber containing the **Yellow Catseye**, the third and final gem that fits into the Beerstein, increasing its value.

Return to the stairs, command Ashley to follow, and descend to the bottom. Follow the path to meet up with another merchant.

Collect the **Shotgun Shells** and **TMP Ammo** resting on the boxes next to the merchant. This is another moment when you should tune up weapons as much as possible and make sure Leon has plenty of recovery items. Purchase First Aid Sprays if needed.

TORTURE SHED

ITEMS FOUND

Item	Occurrence	Remark
Handgun Ammo	1	
Shotgun Shells	1	
TMP Ammo	1	
Incendiary Grenade	1	
Hand Grenade	1	
Green Herb	2	
Red Herb	1	
Yellow Herb	1	
Gold Bars	1	Village Chief
False Eye	1	Village Chief
Spinel	1	Exploding Barrel

Confrontation

Lead Ashley down the path and approach the massive shed. Leon leaves the girl outside while he enters the building, anticipating some kind of ambush. Unfortunately, none other than the village chief himself greets Leon. During the scene, be ready to press the two dodge buttons when displayed onscreen to avoid instant death!

(barrel)

To Gondola

BITORES MENDEZ

Aim for the village chief's exposed spinal column and keep shooting until the chief separates in two. As the chief is stalking toward Leon, shoot until the creature moves to attack. Press the dodge button displayed onscreen to roll out of harm's way, then run to the opposite end of the room. In the north section of the shed is an exploding barrel Leon can shoot to greatly damage the chief. A Spinel appears in the barrel's place.

Continue fighting the slowly advancing monster in this manner until it separates. The upper torso begins swinging from the beams stretched across the ceiling. Climb the ladder to the upper level and move around the loft to avoid damage from the creature while firing at it. To hit the chief more often, switch to the shotgun and blast it when it tries to get close. If the torso swings in close to Leon, run around the u-shaped loft or drop to the floor if needed to escape. Keep blasting the swinging monster until the creature can withstand no more damage. The village chief drops the False Eye and Gold Bars equaling 30,000 pesetas.

Exiting the Village

Taking the village chief's **False Eye** causes a hole to break open in the side of the torture shed. Leap through the hole and command Ashley to follow Leon out of the area. Return to the gondola and ride back to the upper station. Approach the village exit and use the False Eye to finally leave the village.

CASTLE ENTRANCE RANCE

ITEMS FOUND

Item	Occurrence	Remark
Random	2	
Handgun Ammo	1	
Shotgun Shells	1	
Green Herb	1	
Pesetas (Box)	1	
Spinel	1	
Velvet Blue	1	
Gold Bars	1	5500 - Truck, 5000 - Courtyard

To Gondola

Hard Road to the Castle

Take the **Handgun Ammo** on the boxes stacked near the entrance. A crowd of villagers is gathered at the top of the hill. But do not start sniping just yet. Move up the hill until a truck starts up. The crazed driver runs over his fellow villagers and continues toward Leon and Ashley. Shoot the driver to avert disaster, and then run back toward the entrance to avoid being crushed by the overturning vehicle.

Villagers pour from the back end of the wrecked truck. Race to the top of the hill and collect items or money that the villagers who were run down may have dropped. Blast the second wave of parasitic hosts as they attempt to chase the two of you.

Smash the barrels on the first overlook point near the drawbridge's entrance to obtain **Handgun Ammo** and a more valuable ore type called **Velvet Blue**. Then continue toward the drawbridge to complete Chapter 2.

chapter three

Parasites emerging from cultists' necks in the castle stage are different in appearance and attack manner. They no longer have medium-range whip tentacle attacks. However, if a Plaga body gets close enough, it performs a fatality move that chops Leon's or Ashley's head clean off—instantly. Late in Chapter 3, parasites change form again, gaining the ability to spit acid and separate from the host body. These Plaga scuttle across the floor like huge spiders, but they can be easily killed by a single attack; with the knife for instance.

The castle is swarming with enemies and traps. Use grenades liberally as needed to thin crowds.

CHAPTER 3-1
CASTLE ENTRANCE

ITEMS FOUND

Item	Occurrence	Remark
Random	2	
Handgun Ammo	1	
Shotgun Shells	1	
Green Herb	1	
Pesetas (Box)	3	
Spinel	1	
Gold Bars	1	

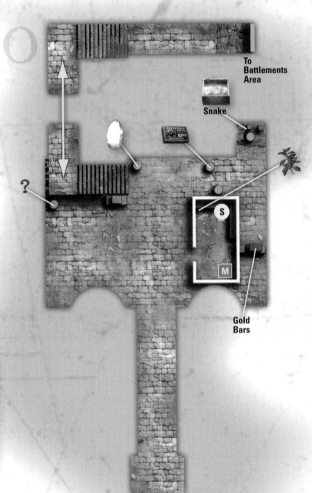

To Battlements Area

Snake

Gold Bars

Preparing for Siege

Smash barrels and crates in the courtyard to find pesetas and refill weapons. Shoot the crates in the upper east corner of the area behind the shop carefully, because one box contains a snake. The red box in the alley east of the shop building contains **Gold Bars** worth 5000 pesetas.

Collect the **Green Herb** inside the shop and use the typewriter if desired. The merchant's list is updated. New items on sale include the Attaché Case L, the Blacktail handgun, the Rifle (semi-auto), the Riot Gun, the Mine Thrower and scopes for the new weapons. Avoid purchasing the Broken Butterfly, because one is provided free inside the castle. New tune-ups are available for the Handgun, Shotgun, Rifle, TMP, and all the new weapons.

Time For A Full Upgrade!

Sell all of your weapons and valuables, and purchase the Blacktail, Riot Gun and semi-auto Rifle. These weapons can be upgraded well beyond the initial set, and should allow you to blast through the rest of the game. Also purchase the Attaché Case L to allow Leon to tote all this stuff.

BATTLEMENT AREA

ITEMS FOUND

Item	Occurrence	Remark
Random	1	
Rifle Ammo	1	
Yellow Herb	1	
Incendiary Grenade	1	
Pesetas (Box)	1	
Spinel	2	
Velvet Blue	1	
Gold Bangle	1	

Covered by Catapults

Run along the path until you reach a box where **Rifle Ammo** is located. Snipe the two cultists on the nearby balcony, and then quickly lead Ashley up the stairs. After the first deluge of flaming projectiles rains down, run through the area and take the first left. Claim any items dropped by the sniped cultist. Continue into the round chamber and examine the large cannon. You must figure out a way to get this weapon to the upper level.

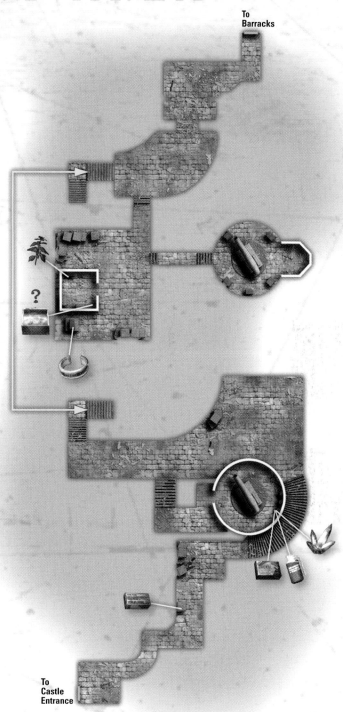

There's gotta be a mechanism somewhere to pull this thing up.

To Barracks

To Castle Entrance

Don't Leave Ashley Behind!

Although Ashley might die and end the mission abruptly, avoid the temptation to make her stay behind anywhere in this area. If Ashley is left alone and Leon proceeds to the next "section" of the battlements, cultists materialize out of nowhere and abduct her. If a cultist manages to carry Ashley to an exit door, the game ends just as well. Keep the girl with you until you reach the small supply building on the upper level.

Sniping in the Quad

Head west under the bridge. Stop at the east edge of the bridge and gaze through the rifle scope at the balcony high above. Pan left and shoot the red exploding barrel to destroy the catapult.

At the top of the stairs, stop and look to the right through a gap in the battlements. Use the rifle to shoot the exploding barrel next to the catapult to the south. Move a little

farther up to the flat area and snipe a cultist with a brass helmet inside a small building. He cannot be killed with a head shot because of the helmet he wears. Shoot him in the chest. This causes him to emerge from the building, where you can shoot him again for the kill.

A Relatively Safe Spot

Quickly lead Ashley to safety inside the small building. Two cultists may follow you in. Step just outside the small building to force the catapults to fire, killing the cultists. If that doesn't work, stay inside the building and blast the duo as they try to enter and snatch your charge.

Look through the north window that can be jumped through and snipe the exploding barrel next to the catapult directly to the north. This leaves only one catapult remaining in the area to the northeast. Collect the items in the small building, including a **Yellow Herb** in the red chest.

Raising the Cannon

Press **R2** to command Ashley to wait inside the small building, and run quickly across the bridge heading east. Even as the last catapult fires, run around a large ring and into the relative safety of a small building. Aim the rifle out of the north window and snipe the cultist

firing the catapult to the north. There is no barrel visible from this location, so you must shoot the cultist. Kill him very quickly or successive catapult attacks may destroy the building in which Leon is taking refuge!

With all the catapults destroyed, you can now safely turn the crank and raise the cannon in the ring-shaped area. Fire the cannon to destroy the castle gates, granting entry. Don't forget to take the **Gold Bangle** from a chest located south of the small building, and visit the merchant just behind the destroyed gate.

BARRACKS

ITEMS FOUND

Item	Occurrence	Remark
Random	1	
Handgun Ammo	1	
Red Herb	1	
Pesetas (Box)	3	
Gold Bars	1	4500 - Red enemy
Golden Sword	1	
Platinum Sword	1	

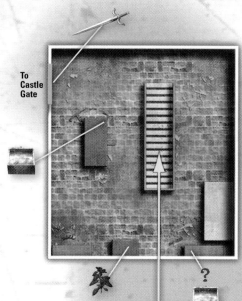

To Castle Gate

To Battlements Area

Exchanging Swords

Take the **Handgun Ammo** on the table and open the cabinet by the entrance to claim **2000 Pesetas**. Take the **Platinum Sword** off the gold plate and start ascending the stairs. When the cultists on the level above cry out, let them funnel down the steps so you can blast them.

Head upstairs with Ashley following. Additional cultists enter through the downstairs door after a few seconds. Stand west of the archway and shoot the cultists as they reach the top of the stairs. Move to the top of the steps and use the rifle to snipe the red cultist lingering near the entrance. Take out the grotesque Plaga emerging from his neck as well. The cultist in red drops **Gold Bars** worth 4500 Pesetas.

Collect the **Pesetas** on the table and take the **Golden Sword** from the plaque in the northwest corner. Replace it with the Platinum Sword, and then go

downstairs and set the Golden Sword in the gold plaque. The upstairs exit is revealed. Collect the other supplies and treasures in the barracks and exit.

CASTLE GATE CASTLE GATE

ITEMS FOUND

Item	Occurrence	Remark
Handgun Ammo	2	
Green Herb	1	
Pesetas (Box)	1	
Spinel	1	
Velvet Blue	1	
Castle Gate Key	1	

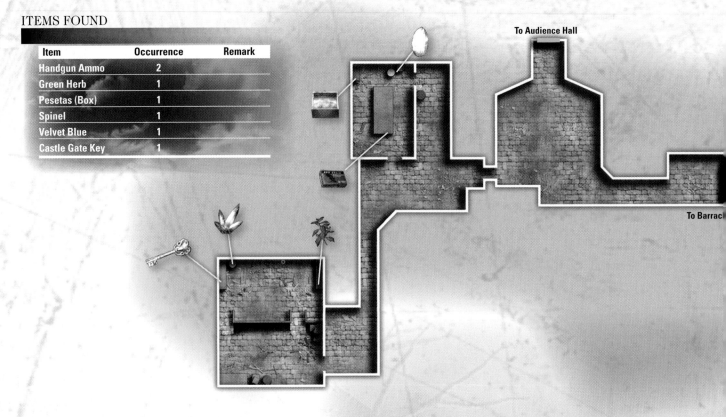

To Audience Hall

To Barrack

Barred from Entrance

The castle gate is unsurprisingly locked, so head west and open the door. Use the rifle to blow the head off the guy a few feet away and then his Plaga if needed. The commotion should alert the enemies inside the building. Either back up and allow them to funnel through the doorway, or charge in and take them head on. One grenade tossed into the building causes some serious damage. Be careful not to stand near the exploding red barrel outside the building since it may go off as well.

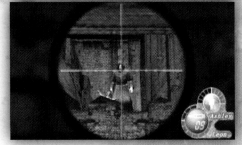

Enter the room through the open rear doorway and kill any cultists lingering inside. Move to the window at the front of the building and use the rifle to snipe the cultist with a crossbow positioned atop the adjacent battlements. Take a moment to scour the room for ammo and treasure.

Cultists with Shields!

Move south under the archway and approach the corner cautiously. Two cultists positioned here hold wooden riot shields. The shields are resistant to handgun fire, but can be obliterated with a single shotgun blast at close range.

A crazy strategy for dealing with these two guys is to lead them back through the small room nearby. When they enter the room, lead them through the open back door. Run a few feet south of the exploding barrel and shoot it when the cultists are standing right beside it.

Create a Good Continue Point

At this point, it's a good idea to return to the barracks and reenter the area. That way, if you don't like how things go in a moment, you can retry without having to do the whole area over.

The Castle Gate Key

Enter the guardhouse and collect the items, including the **Green Herb** on the shelves and the **Velvet Blue** in the barrel. Open the red chest and take the **Castle Gate Key**, then immediately turn back toward the door. Enemies rush the room at such speed that the exploding barrel near the door really doesn't help. The most useful strategy is to throw hand grenades or incendiaries toward both ramps, since the cultists try to approach Leon and Ashley from both sides. This tactic should greatly reduce the amount of damage taken. Return to the castle gate and use the Castle Gate Key to unlock it.

AUDIENCE HALL

ITEMS FOUND

Item	Occurrence	Remark
Random	2	
Handgun Ammo	2	
Shotgun Shells	1	Beam
Green Herb	1	
Yellow Herb	1	
Incendiary Grenade	1	
Pesetas (Box)	2	
Prison Key	1	
Spinel	1	
Velvet Blue	1	
Green Gem	1	Wall above Arch
Gold Bars	1	

The Castellan

Proceed into the hall. Leon and Ashley encounter Ramon Salazar and his creepy bodyguards. After the scene, ascend the steps and continue forward a few more paces until a wall rises in the archway. Examine the wall to see a chimera-shaped indentation. Standing at the chimera wall, turn around and aim extremely high on the wall above the archway. Shoot the shiny object to obtain a **Green Gem**. Smash the pots to obtain a **Velvet Blue** and other items.

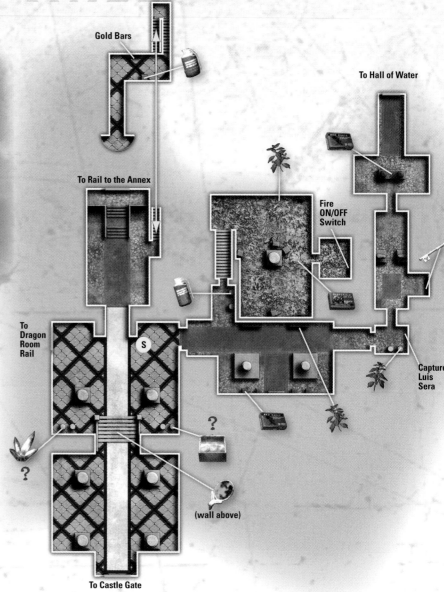

Horses of Fire

Use the typewriter if desired and head through the east door. Smash the barrels and pots and examine the chairs along the south wall to procure items. Check the portrait of Saddler to obtain **Gold Bars** worth 5000 pesetas. Continue east and smash two barrels at the corner to obtain a **Yellow Herb**. Read the **Capture Luis Sera** note on the wall. Head north toward the fire-breathing horse heads and turn right. Examine the painting in the alcove to obtain the **Prison Key**.

The Prisoner

Head back toward the entrance and look through the archways on the right. Notice the **Shotgun Shells** on the beam. Use the handgun or rifle to knock them off the beam to the ground below. Return to the greenish door near the entrance from the audience room and use the Prison Key to unlock it. Command Ashley to stay put and descend the stairs.

Move into the room and collect the Shotgun Shells you shot off the beam as well as the **Green Herb** near the north wall. Approach and open the cell door. The switch to the right shuts off the fire-breathing horses in the corridor above. However, a creature with claws called a Garrador breaks free of captivity in the cell. The Garrador is blind, so as long as you *walk*

instead of run, it should have some trouble finding you. Its weak spot is the parasite on its back. Navigate slowly around the room and try to shoot the Garrador from behind with the shotgun or rifle.

Shoot the bells to drive the Garrador berserk, causing it to lunge for the bell. This creates an opportunity to run up behind the monster and deliver a hard shotgun blast to its Plaga. The Garrador drops 15,000 pesetas when killed, but keep in mind that slaying the creature is completely optional. Once it moves away from its cell, it's possible just to walk quietly into the niche and throw the switch to turn off the fire-breathing horses in the room above. Then you can leave the Garrador in the sub-level and flee. Do so quickly, though! The door only stays open for a limited time. Otherwise, you'll have to battle the creature.

Beyond the Steeds

Stopping the fire emissions of the horses allows a squad of cultists to enter the corridor. Rejoin Ashley quickly and command her to follow you. Move east a few steps and use the gas lantern hanging from the ceiling to set the approaching group of cultists aflame. Command Ashley to wait at the corner and then proceed through the doorway alone. Try to shoot down a dynamite-tossing cultist before he manages to throw a stick. Two cultists with crossbows are best dealt with using the rifle. A last cultist usually remains in the room beyond, where **Handgun Bullets** lie.

HALL OF WATER

ITEMS FOUND

Item	Occurrence	Remark
Random	3	
Handgun Ammo	1	
Shotgun Shells	2	
Rifle Ammo	1	
Green Herb	1	
First Aid Spray	1	
Hand Grenade	1	
Incendiary Grenade	1	
Pesetas (Box)	5	
Velvet Blue	1	
Gold Bangle	1	

Assaulting the Aisles

Enter prepared for all-out war, because this area has to be **taken**. Rush forward immediately and toss a hand grenade or incendiary at the line of cultists in the center of the room before they break formation and try to surround you.

Collect what items you can from this attack, especially from any smashed pots in the center aisle. Lead Ashley to one of the lower corners of the room and toss grenades at clusters coming from both sides. A second wave of attackers pours from the two doors, and there are more cultists in the passage at the bottom of the stairs to the north. The cultist leader in red robes drops **4500 pesetas**.

When the first section appears to be clear of enemies, smash the pots and jars around the area and collect items. Descend the stairs and take out the cultist standing guard in front of the central doorway. Enter the room.

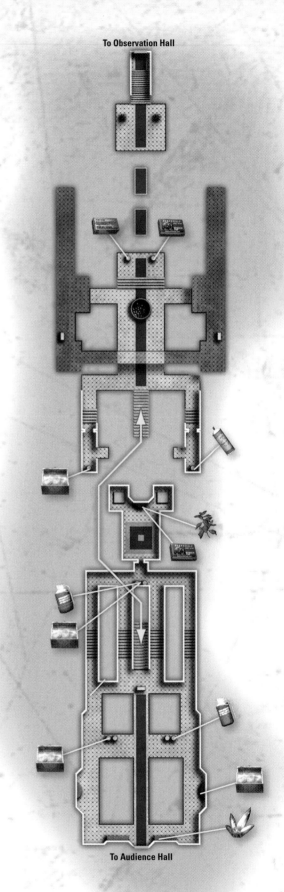

To Observation Hall

To Audience Hall

The Blue Room

Collect the **Green Herb** on table and the **Shotgun Shells** on chair. Walk onto one of the yellow pressure pads with Ashley following. When Ashley is standing on the pad, command her to wait. Then go stand on the other pad.

This action raises a crank out in the main room. But do not be too hasty to leave. Stand at the back of the blue room and command Ashley to stick close to you. Enemies charge through the door and drop out of the hole in the ceiling. Mow them down as they come. When the chanting sounds subside a bit, it means all the enemies in the squad are dead.

The Mezzanine

Return to the south area and turn the crank. Either Leon or Ashley can turn the crank; if enemies are still present, Leon can shoot them while Ashley lowers the stairs.

Ascend to the mezzanine level. Smash the pots in the overlook points to the southeast and southwest to collect **Shotgun Shells** and a **First Aid Spray**. Then move north until Ashley points out a crank on the level above. Prepare for the next shooting event by smashing the clay pots on the northernmost rise to obtain **Rifle Ammo** and **Shotgun Shells**.

Ashley Raises the Platforms

Approach either fresco to the far west or far east until the "piggyback" action appears onscreen. Lift Ashley up to the level above, and then run to the raised north point and equip the sniper rifle. Snipe the ghouls that emanate from the side door and try to grab Ashley. The better you are at keeping the cultists off Ashley, the more often she can turn the crank and raise the platforms in the water.

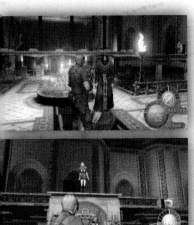

Meanwhile, cultists rush at Leon on the ground as well. Switch to grenades or the shotgun as needed and blow them away. Ashley is a priority however, so if she cries out, switch back to the rifle and immediately kill any cultist trying to carry her off, even if enemies are still coming at Leon.

When Ashley manages to raise both platforms, she runs to the nearest edge and calls for Leon. Quickly go catch her as she drops, and lead her north across the platforms to the exit.

OBSERVATION HALL
OBSERVATION HALL

ITEMS FOUND

Item	Occurrence	Remark
Random	1	
Handgun Ammo	1	
Shotgun Shells	1	
Green Herb	1	
Hand Grenade	1	
Pesetas (Box)	1	
Spinel	2	

Beautiful Silence

Finally, Leon and Ashley find an empty place to rest. Move to the center of the hall, turn south and look at the head of the upside-down goddess. Shoot the sparkly thing out of her eye to obtain a **Spinel**. Collect the other items around the room, including the **Hand Grenade** in the glass display case to the northeast. Use the typewriter and then head north up the narrow corridor where Ashley is abducted!

The Shooting Gallery

The merchant offers new tune-ups for the Handgun, Rifle, TMP, Punisher, Red9, the Rifle (semi-auto) and the Riot Gun. A blue door inscribed with golden guns is right next to the merchant. This door leads to the shooting gallery, a special place where Leon can practice his gun skills and earn points. Prizes are awarded for earning more than 3000 points, and by exhibiting skills such as shooting all of the targets, scoring more than 4000 points, etc. Instructions regarding **Target Practice** are available on the clerk's desk. Target practice game type A is available, enabling you to obtain the six bottle caps in the bottom row of the diorama. More target practice types become available as you enter other shooting galleries in later stages of the game.

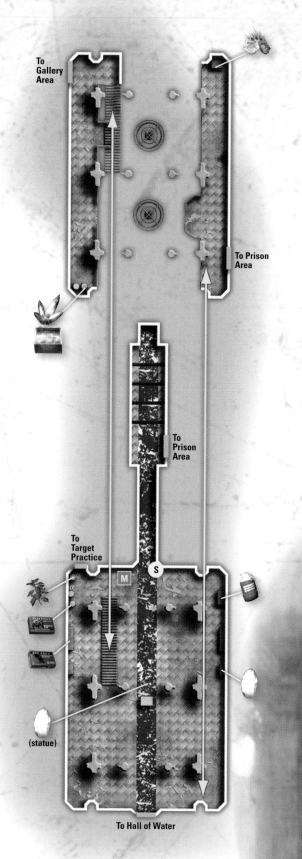

To Gallery Area

To Prison Area

To Prison Area

To Target Practice

To Hall of Water

(statue)

CHAPTER 3-2

PRISON AREA

To Observation Hall

To Observation Hall (2F)

Luis' Memo

Water Valve

ITEMS FOUND

Item	Occurrence	Remark
Random	2	
Handgun Ammo	1	
Shotgun Shells	1	
TMP Ammo	1	
Green Herb	1	
Yellow Herb	1	
Incendiary Grenade	1	
Flash Grenade	1	
Pesetas (Box)	2	
Spinel	1	
Velvet Blue	3	
Novistador Eye	2	Novistadors
Butterfly Lamp	1	

Dungeon Critters

Backtrack south in the corridor where Ashley disappeared and go through the wooden door to the dungeon area. Proceed around the corner and drop over the ledge. Head up the corridor and ignore the creepy sounds on the left.

At the corner, aim through the sniper rifle's scope and zoom to the next corner. See the wisps of cold breath emanating from thin air? That's an invisible monster that you do not wish to fight at close range. Aim for the breath to blow its head off. Novistadors sometimes drop valuable Red Eyes, Green Eyes and rare Blue Eyes. Pick these items up quickly before they disappear.

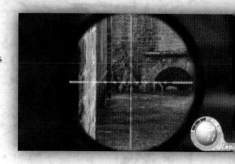

Walk slowly into the next chamber, so as not to attract attention. Move quietly up to the north end of the pool and aim down at the water with the scope. Snipe the two Novistadors waiting quietly in the water. Then jump down and collect the **TMP Ammo** in the pipe. Search the water to find a **Velvet Blue** and **Handgun Ammo**. Climb the ladder and continue to the next room.

Pest Extermination

Open the next door quietly and back up against the north wall. Aim up at the skylight and shoot the Novistador perched the hole. The sound should draw another monster into the room from the left. When Novistadors move, their eyes glow. Shoot th creature before it reaches Leon.

Walk carefully down the east passage and turn the corner. Another invisible Novistador starts moving in, but you should be able to take care of it before it gets too close. That takes care of the enemies in this sector. Head back to the cells in the main area and kick down doors to obtain items. **Luis' Memo** in the northeast cell should be of particular interest.

Draining the Water

Move through the destroyed cells and enter the control room. Smash the crates on the shelves to obtain items, and open the red box to obtain a **Butterfly Lamp**. By setting three Novistador Eyes of three different colors in the lamp, the value of this object increases dramatically. Turn the red valve in the corner to drain the water out of the lower area south of the prison cells.

Fighting Toward the Exit

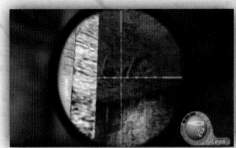

Exit the control room softly. There are now Novistadors positioned on the roof at the corner across from the door and inside the destroyed cells. Snipe the first one while standing in the control room doorway, then move to the south wall, turn and try to snipe the other before it spots Leon.

As you head back to the main area of the prison, a Novistador breaks out of the cell across the way. Shoot it with the rifle before it reaches Leon. Another leaps out of the drained pool, and there's not much to do except put your back in a corner and scan the floor, walls and ceiling for signs of movement.

Drop into the pool and kick the gate down. This triggers another Novistador to come at Leon from behind. Charge up the stairs to narrows its gap of approach, and blast it with the shotgun repeatedly. When all monsters are dead, go back downstairs and search the water near the drain to find a **Velvet Blue**.

Optional Encounter

If you love collecting Novistador Eyes, another insect man has appeared near the entrance, in the area where the wall is smashed in and the strange noises were heard.

Pit of Pendulums

Head upstairs into the last room of the area, in which three deadly pendulums swing back and forth. Move between the pendulums carefully, dashing forward at the instant the blade passes directly in front of Leon. Jump the gap using the same timing as well.

Collect the **Velvet Blue** at the end of the area and go through the door. Climb the ladder and smash the barrels to find **Pesetas** and a **Spinel**. Exit back to the upper level of the Observation Hall.

OBSERVATION HALL (BALCONY)

ITEMS FOUND

Item	Occurrence	Remark
Random	1	
Pesetas (Box)	1	
Spinel	10	Enemies
Velvet Blue	1	
Elegant Mask	1	
Illuminados Pendant	1	Red Enemy

Leon's Turn to Ambush Enemies

A group of acolytes are now performing some kind of dark ritual on the lower level. All of them have jewels around their necks, and the leader in red wears a valuable **Illuminados Pendant**. The leader will spot you if you drop from the balcony or approach too closely to the edge. If the enemies are alerted to your presence, they try to escape and seal themselves in the north passage, behind metal doors.

To take the group down, fire a rocket into the middle of the cluster. With the rocket launcher method, the cultists should drop all ten **Spinels**, plus the cult leaders' pendant. Now you can sell these items for just enough money to replace the rocket launcher you used…

If no rocket launcher is available, move north toward the balcony's edge. Stop just a few steps from the edge and toss a Flash Grenade into the room below. While the entire group is stunned, drop to the level below and toss a hand or incendiary grenade in their midst. This will not be enough to kill the leader, who usually reveals a Plaga after the host body dies. Be sure not to let the leader get away, since he wears the most valuable piece. Using the grenade method, you should be able to make enemies drop up to four Spinels as well as the pendant.

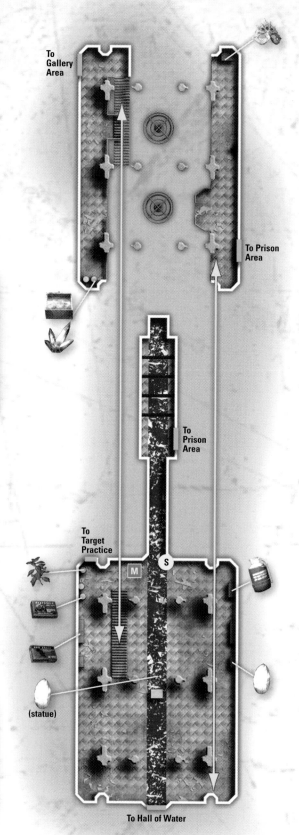

To Gallery Area

To Prison Area

To Prison Area

To Target Practice

M

S

(statue)

To Hall of Water

...eaping Across the Upper Level

...er taking down as many fleeing cultists as possible, climb the ladder back to the ...per level and use the chandelier to swing across to the western balcony. Smash the ...y pots at the south end to obtain a **Velvet Blue** and a few **Pesetas**.

Use the north chandelier to swing back to the east balcony. Raise the switch on the wall to open the gates on the upper level. Move north and smash the display case. Open the red box to obtain an **Elegant Mask**.

...e merchant has moved to the top of the stairs in the northwest corner of the ...om. New tune-ups are available for the Handgun, Rifle, TMP, Punisher, Red9, and ...e semi-auto Rifle. Generally, it is fine to sell all but two of the Novistador Eye gems ...nd. Two gems of each color are needed to fit in the two Blind Butterfly Lamps ...ailable in the game. Go through the pink door when finished.

GALLERY AREA

ITEMS FOUND

Item	Occurrence	Remark
Random	4	
Handgun Ammo	4	
Shotgun Shells	2	
Rifle Ammo	1	
Green Herb	2	
Red Herb	1	
Yellow Herb	1	
Pesetas (Box)	8	
Spinel	1	
Velvet Blue	2	
Goat Ornament	1	Raise Platform
Gallery Key	1	Red Enemy

Security Switch

...ernal ...ll ...ea

Center Column Switch

?

x4

(deer head)

To Observation Hall

Castellan Memo

A Grueling Obstacle Course

Take the **Red Herb** on the table and head upstairs. Collect the **Castellan Memo** on the center table and the **Handgun Ammo** on the chair. Open the green door and use the sniper rifle to kill everyone on the balcony. Some cultists may be able to run into the side room, and that's all right for now. Two cultists on the ground floor can be taken out by sniping them or by leading them toward one of the exploding barrels.

Enter the southwest room and ascend the stairs a short distance. Kill the masked cultist at the top of the stairs. Open the upstairs door and head left to find **Rifle Ammo**.

Chasing the Red Cultist

Cross the balcony to the other corner, and notice the sealed door. You must jump over the ledge to the right. Only then will the cultists open the door, allowing the leader in red to flee across the balcony. Rush through the doorway, go up the stairs and chase after him. Us

the shotgun to knock down any cultists in your path, but stay on the tail of the man in red. Ignore the four boxes of **Pesetas** on the shelf as well as the **Shotgun Shells** and return to the balcony.

As the leader attempts to flee across the balcony, try to snipe him with the rifle. If he makes it inside the southeast door, chase after him. A shielded cultist tries to prevent you from following the main target. Run around this obstacle and chase the red robed culti downstairs. Blast him with the shotgun and prevent him from reaching the center of the lower gallery floor.

If the cult leader manages to get to the center platform, he raises a powerful, but slow-to-rotate machinegun. A rocket launcher makes quick work of him, but otherwise you can circle around the platform as he reloads and give him a shotgun blast to his exposed back. About seven shots will finish him. If you successfully prevent the leader in red from reaching the platform or kill him afterwards, he drops the **Gallery Key**.

[S]ix Must Die

[Ma]ke your way back up to the west balcony, picking up any missed items [alo]ng the way. Use the Gallery Key to unlock the door and proceed into the [ne]xt room. Shoot the eye out of the deer head to obtain a **Velvet Blue** and [sm]ash the clay pots to obtain other items.

[Ex]amine the central panel to solve the puzzle in this room. Each portrait on [th]e wall swivels in place, revealing a second portrait on the backside. Arrange [th]e portraits so six people are depicted dying.

[P]ORTRAIT SWITCH FUNCTIONS

[S]WITCH	FUNCTION
[S]witch 1	Swivels the left 2 portraits.
[S]witch 2	Swivels the left 3 portraits.
[S]witch 3	Swivels the right 3 portraits.
[S]witch 4	Swivels the right 2 portraits.

Death Portrait Puzzle

Push switch 1.

Push switch 3.

Push Switch 2.

Push Switch 4, then choose Ok or quit to solve the puzzle.

[G]allery Shootout

[Co]ntinue into the next room. Salazar has set [up] a little trap for Leon. After the scene, turn [to] Leon's right and bolt through the rusty door. [Sh]oot the enemies as they try to follow him up [th]e stairs.

Enemies then appear on the upper level. A couple should try to enter the stairwell in which Leon is hiding. The rest are crossbow snipers that basically stand their ground. Run in and out of the two stair doors to try and bait more enemies into coming in after you.

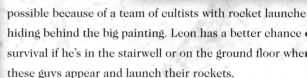

When enemies stop trying to enter the stairwell, open the upstairs door. Standing in the doorway, shoot the gas lamps hung over sniper's heads to take them out. Avoid moving around the upper

level as much as possible because of a team of cultists with rocket launche hiding behind the big painting. Leon has a better chance survival if he's in the stairwell or on the ground floor whe these guys appear and launch their rockets.

Security Deactivation

When the arrows stop flying and the body parts hit the floor, move around the room, smash jars and collect items. Press the switch near exit door on upper level to deactivate security system and raise central platform. The guys behind the painting pop out to try and use rocket launchers on Leon again. Run around the corner to avoid the blast or toss a flash grenade to stop the attack.

Enter the south door, smash the pot at the end of the narrow chamber and press the switch. This action extends a walkway to the central platform in the main room. Wait for two enemies outside to fire rocket launchers before exiting. Then burst out of the room and shoot them both Both enemies die from one shot each. Open the blue chest on the platform to obtain the **Goat Ornament**. Go through the exit to the next area.

EXTERNAL WALL AREA

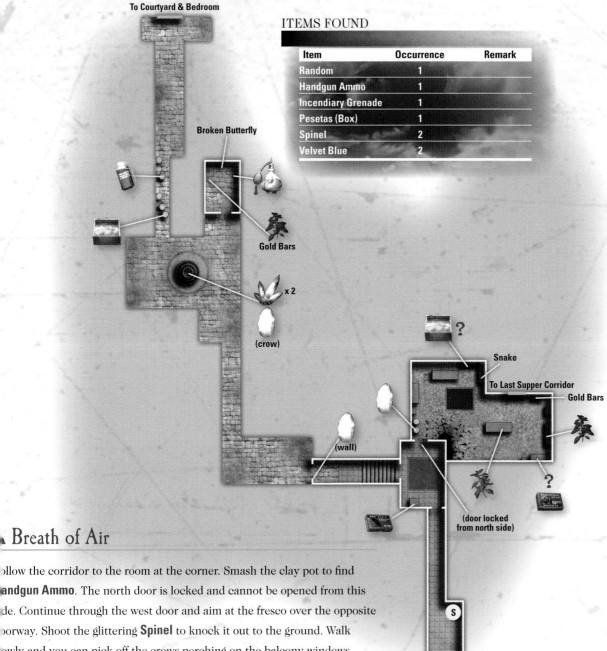

To Courtyard & Bedroom

Broken Butterfly

Gold Bars

x 2

(crow)

(wall)

Snake

To Last Supper Corridor

Gold Bars

?

?

(door locked
from north side)

S

To Gallery Area

ITEMS FOUND

Item	Occurrence	Remark
Random	1	
Handgun Ammo	1	
Incendiary Grenade	1	
Pesetas (Box)	1	
Spinel	2	
Velvet Blue	2	

A Breath of Air

Follow the corridor to the room at the corner. Smash the clay pot to find **Handgun Ammo**. The north door is locked and cannot be opened from this side. Continue through the west door and aim at the fresco over the opposite doorway. Shoot the glittering **Spinel** to knock it out to the ground. Walk slowly and you can pick off the crows perching on the balcony windows.

Head north up the balcony. Stop a distance back from the fountain and use a handgun to pick off the three crows drinking the water. Then examine the fountain to find two **Velvet Blue** ores and all the coins the crows dropped. Examine the locked door on the nearby room to learn a clue on how to get inside the room later with Ashley's help.

COURTYARD & BEDROOM

ITEMS FOUND

Item	Occurrence	Remark
Handgun Ammo	3	
Shotgun Shells	1	
TMP Ammo	1	
Green Herb	1	
Yellow Herb	1	
First Aid Spray	1	
Incendiary Grenade	1	
Spinel	2	
Velvet Blue	2	
Red Gem	1	
Mirror	1	
Moonstone (Left Half)	1	
Moonstone (Right Half)	1	

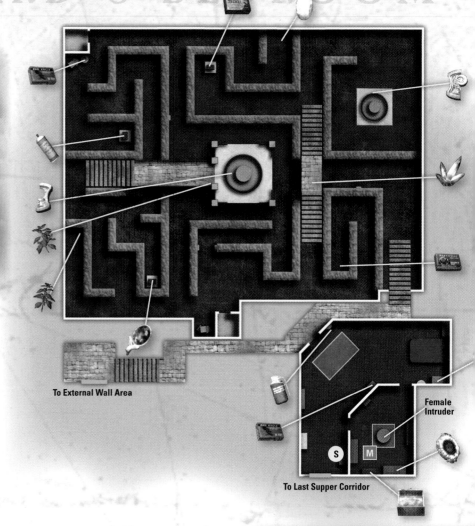

To External Wall Area

Female Intruder

To Last Supper Corridor

S   M

Where Demon Dogs Dwell...

Head east down the stairs and across the balcony. Examine the bedroom doors to see the shape of the indentation there. After a warning transmission from Salazar, continue east and down into the hedge maze.

Open the gates and smash the barrels on the left to obtain a **Velvet Blue**. Colmillos attack as you proceed under the bridge. The area is filled with these abominations, but they do not appear unless entering certain areas. Use the shotgun to kill lone Colmillos and incendiary grenades on packs. Head under the bridge behind the platform and smash the barrel to obtain a **Green Herb**.

Killing in the Kennel

Head south from the entrance and move inward to a closed gate. **Do not open the gate!** Beyond the gate, two Colmillos can be seen locked in a pen. Use the rifle to snipe one of them. The other breaks loose once its partner is dead. Blast through the gate with the shotgun until the hellish hound is dead.

...en the gate and head east. Ignore the stairs on the left for the moment and
...ntinue to the corner. Follow the spiral-shaped path inward to a red box containing
...otgun Shells. Be ready for an ambush when taking the ammo.

The First Moonstone Half

Return to the stairs, ascend them and cross the bridge. Head left from
the bottom of the stairs to a red box containing **TMP Ammo**. Then
return to the base of the stairs and head northeast to the fountain
where the **Moonstone (Left Half)** is located. Equip incendiary
grenades for the trip back...

...easures and Tribulations

...back across the bridge and return to the kennel area. Continue
...ading toward the southwest corner of the area. At the corner, head
...rth to find a **Yellow Herb**. Backtrack a few feet and take the zigzag
...th heading north. Take a few steps east and then head south to a red
...x containing a **Red Gem** that fits into the Elegant Mask.

Head north from the Red Gem's
location and follow the path
under the bridge. Continue toward the northwest corner of the area to find another
kennel with a Colmillos inside. Blast the dog in its cage, then head south to find a red
box containing a **First Aid Spray**. Return to the kennel and head east. Ignore the gate
for the moment and continue east to find a **Spinel**.

...he Second Moonstone

...turn to the kennel and go back under the bridge. This time, go up the stairs and collect the **Moonstone (Right Half)**. Move
...ward the east side of the platform and jump down to the ground below. Make a dash for the entrance gate.

...edroom Encounter

...turn to the bedroom and examine the door. Combine the two puzzle pieces to create the Blue Moonstone and insert it into
...e door. Enter the bedroom to encounter an old flame. Afterwards, collect the items around the bedroom and then enter the
...ea where the merchant stands.
...llect the **Female Intruder**
...e on the table and open the
...noire behind the merchant to
...d the **Mirror**. The merchant
...ers brand new tune-ups for the
...cktail, Broken Butterfly, Riot
...n and Mine Thrower.

THE LAST SUPPER CORRIDOR

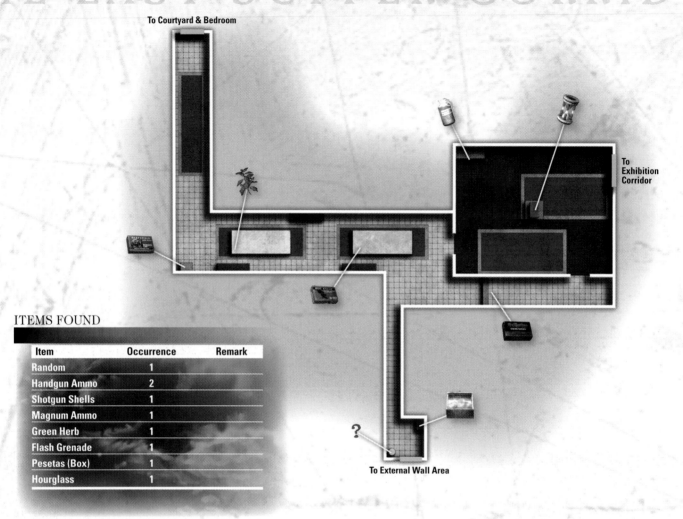

To Courtyard & Bedroom

To Exhibition Corridor

To External Wall Area

ITEMS FOUND

Item	Occurrence	Remark
Random	1	
Handgun Ammo	2	
Shotgun Shells	1	
Magnum Ammo	1	
Green Herb	1	
Flash Grenade	1	
Pesetas (Box)	1	
Hourglass	1	

Elegance in Dining

Head to the south corner and smash the clay pot to obtain **Shotgun Shells**, and read the clue inscribed on the wall to the left. There are three other clues in the room, indicating the order in which to shoot the food items on the painting nearby.

Brief Sojourn for Supplies

Before doing anything else here, head down the south corridor and enter the next room. This is the chamber of the Exterior Corridor that was locked. Open the cabinets and smash the crates to obtain items. A crate on the north wall contains a snake, so avoid it. Break the padlock on the south door if you like, but then head back to the Last Supper Corridor.

Shooting Dinner

Ring the bell on the east counter. The painting at the end of the aisle flips over, revealing a four-course meal. *Shoot the bread, then the chicken, then the desert, and finally the wine, in that exact order.* At this point, the bars are removed from the nearby red room.

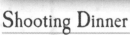

Gladiator's Cage

Walking a short distance into the room, Leon finds himself trapped. Cultists surround the cage, occasionally firing arrows into the melee or dropping into the action from above.

The first order of business is get out of the cage, which is easily accomplished by tossing a grenade toward one of the doors. When the padlock on a door is destroyed, kick it down and blow cultists out of your way as needed.

Rewards for Victory

When the chaos finally ends, collect the **Flash Grenade** from the cabinet and the **Hourglass** from the central red box. Enter the shooting range where the wine-soaked painting hangs and search behind the desk to find **Magnum Ammo**. Then exit via the door in the red room.

EXHIBITION CORRIDOR

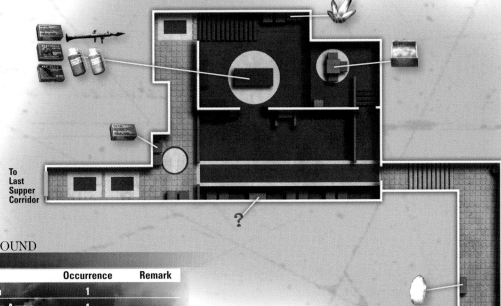

To Last Supper Corridor

?

To Central Hall

ITEMS FOUND

Item	Occurrence	Remark
Random	1	
Handgun Ammo	1	
Shotgun Shells	1	
Rifle Ammo	2	
Flash Grenade	1	
Incendiary Grenade	1	
Rocket Launcher	1	
Pesetas (Box)	1	
Spinel	1	
Velvet Blue	1	

Restricted Access

Walk into the room quietly, trying not to be seen by the enemies on the floor below. Use the rifle to snipe them, as well as the enemy that patrols on the raised platform on the far side of the room. Smash the clay pot on the nearby table to obtain **Rifle Ammo**, then drop to the level below. Throw the switch to raise a bridge connecting the two halves of the upper level.

Retribution for the Rise

Climb the ladder to the upper level, and expect trouble to follow you into the roo from the north door. Note that Plagas emerging from cultists heads are now acid-spitting, head-decapitating insect-like creatures. After the parasite is separated from the host body, it scuttles across the floor toward Leon. Remember to take o multiple parasites with Flash Grenades.

After taking down the group near the entrance, head down the bridge. Another group with shields enters from the far door. Shoot the oil lantern above them to burn them up.

Weapons on Display

Descend a few steps down the stairs and use the rifle to take out a crossbow snipe in a window across the room. Take the **Pesetas** on the table and drop to the level below. Smash open the clay pot on the corner to obtain a **Velvet Blue**.

Break the glass on the display case and take the various items. If the **Rocket Launcher** does not fit into your inventory, do not discard items trying to cram it into Leon's case. The merchant in the next passage sells the Attaché Case XL, which should provide enough room to tote the launcher.

To get out of the room, ascend the stairs near the display case and break the padlock on the door. Cross the platform you raised and proceed down the corridor. Smash the pot on the table to obtain a **Spinel**. Enter the next room for a chilling scene.

CHAPTER 3-4
CENTRAL HALL (MEZZANINE)

ITEMS FOUND

Item	Occurrence	Remark
Random	2	
Handgun Ammo	2	
Rifle Ammo	1	
Flash Grenade	1	
Pesetas (Box)	2	
Gold Bars	1	5000 - Portrait
Spinel	1	

In Memoriam...

Smash the pots surrounding the mezzanine level and collect the various types of ammo and money. Smash the pot to the left of Saddler's portrait to obtain Pesetas, knock his picture aside to obtain **Gold Bars** worth 5000 pesetas. Smash the pot to the right to obtain a **Spinel**.

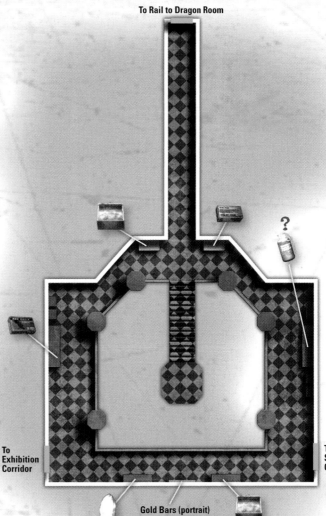

To Rail to Dragon Room

To Exhibition Corridor

To Servant Quarters 1

Gold Bars (portrait)

Sniper's Mission

By this point you should have noticed Ashley, bound to the wall on the level below. Aim to either side and carefully shoot the bands that hold her to the wall. Cultists enter the room and give chase. Aim toward Ashley's position and take their heads off as they try to reach her. Do not allow the cultists to carry her out of the room, or the game ends.

Stay on the central platform and watch Ashley move toward the door. When she finds the exit locked, cultists flood the room. Quickly aim down and shoot the red-robed cultists to release the key to the room. Then take out any crossbow

snipers that may be firing on your position. Meanwhile, shoot any cultists that grab Ashley, and take out all enemies. When clear, Ashley picks up the cultist's key and exits the room.

ITEMS FOUND

Item	Occurrence	Remark
Green Herb	1	
Red Herb	1	
Yellow Herb	1	
Spinel	1	
Velvet Blue	1	
Pesetas (Box)	3	

To Central Hall

Butler's Memo

To Servant Quarters 2

Ashley's Adventure

The player must now control Ashley. Move northwest and collect the **Spinel** by the table. Don't miss the **Yellow Herb** in the northeast corner. Use the typewriter if desired and then proceed into the next room.

Prevent the enemy from attacking Ashley by grabbing the three lanterns around the room and throwing them at the cultist, or by crawling under tables where the cultist cannot follow. A crank in the southeast corner can be turned to raise the bars blocking the archway into the next room, but this is unnecessary. Ashley can crawl through the small hole between rooms in the southwest corner.

Room Full of Clues

…ove forward from the crawl …ole and open the table drawer …o obtain a **Spinel**. Open the …tch in the southwest corner …f the second room to obtain a …w **Pesetas**. After dealing with …e second cultist, rotate the two …anks to remove the two sets of …rs blocking the next passage.

Head down the passage and take the **Red Herb**. Open the door at the opposite corner. In the drawer of the desk near the entrance is a **Velvet Blue**. A **Spinel** is on a table within. Open the bureau on the north wall to obtain **Handgun Ammo**. Take the document on the south bureau titled **Butler's Memo**. Examine the painting and the wheel in the center of the room for clues. Return to the corridor and head south.

SERVANT QUARTERS 2

ITEMS FOUND

Item	Occurrence	Remark
Green Herb	1	
Spinel	2	
Velvet Blue	1	
Pesetas (Box)	1	
Gold Bangle	1	
Stone Tablet	1	
Serpent Ornament	1	
Salazar Family Insignia	1	

Series of Gates

Turn to Ashley's left and crawl under a table. Proceed to the end and press the switch to raise the nearby gate. Enter the middle section and examine the fireplace to find the **Stone Tablet**. Press the switch in this area to raise another gate.

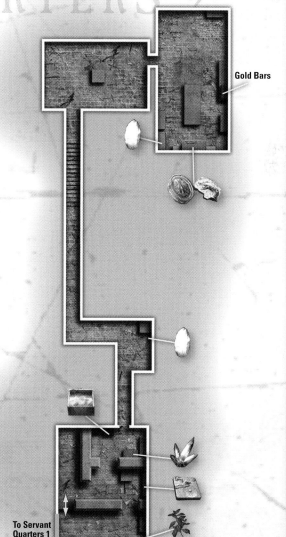

Gold Bars

To Servant Quarters 1

Head into the area you opened and collect the **Green Herb** from the table. Push aside the bookshelf on the south wall to reveal a switch. Press this switch to open the final gate. Collect the **Pesetas** and **Velvet Blue** from the furniture near the exit before going into the next room.

The Knights' Puzzle

Proceed down the dark corridor and collect the **Spinel** from the chair. Note the positions of the suits of armor in the hallway as you proceed to the room at the end. Check the central pedestal in the dark room to find a sliding-tile puzzle. This puzzle can be solved by several methods, but outlined below is one solution that *definitely works*.

Sliding Tablet Puzzle

Move the right center tile inward to the center.

Move the upper right tile down.

Move the top center tile right.

Move the center tile up.

Move the left center tile inward to the center.

Move the lower left tile up.

Move the bottom center tile left.

Move the lower right tile left.

Move the right center tile down.

Move the center tile right.

Move the top center tile down.

Move the top left tile right.

Move left center tile up.

Move the left bottom tile up.

Move the bottom center tile left.

Move the center tile down.

Move the right center tile inward to the center.

Move the bottom right tile upward.

Insert the Stone Tablet.

Treasures of the Armaduras

After solving the stone tablet puzzle, enter the revealed room. Open the box by the east wall to collect a **Gold Bangle**. The cupboard in the southwest corner of the room contains a **Spinel**. Taking the **Salazar Family Insignia** from the statue causes a secret panel to revolve, producing a blue box containing the **Serpent Ornament**.

Taking the object causes all of the armors in the area to come to life and attack. Use the table in the room to outmaneuver the walking suits, and then escape down the corridor. Press the dodge buttons with the right timing to avoid the Armaduras that attack Ashley in the corridor. In the room with the gates, quickly press the switch to shut the nearest barrier and prevent the Armaduras from following. Yet another Armadura attacks as Ashley attempts to leave.

Rejoining Leon

Head back to the previous room and use the Salazar Family Insignia in the wheel. Turn the wheel to open a secret door in the wall. Climb the ladder and take the two boxes of pesetas from the table and then head south. Follow the winding passage out to the upper level of the Central Hall, where Leon awaits.

chapter four

With Chapter 4, the action starts rolling along at a roller coaster's pace. Merchants gradually allow weapons to be upgraded to the maximum levels. When certain guns are maxed out, special "Exclusive" upgrades become available allowing weapons to be improved to incredible strength. Pour every peseta into weapon customization, because money is useless if not spent.

CHAPTER 4-1
EXTERNAL WALL AREA

To Courtyard & Bedroom

Gold Bars

x2

(crow)

(wall)

(door locked from north side)

? Snake Gold Bars

To Last Supper Corridor

S

To Gallery Area

ITEMS FOUND

Item	Occurrence	Remark
Red Herb	1	
Novistador Eyes	2	Enemies
Velvet Blue	1	
Gold Bangle	1	
Elegant Perfume Bottle	1	
Magnum	1	

Now That There Are Two...

Lead Ashley through the Exhibition and Last Supper Corridors. New enemies appea in both areas. Head south in the Last Supper Corridor and go through the south mess hall.

Return to the External Wall Area, and navigate northward to the room Leon coul not previously enter. Stand under the high opening and give Ashley a piggyback. After she unlocks the door, go inside and pilfer the **Elegant Perfume Bottle**, the **Gold Bangle** and the **Red Herb** from the chests to the sides. The big box contains a **Broke Butterfly** magnum handgun. Now return to the Central Hall and head north up the narrow passage.

134

RAIL TO THE DRAGON ROOM

ROOM

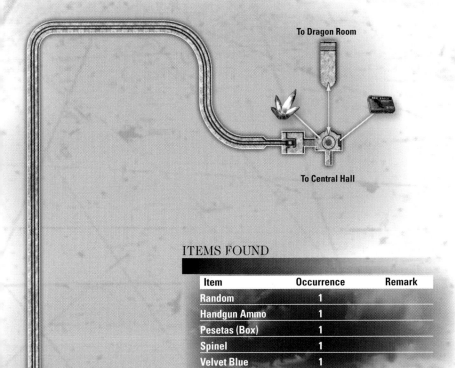

To Dragon Room

To Central Hall

To Audience Hall

ITEMS FOUND

Item	Occurrence	Remark
Random	1	
Handgun Ammo	1	
Pesetas (Box)	1	
Spinel	1	
Velvet Blue	1	

Separated by Machinery

Proceed into the room, head to the right and collect the
Handgun Ammo. Smash the clay pots on either side of the
doorway opposite to obtain a **Velvet Blue**. Although an
interesting railcar is parked at the bottom of the stairs, do not
board it just yet. Step on the square platform and ride the big
wheel device north. Leon must enter the next room alone.

DRAGON ROOM

DRAGON ROOM

ITEMS FOUND

Item	Occurrence	Remark
Illuminados Pendant	1	
Gold Bars	1	5000
Lion Ornament	1	

Fields of Fire

Cultists piloting giant dragon machines slowly move the devices to Leon's position and cause the monstrous machines to intermittently breathe fire. Quickly aim the rifle and snipe both dragon wranglers. Killing the machinists raises two red boxes in the area, containing **Gold Bars** worth 5000 pesetas and an **Illuminados Pendant**.

Tricky Tactics

If sniping the dragon wranglers proved tricky, the strategy required for the next part could prove even more complex. Continue north and jump across the gap when the opening of the spinning circular cage passes by. Before leaping to the next platform, snipe the cultists waiting in the area beyond.

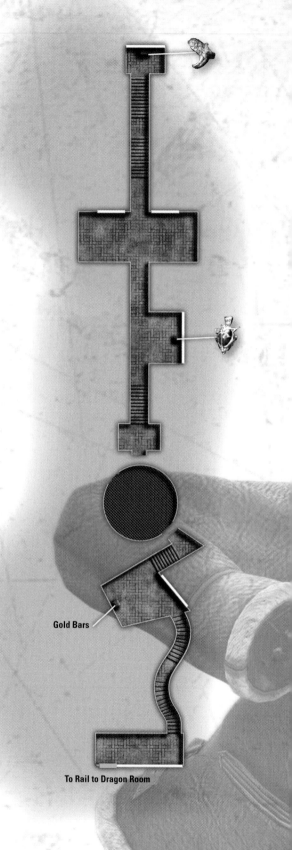

Gold Bars

To Rail to Dragon Room

oceed forward and collect the **Illuminados Pendant**, then dash to the north end of the area. When the third dragon achine rises, stand in front of the heat shield to the right to prevent fire damage from the last dragon. Quickly turn and ce south. Snipe the cultists at drop from the tower below eon's position as soon as they t the platform.

When the cultists stop emerging from the tower, run to one corner of the northern platform. When the dragon turns to face that direction and starts to emit flame, sprint to the other end of the platform and snipe the dragon wrangler before he is able to turn the dragon to face Leon.

Proceed up the steps to the blue box and collect the **Lion Ornament**. Navigate back out of the dragon's lair and rejoin Ashley. Board the railcar and ride back to the audience hall near the castle's entrance.

AUDIENCE HALL HALL

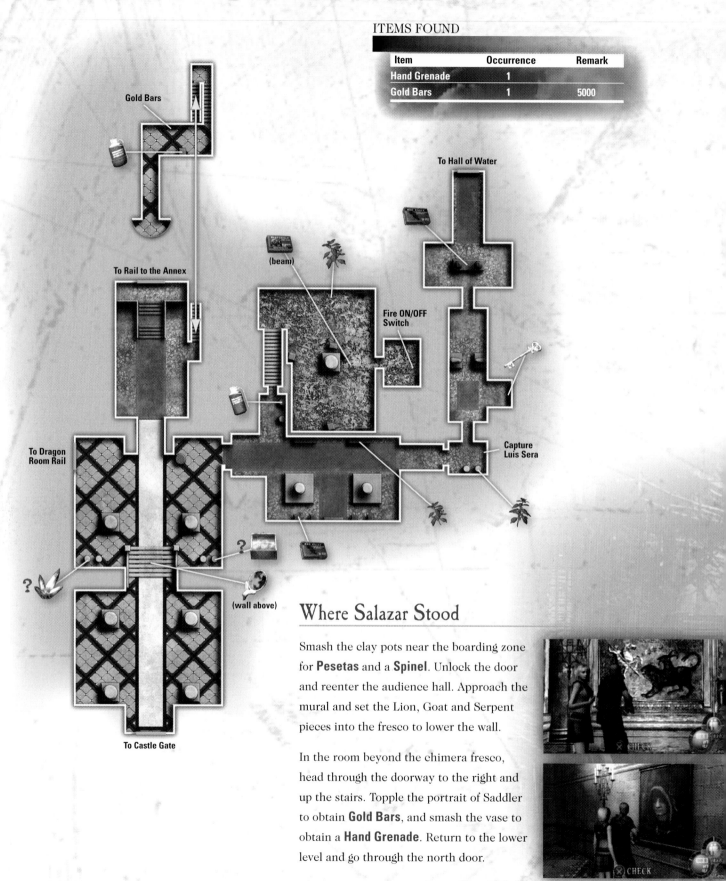

ITEMS FOUND

Item	Occurrence	Remark
Hand Grenade	1	
Gold Bars	1	5000

Gold Bars

To Hall of Water

(beam)

Fire ON/OFF Switch

To Rail to the Annex

Capture Luis Sera

To Dragon Room Rail

?

? (wall above)

To Castle Gate

Where Salazar Stood

Smash the clay pots near the boarding zone for **Pesetas** and a **Spinel**. Unlock the door and reenter the audience hall. Approach the mural and set the Lion, Goat and Serpent pieces into the fresco to lower the wall.

In the room beyond the chimera fresco, head through the doorway to the right and up the stairs. Topple the portrait of Saddler to obtain **Gold Bars**, and smash the vase to obtain a **Hand Grenade**. Return to the lower level and go through the north door.

RAIL TO THE ANNEX

ITEMS FOUND

Item	Occurrence	Remark
Random	2	
Pesetas (Box)	2	
Spinel	1	
Velvet Blue	1	

Private Transport

Hop over the fence to the sides of the tramcar and smash the vases to obtain the available items. Board the tramcar and ride to Salazar's private annex. At the arrival point, smash the vases to procure a **Velvet Blue**. Check behind the hung portrait of the man in contemplation to obtain **Gold Bars** worth 5000 pesetas. Enter the annex.

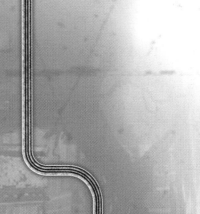

To Annex
Main Corridor

Gold Bars
(portrait)

?

To Audience Hall

?

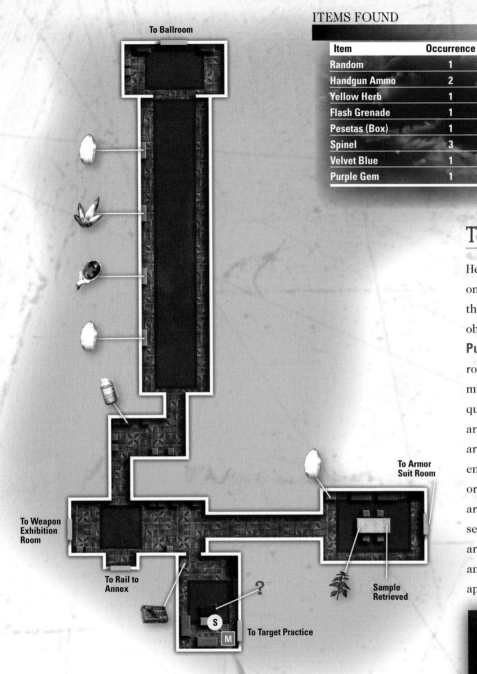

To Ballroom

To Armor Suit Room

To Weapon Exhibition Room

To Rail to Annex

Sample Retrieved

To Target Practice

ITEMS FOUND

Item	Occurrence	Remark
Random	1	
Handgun Ammo	2	
Yellow Herb	1	
Flash Grenade	1	
Pesetas (Box)	1	
Spinel	3	
Velvet Blue	1	
Purple Gem	1	

Toasting To Royalty

Head north and pick up the **Flash Grenade** on the chair. Continue north and shoot the shiny stones set in the column to obtain two **Spinels**, a **Velvet Blue** and a **Purple Gem** for the mask. Examine the royalty busts at the end of the hall. Grails must be set in the hands of the king and queen busts to unlock the exit to the next area. The two grails are located in two areas to the east and west of the annex entrance. The areas can be visited in any order. In the sections below, the west area is described first and the east area second. After surviving the trials in each area, return here with the Queen's Grail and the King's Grail, and set them in the appropriate royal's hands.

Shopping Break

[En]ter the door just east of the entrance to find a merchant. Open the cabinet [in]side the door to obtain **Handgun Ammo**. Be careful to *break* the clay pot on [th]e counter instead of *shooting* it; you might shoot the merchant by accident! [T]he merchant offers new tune-ups for the shotgun, TMP, and the semi-auto [rif]le. The blue door leads to the shooting gallery, where two game types are [n]ow available.

WEAPON EXHIBITION ROOM

[I]TEMS FOUND

Item	Occurrence	Remark
Random	1	
Handgun Ammo	2	
Rifle Ammo	1	
Pesetas (Box)	1	
Spinel	1	
Velvet Blue	1	
Elegant Chessboard	1	
Queen's Grail	1	

[F]our Knights on [F]our Pressure Pads

[T]his description details the area *west* of [th]e annex entrance. Examine the locked [do]or at the north end of the room to learn [h]ow to open the portal. Lead Ashley onto [o]ne of the four pressure pads, and then [p]ush the two knight statues in the room [o]nto two other pads. Finally, stand on the [r]emaining pad to open the door.

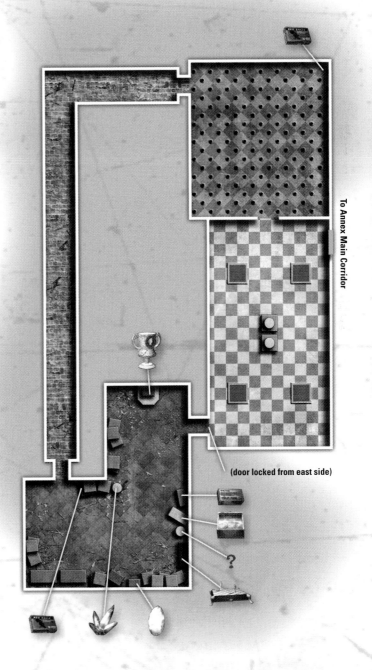

To Annex Main Corridor

(door locked from east side)

Death from Above

Salazar triggers the old crushing ceiling trap. Shoot the four jewels in the ceiling to stop the roof from descending. Collect the **Handgun Ammo** in the corner and follow Salazar into the corridor.

Crazy Cultist Drivers!

Proceed through the stone corridor, and be sure to equip the sniper rifle before entering the room at the end. Leon is separated from Ashley by a gate, and a giant wrecking machine threatens to kill her. Quickly aim through the bars at the two drivers of the machine and kill them. Slaying the pilots opens the gate, but does not stop the machine. Back up so that Ashley can get into the room.

Break open crates and barrels to collect various items and treasures. The **Queen's Grail** is stored in the red box. Open the cabinet in the southeast corner to find the valuable **Elegant Chessboard**. Break the padlock on the door and exit the area.

ARMOR SUIT ROOM

ARMOR SUIT ROOM

ITEMS FOUND

Item	Occurrence	Remark
Handgun Ammo	2	
Shotgun Shells	1	
Green Herb	1	
Pesetas (Box)	3	
King's Grail	1	

Don't You Hate When Armor Attacks?

This description details the area *east* of the annex entrance. Proceed to the corner and take the **Handgun Ammo** set on the base of the lion statue. Command Ashley to wait, then walk down the corridor. Press the dodge buttons to escape the axes of the Armaduras that suddenly attack from either side. This little exercise in terror happens twice.

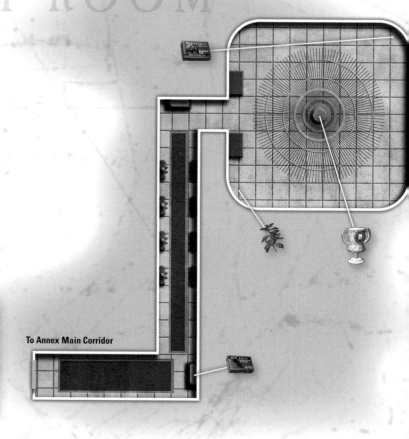

To Annex Main Corridor

Hall of Wrath

...ommand Ashley to stay put as you enter the next room. Collect the **Green Herb** in ...orner near the entrance and the **Shotgun Shells** in northeast corner. Equip hand ...enades if available or the shotgun if not, and take the **King's Grail** on the center ...edestal.

...king the grail triggers the appearances of three Armaduras. As they approach, back up to one corner of the room and allow ...em to advance. Just before there is no room to get out, slip between them, spin around and toss a grenade into the cluster. ...low the Armaduras to kneel in pain and then rise, and toss another. The Plaga in each suit should appear at this point.

Toss a flash grenade to kill them all simultaneously. Accomplish this with full health, and each enemy should drop supplies. The second three Armaduras each drop a box of **6500 Pesetas**!

BALLROOM

...EMS FOUND

Item	Occurrence	Remark
Random	1	
Handgun Ammo	1	
Shotgun Ammo	1	
Red Herb	1	
Pesetas (Box)	3	
Spinel	1(2)	
Green Eye	4	Enemy x9
Red Eye	3	Enemy x9
Blue Eye	1	Enemy x9
Butterfly Lamp	1	

...hattered Glass

...hoot the pots to either side to claim items, just ...e careful of a snake planted in one. Proceed down ...e corridor, opening the cabinets on the left to ...btain money.

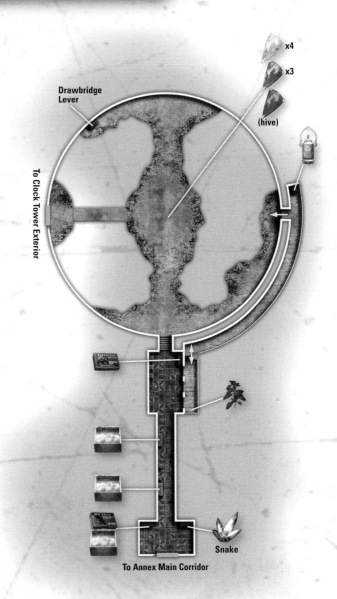

Drawbridge Lever

x4

x3

(hive)

To Clock Tower Exterior

Snake

To Annex Main Corridor

Reaching the double doors, turn right and jump through the smashed window to the balcony outside. Collect the **Red Herb** at the corner, and climb the ladder. Follow the circular ledge to the end, where another **Butterfly Lamp** is located inside a red box. Drop from the ledge into the ballroom, and then catch Ashley.

Home Is Where the Hive Is

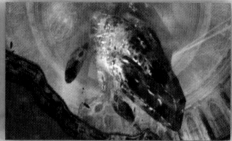

The Novistador hive is in the center of the room. Shooting the hive down causes the Eye gems listed in the table above to appear in the central area. Novistador enemies encountered in this area may drop addition Green, Red and Blue Eyes. Unfortunately, Ashley won't be around to share...

When a swarm of Novistadors appears, run through the south door and allow the enemies to funnel into the corridor, where you should be able to blast them easily with a shotgun. Reenter the room, throw the lever to try and lower the drawbridge, and then shoot the mountings of the chains that strain to hold the platform up. Exit the annex.

CLOCK TOWER EXTERIOR

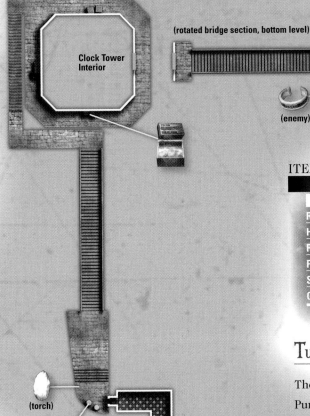

Clock Tower Interior

(rotated bridge section, bottom level)

To Watchman's Hallway

(enemy)

(torch)

?

To Ballroom

S M

ITEMS FOUND

Item	Occurrence	Remark
Random	1	
Handgun Ammo	1	
Rifle Ammo	1	
Pesetas (Box)	1	
Spinel	1	Torch
Gold Bangle	1	Enemy

Tune-Up to Take the Tower

The merchant offers new tune-ups for the Handgun, Rifle, Punisher, Red9, Blacktail, Broken Butterfly, Riot Gun and the Mine Thrower. Use the typewriter if desired and collect the **Handgun Ammo** on the chair. Smash the barrels to obtain a **Velvet Blue**, and shoot the torch at the top of the stairs to obtain a hidden **Spinel**.

Infiltration under Fire

Race toward the tower before the catapults firing from the right slow Leon down. Move west and quickly ascend the stairs. Take out the cultists on the balcony behind the tower. Then navigate to the front of the building and smash the barrels for items, if the catapults haven't done the job already. Whether you snipe the catapult operators is up to you, because you can slip around to the east side of the tower and easily get inside.

CLOCK TOWER INTERIOR
CLOCK TOWER INTERIOR

ITEMS FOUND

Item	Occurrence	Remark
Random	2	
Handgun Ammo	2	
Green Herb	1	
Hand Grenade	1	
Pesetas (Box)	2	

Clogs in the Cogs

Take a step toward the balcony rail and aim upward. A wooden
block is wedged into the clock tower gears. Shoot it to clear
the mechanism. Aim even higher up to spot another. Move to
the right and climb the ladder to the level above. Head to the
southeast corner and shoot the crate to obtain a random item.
Move around the balcony to the other side of the blockage to
find **Handgun Ammo**. Climb up to the next level.

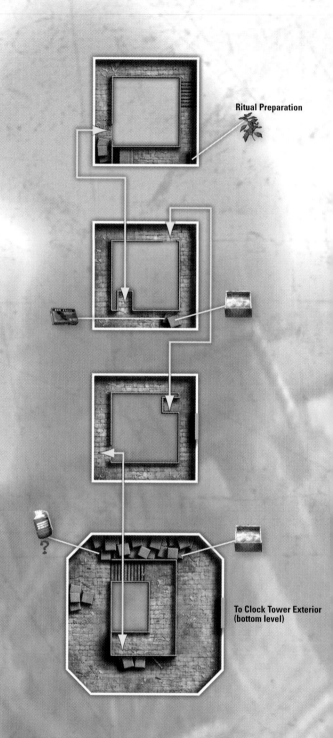

Ritual Preparation

To Clock Tower Exterior
(bottom level)

Navigate around the balcony and up the steps to a table.
Collect the **Green Herb** and the **Ritual Preparation** file.
Approach the lever at the end of the balcony, look to the
right and shoot the final block of wood out of the mechanism.
Throw the lever to rotate the bridge outside the tower.

Clockwork Firefight

The tower becomes suddenly flooded with enemies. Take out the snipers as you descend to the bottom level of the tower. Dropping down to the bottom level fills the tower with enemies over again. Climb back up and take out

those throwing dynamite, and then contend with those climbing up the ladders in pursuit of Leon.

Drop back down to the bottom level and shoot the sniper that likes to hide near a couple of crates. Destroy the crates to obtain a **Hand Grenade**. Navigate around the bottom level to the exit.

A Bridge Too Far

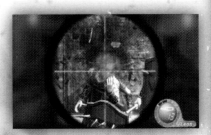

Exit the tower and take out the group of shield-bearing zealots that are approaching. Estimate where their heads are behind the shields, and use the sniper rifle to kill them in one shot.

Proceed onto the bridge until a much larger group emerges, both in front and behind Leon. Turn around and head back toward the clock tower, blasting the enemies out of the way with a shotgun. Make your stand at the clock tower doors, and toss grenades at the group crossing over the bridge. When Plagas emerge from cultists' necks, toss flash grenades to take out several parasites at once. The leader, wearing the goat mask, tends to hang back near the entrance of the anti-castle. Kill him to obtain a **Gold Bangle**.

WATCHMAN'S HALLWAY

WATCHMAN'S HALLWAY

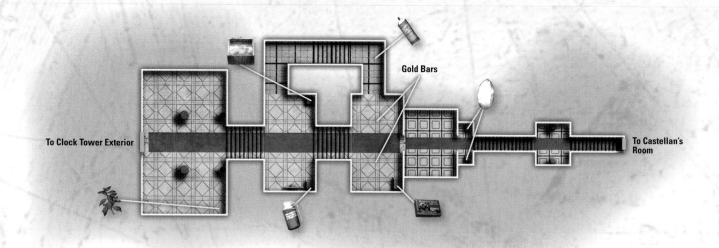

To Clock Tower Exterior

Gold Bars

To Castellan's Room

ITEMS FOUND

Item	Occurrence	Remark
Random	1	
Shotgun Shells	1	
Green Herb	1	
First Aid Spray	1	Enemy
Incendiary Grenade	1	
Pesetas (Box)	1	
Spinel	2	

Double Garradors!

The combination of cultists and two Garradors in this room makes survival extremely tough. Although it is possible to stay away from the Garradors and snipe them from a distance, the cultists constantly approach too close and require you to make noise, alerting the Garradors.

Fortunately, there are two simple words that allow you to get through this room with your sanity intact: *rocket launcher*. Stand just inside the entrance and aim a missile at the door between the two Garradors positioned at the back of the room. The explosion scorches the Plagas on both their backs, killing them both instantly. Now only the cultists remain, and you are free to shoot without fear of alerting the blind.

Without a rocket launcher to help, use the sniper rifle to take out the two cultists on the midlevel. Allow the Garradors to charge toward Leon and stab their claws into the entry doors. Throw grenades to damage the Garradors and take out the second wave of cultists. Shoot the bells in order to drive the Garradors to the sides of the room, where their parasites can easily be targeted.

Salazar Cornered

The east passage of the room opens when the two Garradors die. Killing the cultist in the mask who hangs out in the side corridor nets a **First Aid Spray**. When the first three cultists die, another four emerge from secret doors near the entrance. Have fun.

mash the pots in the room to obtain items, and collect the ammo
ring around the area. In the corridor beyond the initial room, two
pinels are affixed to knightly busts.

Enter the next room.
Whimsical Salazar drops Leon
into a deadly pit. Press the
dodge buttons on cue to save
Leon's life.

TRAITOR'S PIT

ITEMS FOUND

Item	Occurrence	Remark
Handgun Ammo	1	
Yellow Herb	1	
Spinel	1	
Velvet Blue	2	
Crown	1	

The Impaled

Leon finds himself in Salazar's disposal pit where
the little master does away with servants that no
longer suit his whimsy, including cultists who try
to steal from him. Examine the body impaled on
the spike near the waterfall to obtain a **Velvet
Blue**. A dead cultist slumped against the back wall
holds the **Crown**. Two other pieces fit into this
crown to increase the overall value so do not sell it
immediately.

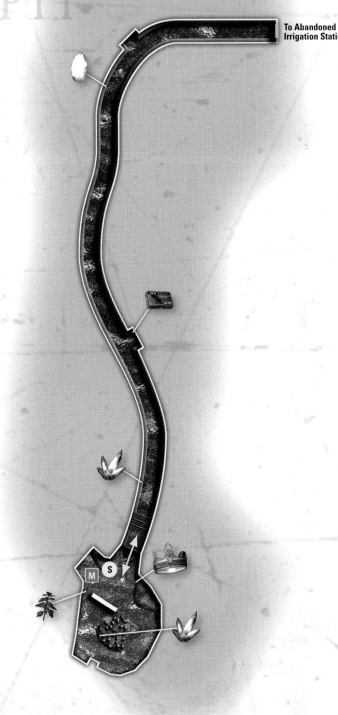

To Abandoned
Irrigation Station

The merchant now sells the fast firing Striker, which is less powerful at long range than other shotguns but more powerful up close. We highly recommend you upgrade to this awesome weapon if funding allows.

Wading Upstream

Climb the ladder head up the corridor.
Check the first drain on the left for a **Velvet Blue**, and take the **Handgun Ammo** at the next corner. Continue up the tunnel and take a **Spinel** from another drain on the left.

ABANDONED IRRIGATION STATION

ITEMS FOUND

Item	Occurrence	Remark
Handgun Ammo	1	
Shotgun Shells	1	
TMP Ammo	1	
Green Herb	1	
First Aid Spray	1	
Crown Jewel	1	Verdugo

Hunted from the Shadows

Proceed down the tunnel and follow the first branch on the right. Examine the liquid nitrogen container just inside the door, and collect the **Handgun Ammo** and **First Aid Spray** on the desk. The elevator at the back of the room cannot be called to this level because the power

is out. You must restore the power to call the elevator and escape.

Upon leaving the room, you may need to dodge a tail attack by the "executioner" Salazar sent after Leon. Quickly make your way to the north room, and stay ready to crouch or dodge at an instant's notice.

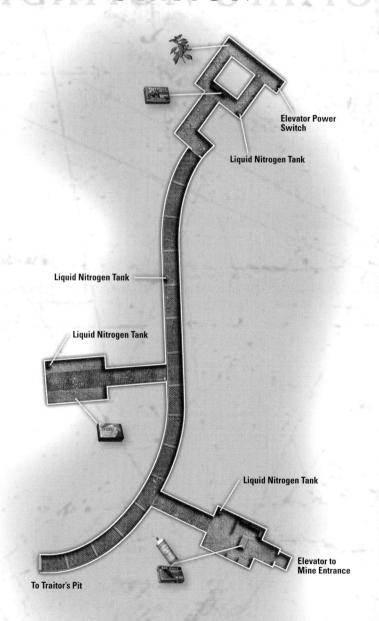

Elevator Power Switch

Liquid Nitrogen Tank

Liquid Nitrogen Tank

Liquid Nitrogen Tank

Liquid Nitrogen Tank

To Traitor's Pit

Elevator to Mine Entrance

…avigate left around the fenced area and collect the **Shotgun Shells** on the console. …ead northwest to find a **Green Herb**. Then follow the back wall of the room to the …ortheast corner and throw the switch to restart the power. The elevator appears in a …w minutes.

Turn on the power?
▶Yes No

The area must be locked down for safety reasons. I hope it's temporary.

Head back toward the closed entrance and press the button. The shutter takes some time to open as well. Until then, you must survive a difficult battle against Salazar's vicious bodyguard.

VERDUGO

…his entire strategy assumes that you do not have a rocket …auncher, which makes the battle a very simple matter. Press …he dodge buttons to try to survive the Verdugo's initial attacks, …hen make your way to the back of the power room and stand …ext to the liquid nitrogen tank. When the Verdugo approaches, …ress ✖ to knock over the tank. While the creature is frozen and …hivering, damage done to the monster is tripled. Use the rocket …auncher at this point to shatter it into a hundred shards of …rozen bug man.

…ithout a rocket launcher, blast Verdugo with the shotgun or shoot several mines into it with the mine …hrower and run away. When a certain amount of damage is inflicted on the creature, it shrugs off its icy …oating and returns to full speed and strength. Soon after inflicting so much damage to it, the shutter room …oor should open and …ou can dash down …he corridor. Be ready …o dodge up to three …eiling tail attacks in … row on your way to …he next attack point.

Run to the next liquid nitrogen canister in the corridor and wait for Verdugo to approach. Knock the canister over to freeze the beast and attack it, then run away. Continue south and then west into a small room where TMP Ammo is located. Use the liquid nitrogen tank in this room against the monster, and then head back to the room where the eagerly awaited elevator is expected to arrive. Use the last liquid nitrogen tank against it, and then either board the elevator and flee, or stay and finish the monster. Continue blasting it with a shotgun and throwing grenades, and press the action buttons to dodge its attacks when possible. Sticking around to execute the executioner has its advantages, since the monster drops the Crown Jewel.

CHAPTER 4-2
MINE ENTRANCE

ITEMS FOUND

Item	Occurrence	Remark
Handgun Ammo	2	
Rifle Ammo	1	
Green Herb	1	
Hand Grenade	1	
Spinel	1	

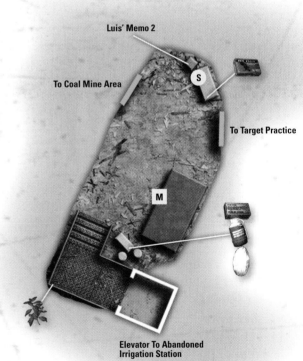

Luis' Memo 2

To Coal Mine Area

S

To Target Practice

M

Elevator To Abandoned Irrigation Station

Gear Up at the Depot

Step off the elevator and collect the **Green Herb** at the corner of the platform. Smash the three barrels at the bottom of the stairs to obtain **Rifle Ammo**, a **Hand Grenade** and a **Spinel**. More **Handgun Ammo** lies by the typewriter, and **Luis' Memo 2** waits to be read near the exit. Enter the shooting gallery if desired to play Target Practice game types A, B, or C.

COAL MINE AREA

Introduction
Characters
Enemies
Weapons and Ammunition
Key Items and Treasures
Game System and Strategies
Walkthrough
Secrets and Bonuses

Dynamite (move trolley)

Trolley Control

To Blast Furnace

Circuit Breaker Switch

Gold Bars

ITEMS FOUND

Item	Occurrence	Remark
Random	2	
Handgun Ammo	1	
Shotgun Shells	1	
Green Herb	1	
Flash Grenade	1	
Pesetas (Box)	4	
Velvet Blue	2	
Gold Bars	1	5000 - Behind Circuit Breaker
Dynamite	1	

To Mine Entrance

nto the Mine

llow the tunnel and kill the two villagers standing idle in the cave. xamine the first coal cart on the right to obtain a **Velvet Blue**. Smash e barrels to obtain **Handgun Ammo** and **Pesetas**. Read the warning the nearby board, and proceed down the passage.

Maintain the High Ground

Snipe as many of the villagers as you care to, then drop to the level below. A few more enemies drop to the ground with you. However, with improved weapons, the villagers should prove easier than ever to kill. Collect the items and pesetas scattered around the area.

Boulder Blasting

A massive boulder blocks the path to the exit. Pull the lever in the northwest corner of the mine to move the trolley. Before the trolley is fully lowered to the ground floor, the circuit breaker shorts out. Take the **Velvet Blue** lying in the mine cart near the lever, then head toward the circuit breaker on the upper level and flip it back on.

Defeat the angry group of villagers now coming down the entrance tunnel and a chainsaw maniac positioned near the trolley lever. The chainsaw man drops **10,000 Pesetas** upon dying.

When the coast is clear, pull the northwest lever a second time to lower the trolley to the bottom level. Take the **Dynamite** from the cart and place it upon the boulder blocking the path. Be sure to move back, or Leon could die from the blast. Head into the next room.

BLAST FURNACE

ITEMS FOUND

Item	Occurrence	Remark
Shotgun Shells	2	
First Aid Spray	1	
Flash Grenade	1	
Incendiary Grenade	1	
Pesetas (Box)	1	

Magma Battle

Search along the walls of this fiery chamber and collect the ammo and **First Aid Spray** located in the south half or the room. Then approach the massive doors. Not one, but *two* Gigantes storm into the room! During the battle, smash the barrels beyond the big doors if needed to obtain an **Incendiary Grenade** and **Shotgun Shells**.

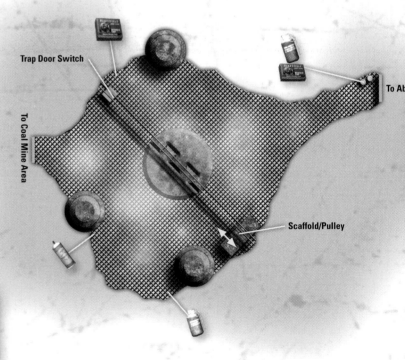

Trap Door Switch

To Ab

To Coal Mine Area

Scaffold/Pulley

LOS DOS GIGANTES

Consider the reward options before choosing a strategy in this intense battle. Each Gigante is worth 15,000 pesetas, but you must kill them the old fashioned way by shooting them and then climbing onto their backs to cut the parasite. If you dump one of them into the magma with the central trap door, the potential reward drops by half. However, fighting two giants at once is probably more trouble than the double reward is worth.

Whichever option you choose, separate Leon from the Gigantes by climbing the scaffold on the east side of the room. Wait until the Gigantes approach and begin to strike the scaffold. Before they shake Leon off the platform, grab the

winch and swing down to the floor. Leon lands directly in front of the lever that opens the trap door in the center. Press ✗ to grab the lever. Leon looks over his shoulder as the Gigantes approach. One of them is smart enough to always avoid the trap door, but the darker skinned one walks right over the trap door. If you are not interested in doubling the reward, pull the lever to open the trap door and drop one of the Gigantes in the magma. Be sure to stay clear of the pit's edge until the door closes a moment later. Otherwise, the dying Gigante leaps out and drags Leon to a fiery death.

Use the winch to escape from the monsters even if you don't wish to use the magma pit trap. As the monsters turn and close in, shoot them to weaken the monsters and force them to reveal their parasites. Avoid climbing onto a Gigante while the other is present, or the second creature may snatch Leon off the top of the target Gigante. When one Gigante bows, toss a flash grenade to stun the other and then go after the exposed Plaga. When this attack is done, climb the scaffold and slide down to the other side of the chamber again. Repeat the entire process until one and then the other Gigante is killed.

ABYSS

ITEMS FOUND

Item	Occurrence	Remark
Shotgun Shells	1	
TMP Ammo	1	
Green Herb	3	
Red Herb	1	
Flash Grenade	1	
Novistador Eyes	1	Enemy x29
Royal Insignia	1	

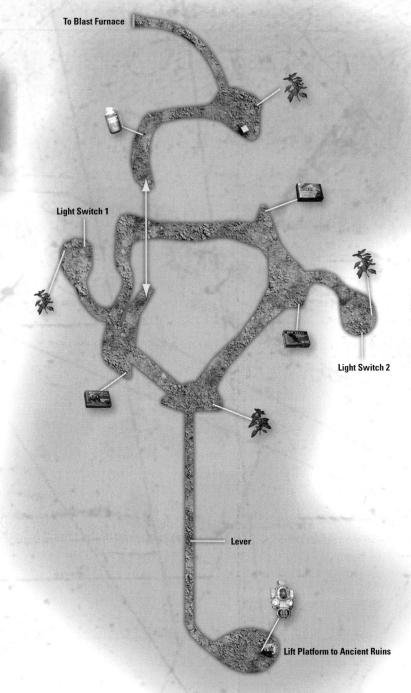

To Blast Furnace

Light Switch 1

Light Switch 2

Lever

Lift Platform to Ancient Ruins

From the Bottom Up

Novistadors hover over the pit in the open area. Snipe them out of the air with the rifle, or fire a warning shot to bait them into flying over solid land. Then you have an opportunity to score one of the Novistadors' Eye jewels. In this cave only, Novistadors also drop a variety of ammo and recovery items, and they do not turn invisible. Once you have the enemies' attention, stand in the narrow tunnel and wait for a dozen or more Novistadors to come after Leon.

The Two Light Rays

Grab the **Green Herb** in the corner and read the pedestal inscription regarding "two lights." Continue up the path, collecting a **Flash Grenade** and **Shotgun Shells**. Enter the nearby cave to the west and collect another **Green Herb**. Press the switch to emit a ray of light in the main cavern. Naturally this drives almost a dozen Novistadors into the little cave you hide in. Blast them as they attempt to funnel in.

xit the side cave and head north, then east.
ke the **TMP Ammo** at the corner. Make your
ay to the high cave on the east wall, and take
e **Handgun Ammo** outside the entrance. Blast
e half dozen Novistadors milling around in the
ve. Collect another **Green Herb** and press the
witch to make the second ray of light appear.

Fighting for the Exit

The south exit opens, and another swarm of Novistadors appears.
Sprint for the exit, or stay in the side cave and blast the Novistadors as
they attempt to intrude.

Another swarm flies
out of their hive as
you head toward the
exit. Quickly press the

witch on the revealed door, move a few steps into the cave and turn around
take down your enemies. Or, avoid combat and continue fleeing into the
ve, where the Novistadors cannot follow for obvious reasons.

Pounding Stones

Giant stones mechanically rise and smash into the ground. If Leon is
caught under a falling stone he's going to feel a lot worse about life.
Wait until each stone slams into the ground, then run forward and
underneath as the rock rises. Climb over the rises and quickly drop
over the next ledge before the stone falls.

At the midpoint of
the passage, throw

e switch on the left. The lever deactivates the second of three stones. Run
der the first stone and stop in the pool of light. Wait for the last stone to
l, then cross under it as it rises.

Outta Here!

Take the **Royal Insignia** from the pedestal and combine
with the Crown and Crown Jewel to form a very valuable
treasure. Examine the sarcophagus to raise the platform to
the surface world.

ANCIENT RUINS

Lift to Abyss

Letter from Ada

To Mine Cart Room

(upper level)

Elevator to Cathedral

To Mine Entranc[e]

Message from the Mistress

Smash the barrels to the left of the merchant's shack to obtain a **Green Herb** and **Handgun Ammo**. Examine the paper posted on the merchant's doorway to read a **Letter from Ada**. The merchant offers new tune-ups for every weapon *except* the Riot Gun and Mine Thrower.

ITEMS FOUND

Item	Occurrence	Remark
Random	2	
Handgun Ammo	2	
Green Herb	1	
Flash Grenade	1	
Pesetas (Box)	2	
Spinel	2	
Velvet Blue	2	

Villager Bonfire

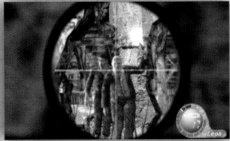

Continue east to lone a tree. Use the sniper rifle to take out the large group of villagers within the ruins. If ammo is scarce, there a key tactical points in the ruins where Leon can climb ladders to escape from clawing hands and blast enemies from above.

The Hidden Mine

Search the ruins for boxes of pesetas lying around as well as other items. The door at the east end of the area is locked and requires a "sacrifice." South of the exit is a dilapidated wooden structure. Hop through the open window behind the building and smash the barrel on the left for a **Green Herb**. Turn the crank to open the pit cover, and climb down.

UNDERGROUND RUINS ENTRANCE

Introduction

Characters

Enemies

Weapons and
Ammunition

Key Items
and Treasures

Game System
and Strategies

Walkthrough

Secrets and
Bonuses

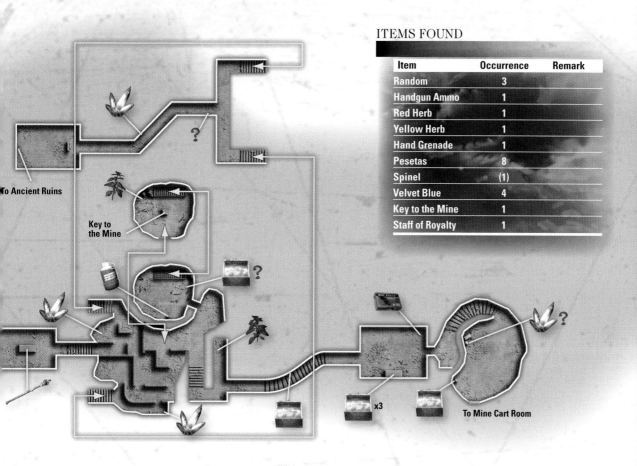

ITEMS FOUND

Item	Occurrence	Remark
Random	3	
Handgun Ammo	1	
Red Herb	1	
Yellow Herb	1	
Hand Grenade	1	
Pesetas	8	
Spinel	(1)	
Velvet Blue	4	
Key to the Mine	1	
Staff of Royalty	1	

The Dig Site

...ad the inscription on the monolith near the entrance, then head down the tunnel and break a crate on the right to ...rner a random item. Stepping out of the tunnel, snipe as many villagers as possible with the handgun and rifle. While ...aneuvering through the maze ...the room, proceed cautiously ...d shoot the bear traps set all ...er the place to prevent leg ...pture. The exit door is locked, ...d the key is well-guarded.

The King's Rod

Open the sarcophagus in the lower chamber under the entrance to obtain the valuable Staff of Royalty. This is also a good place to make enemies funnel into a tight formation where they can be easily picked off.

Slaughterhouse Guards

By now you undoubtedly noticed the chainsaw maniac spinning in circles in the room above. A second chainsaw guy is in the room downstairs. Entering the upstairs or downstairs room triggers the appearance of a mob of villagers. For strategy's sake, open the downstairs door quietly. Snipe the chainsaw man standing idly a few feet away with the rifle. This probably will not kill him, but should weaken him considerably.

Equip the shotgun and quickly blast a path up the interior stairs. Repeatedly topple the ladder outside the structure to prevent villagers from entering, and blast enemies trying to come up the steps.

If the heat gets too hot in the upstairs room, leap out of a window. The villagers will follow, and the chainsaw men will not. Blast the villagers as they exit the enclosed area, then return inside and take down the chainsaw guys for **10,000 Pesetas** apiece. Toss grenades liberally to stun or destroy enemy clusters.

The Mine Key

Smash the crates and barrels in the two-story enclosure to obtain items and pesetas. Take the **Key to the Mine** from the upstairs pedestal, you earned it! Taking the key triggers the appearance of more villagers. Do not collect the item while other enemies still linger. Use the Key to the Mine to open the east door and follow the tunnel.

Ancient Trap

Enter the room with the spiky ceiling and proceed inward a few steps. When the ceiling starts to descend, quickly use a flash grenade to eliminate Las Plagas. Shoot the four gems in the ceiling to stop the spikes' descent. Open the sarcophagus to obtain three boxes of **Pesetas** and search the rubble to left of the exit for hidden **Handgun Ammo**. Continue into the next room and down the ramp.

MINE CART ROOM

ROOM

EMS FOUND

Item	Occurrence	Remark
Random	1	
Handgun Ammo	2	
Shotgun Shells	2	
Green Herb	1	
Pesetas	3	
Stone of Sacrifice	1	

Ride from Hell

Smash the barrels near the entrance for **Shotgun Shells** and **Pesetas**. Collect the **Green Herb** and board the mine cart. Hop from cart to cart up to the front, and use the rifle to snipe the villagers standing on the platforms just inside the tunnel ahead. Move to the middle car, shoot the lever, and then jump to the front car and enjoy the ride. Villagers attempt to jump into the mine cart as it rolls forward on the rails. Try to shoot the villagers with the TMP or shotgun before they have a chance to board the transport.

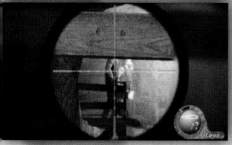

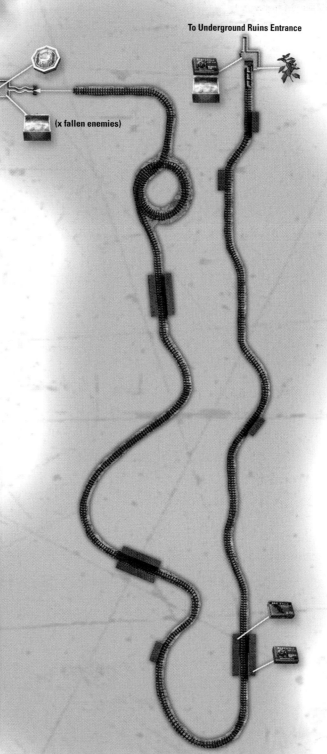

To Underground Ruins Entrance

To Ancient Ruins

(x fallen enemies)

At certain points along the route, Leon is in danger of hitting his head on a board spanning the tunnel. Shoot the board, or press the action buttons with good reflexes to crouch under it.

Derailed

The villagers throw a switch to stop the train between two platforms. One of the attackers is a chainsaw maniac, who drops **10,000 Pesetas** when killed. If you happen to be in position, quickly grab the **Handgun Ammo** to the right of the rear cart and the **Shotgun Shells** to the right of the front cart. Then shoot the lever at the front of the train to get the mine cart back on track. Use the shotgun

to blast the villagers and chainsaw maniac illegally boarding your train.

The mine cart rolls through a few more passenger boarding points, and more board spanning the tunnel threaten to decapitate Leon. When the train reaches a sharp spira descent, it becomes impossible to jump from one cart to another. Face forward and prepare to press the two action buttons displayed onscreen when the cart drops into a chasm. With the right timing, Leon leaps across the gap. Press the action butto displayed rapidly to make convince Leon t climb onto the platform.

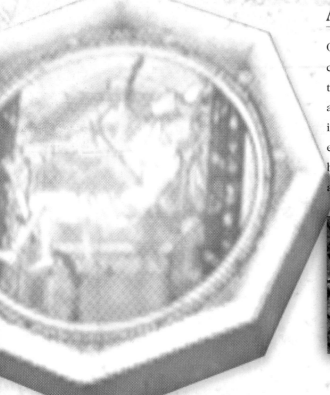

A Suitable Sacrifice

Open the door and enter the chamber. Search the rubble to the left of the door to find small amounts of **Pesetas**, placed here in connection with the number of enemies killed before they could

board the train. Collect the **Stone of Sacrifice** from the central pedestal to revea a secret tunnel. Enter the tunnel and climb the ladder.

Back in the ancient ruins, use the Stone of Sacrifice to open the eas door. Board the lift and operate it

CHAPTER 4-4
CATHEDRAL

ITEMS FOUND

Item	Occurrence	Remark
Random	3	
Handgun Ammo	3	
Rifle Ammo	1	
Pesetas	3	
Gold Bars	1	5000 - Red Enemy
Spinel	1	
Velvet Blue	2	

Hall of Worship

Down passage and to the right, Leon finds one box of **Handgun Ammo** and a typewriter. Continue down the passage and descend the stairs a short distance for a better view of the Salazar statue, the obvious totem of this bizarre religion.

Start heading south. Zealots cut off the exit and set Robo-Salazar in motion. The statue's left hand begins moving up and down like an elevator between the three western levels.

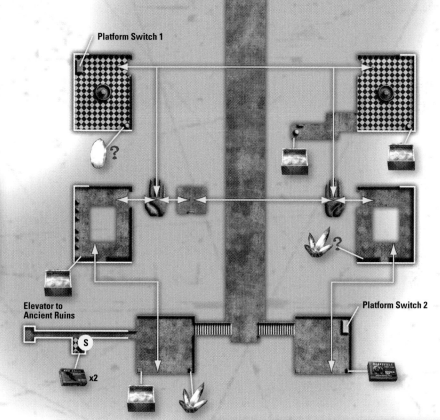

Ascend the west stairs and aim upward to shoot enemies on the platforms overhead. Let your bullets topple them from ledges. Head to the closed east gate and give the cultist in red a blast or two. Just be sure not to kill him, so that you can claim what he drops later.

Rising in Level

Return to the west side of the room and climb the ladder. Jump onto Robo-Salazar's left hand. Allow the hand to raise you to the third level. Blast enemies off of the third level platforms, and then jump across.

Smash the pots at the back of the third level to obtain a **Spinel**. Throw the lever to re-raise one of the platforms in the center aisle of the room. New cultists appear on the east side of the room.

Switching Hands

Jump to the center platform and operate the switch. Robo-Salazar starts moving its right hand. If for some reason you should miss the left hand when leaping toward it, return to the second level of the west side and shoot the central lever to change hands.

Ride the right hand to the third level and break the clay pot to obtain **Pesetas**. Follow the narrow platform behind the statue. Move the lever on Robo-Salazar's back. Now both hands move. The upturned palms also come together at the top so that the third floor can be crossed more easily.

Completing the Path

Ride the right hand to the second level on the east side. Smash the pot to obtain a **Velvet Blue**, and finish off the lone zealot in red for **Gold Bars** worth 5000 pesetas. Smash the pot on the lowest east level for **Shotgun Shells**, and move the nearby lever to open the gate and raise the second platform to the north. A final enemy set appears. Take them out.

The Revenge of Robo-Salazar!

Equip the shotgun, then head north up the center aisle. Robo-Salazar comes to life and threatens to stomp Leon. Press ❌ rapidly to sprint. Press **L1** to dodge a column falling from the left, and **R1** to dodge one from the right. Press both buttons to dodge two columns.

Reaching the end of the path, quickly blast the padlock off the door and kick it open. As the chase continues on the bridge outside, tap ❌ rapidly to sprint and press the two buttons displayed to jump when Robo-Salazar falls, taking out the bridge. Press ❌ rapidly to climb up onto the platform and enter the tower.

OWER

EMS FOUND

Item	Occurrence	Remark
Random	3	
Handgun Ammo	4	
Shotgun Shells	2	
Rifle Ammo	1	
Green Herb	1	
Red Herb	1	
Yellow Herb	(1)	
First Aid Spray	1	
Incendiary Grenade	1	
Pesetas	4	
Velvet Blue	1	

alazar's Last Escape

ring the terse confrontation between Leon and
lazar in the tower, press the dodge buttons to
ck the bodyguard's attack. Salazar rides the
evator, but Leon has no such luck. He has to
e the stairs and deal with numerous enemies in
e tower. Search the left side of the room to find
ndgun Ammo and a Yellow Herb hidden behind
me boxes.

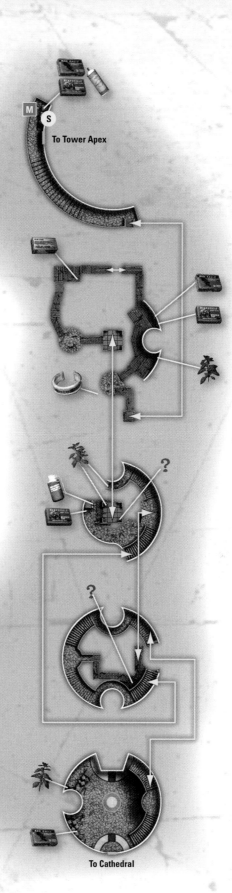

To Tower Apex

?

?

?

To Cathedral

Burning Barrels

Ascend the stairs until enemies begin rolling barrels down the stairs. Damage from the barrels is severe, especially if a burning barrel explodes near Leon. Wait until a barrel crashes, and then quickly run up the stairs. Evade the next barrel by following the suspended scaffold to the left.

Leon's Turn to Roll

Cross the wooden platforms and slay the cultists dropping from above. Climb the ladder to the level above. Leon finds himself right next to the mechanism that issues the barrels. On this cue, a group of cultists enters the tower via the bottom door. Pull the switch on the

column repeatedly to roll barrels down the stairs. When enemies stop screaming and groaning, descend to the bottom level and kill the leader near the entrance to obtain a cool **5500 Pesetas**.

Capacity Load

Follow the spiral stairs back to the top of the tower and take the **Green Herb** next to the crate blocking the path. Then return to the level below and board the lift. A cultist sniper may be standing on a platform above and behind the lift, and you should take his head off with the rifle before boarding. Smash the barrels behind the lift to obtain **Shotgun Shells** and an **Incendiary Grenade**.

The weight capacity of the lift is extremely low, and it will not rise with all of the objects on it. Smash the barrels on the lift and push the two large cargo boxes over the sides. Then press the switch on the panel to begin the slow ascent.

As Leon rides the lift, acolytes drop onto the platform. Exceeding the capacity, the lift stops. Blast the enemies off of the lift to continue rising. Meanwhile, sniper archers positioned on the surrounding ledges and balconies make life hard. Shoot them to knock them from their perches.

Tower Top

When the lift is finally allowed to reach the top, follow the path around the exterior of the tower. Smash the barrels to obtain ammo. Collect the **Red Herb** on the floor at the last corner, and then drop from the side of the platform to find a red chest in a cubby-hole containing a **Gold Bangle**. Climb back out of the hole and board the small lift. Ride it to the level above.

Collect the **Handgun Ammo**, **Shotgun Shells** and **First Aid Spray** next to the typewriter. The merchant offers new tune-ups for the Red9, if you still own that old thing. Purchase a rocket launcher if you want the upcoming battle to end quickly. If funds are insufficient, at least try to upgrade the firepower of a rifle for greater damage per shot.

TOWER APEX

ITEMS FOUND

Item	Occurrence	Remark
Handgun Ammo	5	
Shotgun Shells	2	
Green Herb	2	
First Aid Spray	1	
Flash Grenade	1	
Incendiary Grenade	1	
Pesetas	2	25000 x2 - Salazar

The Transcendent Lord

Salazar decides to make a stand against Leon's advance, and oh what a show he puts on! Both Salazar and his creepy bodyguard are enveloped within some kind of giant parasite organism, mutating into a multi-limbed monster.

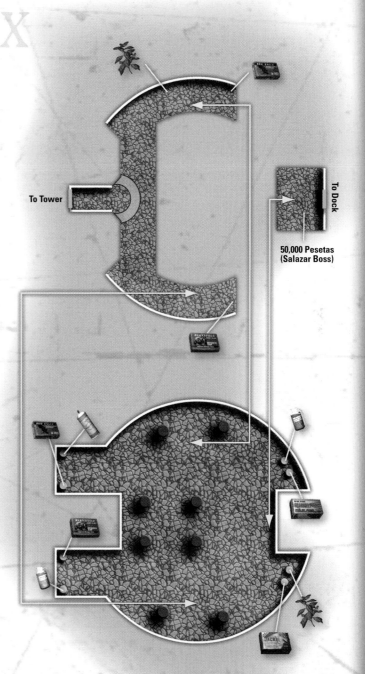

To Tower

To Dock

50,000 Pesetas
(Salazar Boss)

SALAZAR

SALAZAR

Leon faces danger from the central head as well as the two tentacles to either side. The tentacles can be damaged just enough to make them withdraw into the wall. However, shooting both tentacles triggers an attack by the central head. If this attack is successful, Leon dies instantly. Therefore, shoot only one of the tentacles until it withdraws into the wall, and stick to that side of the room so that you are free to attack the central head.

Fight the monster by shooting the large red eye on the center head with a shotgun or the TMP. When the red eye takes enough damage, Salazar emerges from his cocoon. Shoot him with the rocket launcher to end the battle. If you don't have a rocket launcher, shoot him with the rifle until the tentacles block your view. Repeat the entire strategy thus far to defeat the Salazar monster. Attacking Salazar himself is the only way to damage the monster, and everything else serves only to weaken the creature enough to reveal the master.

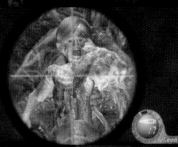

Even if one of the side tentacles is left active, the central head may open wide it jaws and attack. However, it is easier to avoid the attack when one of the tentacles still whips around. Run left or right to avoid the impending attack of the center head. Run toward a clear zone, meaning someplace where a tentacle has been made to withdraw.

If a tentacle hits Leon, he is knocked into the pit full of Plaga below. Toss a flash grenade to kill all the Plaga, and then quickly run to a ladder and climb out of the pit before more Plaga are birthed. Barrels spread all over the pit that can be broken for ammo and supplies if needed, but staying in the pit for any amount of time with all the spawning Plaga is quite a bit of hassle.

When the battle is done, drop into the pit and cross to the eastern platform. Collect the 50,000 Pesetas Salazar drops as well as the remaining items in the room. Proceed through the east door to the next area.

DOCK

ITEMS FOUND

Item	Occurrence	Remark
Random	3	
Handgun Ammo	1	
Flash Grenade	1	
Pesetas	2	
Spinel	1	

Seaside Retreat

Shoot the barrels as you move through the area, being cautious of a snake attack. Climb down the rope to the level below, then ride the lift down to the underground dock.

Follow the passage to encounter a merchant. The shop now offers new tune-ups for the Shotgun, TMP, Punisher, Red9, Blacktail, Riot Gun, Mine Thrower and Striker. Weapons like the Blacktail and TMP can now be improved to their maximum level, at which point an "Exclusive" upgrade can be purchased to take the weapon beyond normal limits. When finished with the weapon dealer, kick open the south door and proceed down the passage. Leon hitches a ride with an old flame to Saddler's impenetrable island fortress.

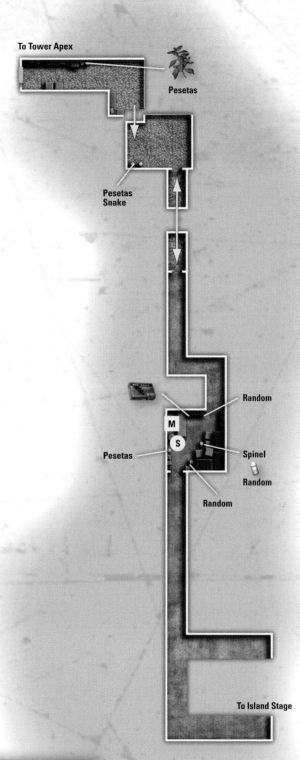

To Tower Apex

Pesetas

Pesetas
Snake

Random

M
S

Pesetas

Spinel

Random

Random

To Island Stage

chapter five

On Saddler's remote island base, the enemies are mainly soldiers and commandos. These are no peasant villagers; they're much stronger and attack with greater ferocity. Certain commandos carry shock sticks that electrocute Leon, an attack from which it takes a few seconds to recover. In fact, none of the enemies on the island have been encountered previously in the game. Be sure to upgrade the firepower of weapons to stay prepared for the coming attacks.

SPECIAL AUTHOR'S NOTE

At the start of the Island stage, the game assesses the player's inventory and automatically adjusts the difficulty level to compensate for the possession or lack of powerful weapons. Therefore, while we've tried to present accurate item locations and enemy strategies, some item placement and enemy appearances may change depending upon the weapons owned and the levels to which they are improved. Generally, item locations are the same as depicted on the maps, but you might find a different item than what is listed.

CHAPTER 5-1
BEACHHEAD

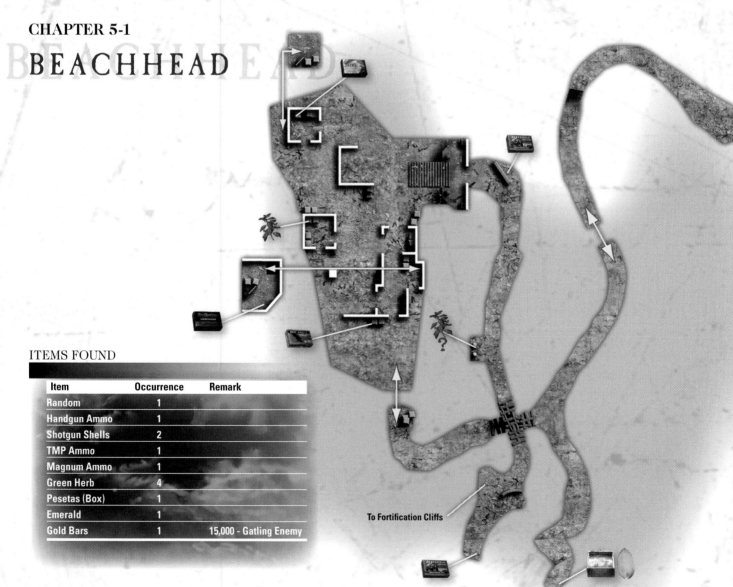

To Fortification Cliffs

ITEMS FOUND

Item	Occurrence	Remark
Random	1	
Handgun Ammo	1	
Shotgun Shells	2	
TMP Ammo	1	
Magnum Ammo	1	
Green Herb	4	
Pesetas (Box)	1	
Emerald	1	
Gold Bars	1	15,000 - Gatling Enemy

X CLIMB DOWN

Landing Zone

Proceed into the area until you reach a fork in the path. Continue south and climb the cliffs. Smash the boxes to obtain **Pesetas** and an **Emerald**. Then return to the planks and follow the west path until Leon sees Ashley being carried through a large door.

[ ]o not shoot out the searchlight [be]fore leaping across the gap [to]ward the buildings. Instead, [al]low Leon to be discovered so [th]at an enemy group emerges [to] attack. Jump back across the [ga]p and shoot the enemies when [th]ey stand at the edge to drop [th]em into the water, causing [in]stant death.

[T]he Gatling Gunner

[Ta]ke the **Handgun Ammo** on the crates and move left to a portion of [th]e wall with a gap. A large enemy toting a Gatling gun drops from the [to]wer above. Stay behind the wall and aim through the gap with the [sn]iper rifle. Shoot the Gatling gunner repeatedly in the head until he [di]es, then collect the **15,000 Pesetas** he drops. Take out the few other [en]emies in the area by leading them back to the gap and dropping [th]em into the water.

[R]eflecting Beams

[A]pproach the stairs and examine the lens on the left to activate a laser beam. Use the mirrors positioned on rooftops around [th]e area to reflect the laser back at the red panel on the right side of the door. Climb to the roof of the northwest building

and turn the mirror to point the reflected beam at the southeast mirror. Press ● or ● to cancel when the laser reflects off the other mirror.

[C]limb the ladder inside the southeast structure and collect the **Magnum Ammo** on the rooftop. Rotate the mirror so that the [la]ser beam hits the red plate on the right side of the doorway to open it.

Attempts to Send Leon Back

Go through the opened door. Hop over the sandbags and collect the **Shotgun Shells** on the ground behind. Follow the path south until commandos attempt to drop a boulder on Leon. Dodge the boulder and continue into the cave.

Break the barrels on the right to find a **Green Herb**. Proceed across the wooden planks bridging the gap. Shoot the archer commando in the next cave, as well as another soldier. Collect the **Shotgun Shells** in the corner nea the opening and climb the ladder to the cliffs above.

FORTIFICATION CLIFFS

ITEMS FOUND

Item	Occurrence	Remark
Shotgun Shells	2	
TMP Ammo	2	
Rifle Ammo	1	
Red Herb	1	
Green Herb	1	
Emerald	1	
Golden Lynx	1	

To Beachhead

To Kitchen
Entrance

The Upper Level

Turn left and examine the nearby boxes to obtain an **Emerald**. Exit the tent, hop over the sandbags and take down the guard standing there. Then turn around, head north and jump over the gap. Hop through the next window on the right and collect the **Rifle Ammo** on the table. A nearby enemy should spot Leon and cry out. Hop back through the same window and let the three guys with shock sticks try to follow. They are easy to gun down as they try to climb through the window.

The Cat Shrine

Head east once in the enclosure, stand back from the red barrel and shoot it to clear the debris out of the way. Climb the raised rock inside the small shrine and open the red box to obtain the **Golden Lynx**. This treasure increases in value when three gems are added to it.

Los Ganados' Last Stand

Stand to the left of the stacked cement blocks north of the building and snipe the crossbow archer on the high ledge and any other enemies that are visible from this position. Continue east to the right side of the other cement block stack and snipe the rest of the enemies from behind cover. Prioritize killing the enemy carrying a rocket launcher before he gets a chance to fire it. Shoot the exploding barrel on the high ledge to take out enemies on the level above, and shoot dynamite-throwers after they've lit their bombs and before they throw them.

Run forward once the initial enemies in this canyon are dispatched. Another group drops from the bridge above. Head west through a tunnel and up a slope, blasting the foes out of the way. Continue across the wooden bridge and into a small cave to find **Shotgun Shells** and a **Green Herb**.

Introduction

Characters

Enemies

Weapons and Ammunition

Key Items and Treasures

Game System and Strategies

Walkthrough

Secrets and Bonuses

Emerge from the small cave quickly and drop off the north side of the bridge. Run to the door at the top of the slope and wait for the enemies to cluster below the bridge. Then shoot the wagon full of barrels to send it rolling down the hill right into the enemies, killing everyone. The exploding wagon reveals a small niche in the rock wall where **TMP Ammo** is stored.

The Back Door

Press the switch to the left of the door bearing Los Illuminados' mark and descend the slope to find the first merchant on the island. The merchant now sells a Treasure Map that reveals the locations of all treasures in the island stage. The Killer7 is also for sale. This is undoubtedly the most powerful weapon in the game next to the rocket launcher—mmmm...Killer7.

Continue south down the passage. Take cover behind the cargo crate on the left and use a rifle to take out the crossbow sniper and other enemies perched on the building at the top of the hill. Enter the back door of the facility.

KITCHEN ENTRANCE

ITEMS FOUND

Item	Occurrence	Remark
Random	1	
Shotgun Shells	1	
Incendiary Grenade	1	
Hand Grenade	1	Sink
Green Herb	1	
Pesetas (Box)	1	

Something Smells...

Open the locker on the left to obtain a **Green Herb**. Head down the corridor and around the corner. Open the white dumpster to find an **Incendiary Grenade**. Proceed through the kitchen door and take out the enemy standing behind the shelves on the left.

Collect the **Green Herb** on the counter and open the duralumin case in the back room to find **Shotgun Shells**.

To Fortification Cliffs

To Stairwell Corridor (locked from the east side)

To Monitor Station

quip a shotgun as you proceed into the kitchen past some rotten
eat toward a roaster. An enflamed enemy bursts out of the roaster.
ast him quickly before he seizes Leon to avoid damage. Examine the
nk full of stagnant water to find a **Hand Grenade**, and then continue
to the next area.

MONITOR STATION

EMS FOUND

Item	Occurrence	Remark
Handgun Ammo	1	
Yellow Herb	1	
Pesetas (Box)	1	
Red Stone of Faith	1	
Gold Bars	1	5000

Up and Down the Stairs

un swiftly around two corners in the
orridor and take out the armored soldier
arrying a pickaxe. Then dash downstairs
nd take out another big guy and a
rossbow archer. Proceed a few steps away
om the bottom of the steps into the lower
oom triggers the appearance of two more
uys, who chase you down the steps.

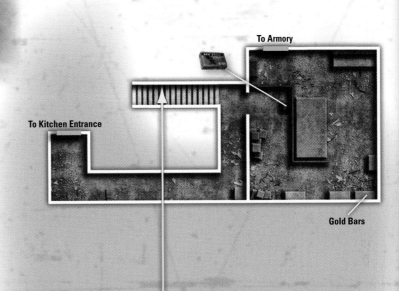

To Armory

To Kitchen Entrance

Gold Bars

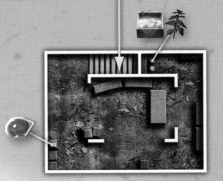

Open the duralumin case in the corner to find the **Red Stone of Faith**, which fits nicely into the lynx statue for a higher overall value. Smash the barrels in the space under the steps to find a **Yellow Herb** and **Pesetas**. Then head back upstairs and enter the room from which Ashley's cries are emanating. Take the **Handgun Ammo** across from the entrance, then head around the corner to see what terrible things are happening to Ashley on the monitor. Continue into the next room.

ARMORY

ITEMS FOUND

Item	Occurrence	Remark
Shotgun Shells	2	
Rifle Ammo	1	
TMP Ammo	1	
Red Herb	1	
Emerald	1	

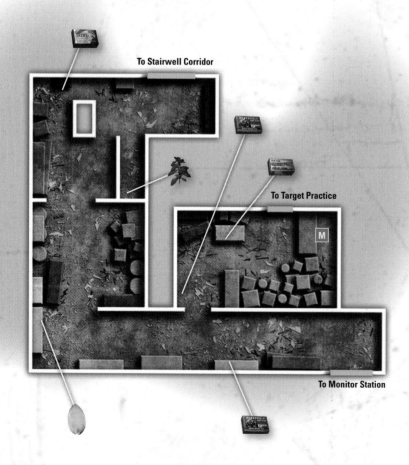

To Stairwell Corridor

To Target Practice

M

To Monitor Station

Welcome Supplies

Proceed down the corridor and open a file drawer on the left to obtain **Shotgun Shells**. Enter the next doorway on the right to find a merchant. Take the **Shotgun Shells** from the boxes stacked in the archway between rooms, and smash the glass cabinet to obtain **Rifle Ammo**.

Let's Get Tactical

The merchant now sells the Tactical Vest, an important piece of body armor that reduces damage by 30% and also changes Leon's look for the rest of the game. New tune-ups are available for the Striker and the Killer7. The Striker's levels can now be improved to maximum. At max, an Exclusive upgrade becomes available for the Striker that increases the magazine capacity to 100 shells! If you can afford this, there should hardly be a need to reload in battle for the rest of the game.

Enter the blue door to the left of the merchant to shoot at the target range if desired. Game types A, B, C, and D are now available, allowing you to finally collect bottle caps on every row of the diorama.

Armory Peek-a-Boo

When proceeding beyond the merchant's section of the area, equip the sniper rifle and aim through the smashed window on the right toward the garage door. A commando looks through the window on the right, and when he sees Leon he opens the garage door to reveal dynamite-tossing enemies. Shoot one of the enemies in the head before he throws his bomb, and the resulting explosion should take out everyone behind the door.

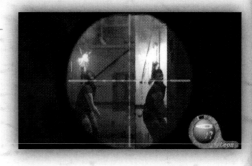

Three crossbow snipers then take up positions behind the shutter. Equip a grenade and move into the room. When the garage door opens, toss the grenade through the door to take out everyone. The enemy who pulled the switch to open the garage door may still be alive, so enter cautiously. Collect the remaining supplies and treasures in the area and proceed through the double doors.

STAIRWELL CORRIDOR

Card Key Required

Collect the items in and outside of the small room to the left. Then head upstairs and collect all of the items marked on the map above. The doors to the freezer and the smelly northwest room are locked, and both require some kind of card key.

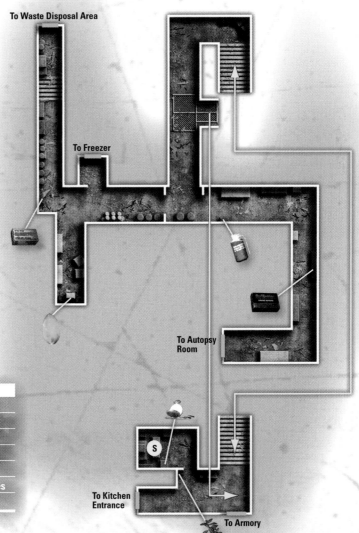

To Waste Disposal Area

To Freezer

To Autopsy Room

To Kitchen Entrance

To Armory

ITEMS FOUND

Item	Occurrence	Remark
Rifle Ammo	1	
Magnum Ammo	1	
Incendiary Grenade	1	
Green Herb	1	
Brass Pocket Watch	1	
Gold Bars	2	5000 x2 - Enemies
Emerald	1	

Introduction
Characters
Enemies
Weapons and Ammunition
Key Items and Treasures
Game System and Strategies
Walkthrough
Secrets and Bonuses

Return to the top of the stairs and head east. Open the red wall cabinet on the right to obtain an **Incendiary Grenade**. Continue north and smash a crate on the shelves to the left to obtain **Magnum Ammo**. Enter the double-doors at the end of the hall.

AUTOPSY ROOM

ROOM

ITEMS FOUND

Item	Occurrence	Remark
TMP Ammo	1	
Emerald	1	
Gold Bars	1	5000 - Enemy
Freezer Card Key	1	

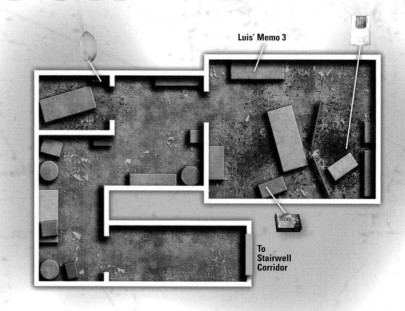

Luis' Memo 3

To Stairwell Corridor

The Colored Light Panel

The door to the operating room is locked. Open the door by examining the panel to the right. Turn the blue panels once, then turn the green panels twice, then turn the red panels three times to form a the correct pattern of moving tiles on the panel.

The Regenerator

Enter the operating room and examine the bed on the left to find **Luis' Memo 3**, regarding Regenerators. Take the **TMP Ammo** on the ground on the opposite side of the room, and then head behind the partition. Take the **Freezer Card Key** from the dead man's hands.

n your way out of the autopsy room, the Regenerator in the side
om returns to life. *The means to take this monster out are not
rrently at your disposal, so flee the room.*

Return to the hallway. Another
Regenerator in the corridor
may knock you to the ground,
but you'll just have to take your
licks and continue. Use the
Freezer Card Key to unlock the
freezer door, and enter.

FREEZER

ITEMS FOUND

Item	Occurrence	Remark
Rifle Ammo	1	
Green Herb	1	
Waste Disposal Card Key	1	Rewrite Freezer Card Key
Infrared Scope	1	Locker
Gold Bars	1	5000 - Enemy

Rewriting the Card Key

ollect the items around the cold storage room. To reach
e **Green Herb** in the glass cabinet at the back of the
om, smash the glass. Enter the small room just east of the
ntrance. Examine the first machine and insert the Freezer
ard Key to rewrite the data. This is how Leon obtains the
Waste Disposal Area Card Key. Deactivate the cryogenic
reezer device in the corner.

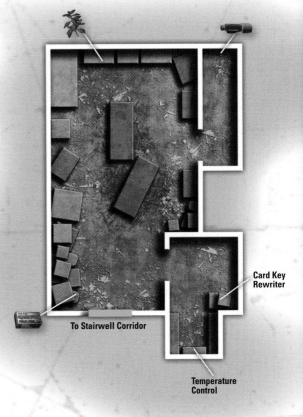

To Stairwell Corridor

Card Key
Rewriter

Temperature
Control

Revealing a Regenerator's Weak Spot

Head to the tiny northeast chamber and open the locker to obtain the **Infrared Scope**. Acquiring the scope causes a Regenerator to come to life in the main room. Equip the sniper rifle and the infrared scope and aim at the monster. With infrared, the parasites on the creature's body are revealed. Shoot all the parasites, and the Regenerator becomes metabolically unstable, exploding into a pile of warm goo. A Regenerator drops **Gold Bars** equaling 5000 pesetas on death.

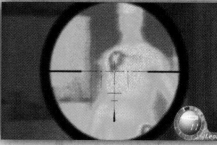

Corridor Regenerators

Exit the freezer to find two more Regenerators in the corridor. Head down the short passage toward the duralumi case, turn around, and use the infrared scope to spot and snipe the parasites on the Regenerator advancing from the north. Then stand in the middle of the corridor and snipe the parasites on the Regenerator advancing from the east.

Reenter the Autopsy Room and eliminate the Regenerator left here previously. Smash the glass cabinet in the small room the Regenerator came out of to obtain an **Emerald**.

Return to the stairwell corridor and head to the northwest door. Use the Waste Disposal Area Card Key to unlock the door marked "Flammable Liquid," and enter it.

WASTE DISPOSAL AREA

Introduction

Characters

Enemies

Weapons and
Ammunition

Key Items
and Treasures

Game System
and Strategies

Walkthrough

Secrets and
Bonuses

ITEMS FOUND

Item	Occurrence	Remark
Random	1	
Shotgun Shells	1	
TMP Ammo	2	
Green Herb	1	
Yellow Herb	1	
Emerald	1	
Hand Grenade	1	

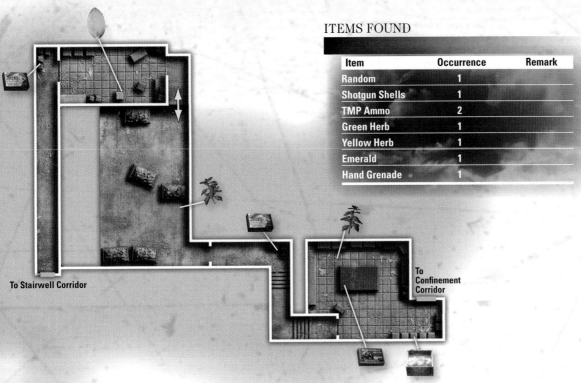

To Stairwell Corridor

To
Confinement
Corridor

Dump the Garbage

Proceed to the next corner and collect **TMP Ammo**. Open the door quietly and collect the **Emerald** in front of the control console. Examine the controls, and

use the grab-it device to pick up the enemies and dump them in the trash. When the device is moved three times, it quits working. The remaining enemies barge into the control room, so stand your ground and take them out.

Drop into the lower section and collect the **Green Herb** behind the dumpster. Examine the edge of the area to learn an important clue. Head through the door in the corner and collect more **TMP Ammo** at the corner.

Proceed upstairs to the security room and collect the various items on the table and in the corner lockers. Continue to the next area.

CONFINEMENT CORRIDOR

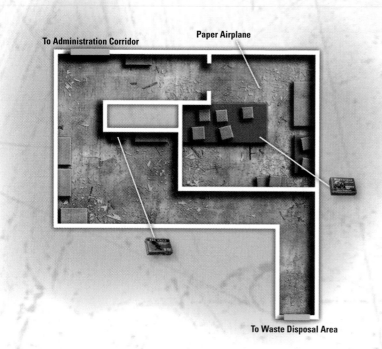

To Administration Corridor

Paper Airplane

To Waste Disposal Area

ITEMS FOUND

Item	Occurrence	Remark
Handgun Ammo	1	
Shotgun Shells	1	
Pesetas (Box)	2	Enemies

Ashley's Holding Cell

Head down the corridor and open the red cabinet on the right to obtain **Handgun Ammo**. Follow the sounds of Ashley screaming to find her cell, guarded by two huge and armored guys. Blow their heads off and collect the **Pesetas**

they drop. Examine the door to make Ashley quiet down, then exit through the northwest door.

ADMINISTRATION CORRIDOR

ITEMS FOUND

Item	Occurrence	Remark
Shotgun Shells	1	
Rifle Ammo	1	
Magnum Ammo	1	
Flash Grenade	1	
Green Herb	1	

Strange X-Rays

Head down the steps and collect the **Shotgun Shells** on the left. Open the door to get the enemies' attention, then retreat into the corridor and let them funnel through the doorway for easy kills. Gather the weapons and ammo on the upper level and descend the steps. Search the area under the stairs to find **Magnum Ammo**.

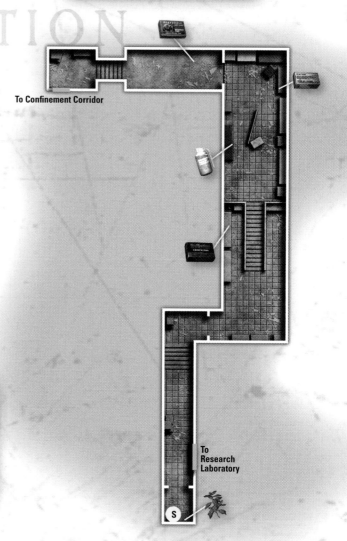

To Confinement Corridor

To Research Laboratory

S

llow the next corridor. At the end, go
rough the south door to find a **Green
rb** next to a typewriter. Then return to
e corridor and go through the east door.

Introduction

Characters

Enemies

Weapons and
Ammunition

Key Items
and Treasures

Game System
and Strategies

Walkthrough

Secrets and
Bonuses

ESEARCH LABORATORY

EMS FOUND

Item	Occurrence	Remark
Shotgun Shells	1	
Rifle Ammo	3	
TMP Ammo	1	
Magnum Ammo	1	
Red Herb	1	
Green Herb	1	
Storage Room Card Key	1	Carried by Enemy
Emerald	1	

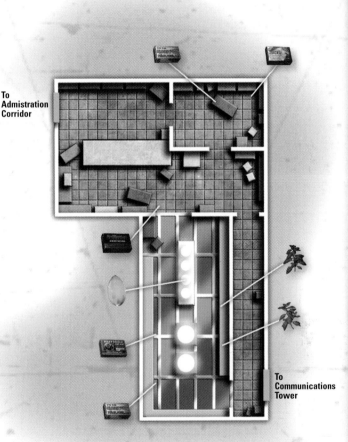

To
Admistration
Corridor

To
Communications
Tower

nter the Iron Maiden

oceed ahead and through the door. An Iron
aiden enters the lab. Note that this version of a
generator has something lodged in its abdomen,
d that merely shooting the many parasites
vering its body is not enough to kill it. Continue
ooting the Iron Maiden or throw a grenade even
er eliminating the parasites. **Rifle Ammo** is
ailable on the corner exam table if needed.

shley's Waiting, but...

hen the creature dies, it drops the **Storage Room Card Key**. Now
u can free Ashley! However, continue exploring the room and pick
the many items and ammunition located around the lab. In the
ecimen area, rotate the red valve to open a compartment containing
ore **Rifle Ammo**. Before going back to save Ashley, go through the
utheast door.

COMMUNICATIONS TOWER

ITEMS FOUND

Item	Occurrence	Remark
Handgun Ammo	1	Crow
Shotgun Shells	1	
Incendiary Grenade	1	
Flash Grenade	1	Crow
Green Herb	1	
Yellow Herb	1	
Pesetas (Box)	3	Crows
Gold Bars	1	5000 - Crow

To Research Laboratory

Gold Bars (crow)

(crow)

M

Comm Tower Crows

Take one or two quiet steps and aim at the lowest beam of the tower support arch. Six crows are perched on the beam. Shoot them one by one to obtain **Pesetas x3**, a **Flash Grenade**, **Gold Bars** worth 5000 pesetas, and **Handgun Ammo**. If you accidentally scare them off, leave and reenter to reset the crows to their initial positions.

Answered with Static

The merchant farther down the path has no new items or upgrades, so tune up the thing you own. Smash the barrels to obtain items and ride the lift to the top of the tower.

Exit the lift and move left to find a **Green Herb**. Enter the control tower and approach th console. Leon's calls for backup go unanswered. Turn left and collect the **Shotgun Shells** on the counter.

Rescuing Ashley

Return to the Administration Corridor. The enemies have cooked up a little ambush for Leon at the stairs. Use the handgun to trip enemies running downstairs and shoot them while they are down. Snipe crossbow archers positioned at the top of the stairs. Continue backtracking to the confinement corridor and use the Storage Room Card Key to open Ashley's cell. Move to the back of the storage room to reunite with the President's daughter.

VASTE PROCESSING PLANT

EMS FOUND

Item	Occurrence	Remark
Rifle Ammo	2	
Green Herb	1	
Gold Bars	2	20,000 x2 - Enemies

xtraction to the scape Point

ide Ashley's holding room, collect
Shotgun Shells on the table and
rt to lead Ashley to freedom. A
per Airplane flies through the
ndow. Read it for a friendly tip.
mmand Ashley to stay inside the
rage room and walk outside to
nfront a party of locals.

urn to the Waste Disposal Area. Kill the three enemies in the security room. A fourth enemy locks the exits from the room.
him and then press the switch on the console to open the exit. Three more enemies charge into the room and are on top

Leon and Ashley in an instant.
rn about face and blast them
h the shotgun. These enemies
m particularly weak, so
s attack should be all that is
eded to kill them. Enter the
bage dump area and proceed
the ledge. Leon and Ashley
np into the darkness below.

he Waste Processing Plant

on and Ashley wind up in a Waste Processing Plant. Equip a sniper rifle and the Infrared Scope. Throwing the lever to
en the gate brings an Iron Maiden to life. Lead Ashley under the gate and throw the switch to lower the bars, slowing the
monster considerably. Run farther back in the
room and command Ashley to hide in the green
dumpster on the right. Collect the **Rifle Ammo**
east of the dumpsters.

To
Incinerator

Open the next gate and close it behind you. Then back up and shoot the parasites on the Iron Maiden. When it opens the gate and heads toward your position, shoot the exploding red barrel to inflict some solid damage. Continue attacking the monster until it implodes.

Push the Container to Build a Bridge

Whistle for Ashley. Lead her to the large red container blocking the bridge across the sewage. Stand on the right side of the container and start pushing. Ashley helps, and the two of you push it into the muck. The sewage can now be crossed.

The Second Iron Maiden

Make Ashley hide in the green dumpster in this area. Collect the **Rifle Ammo** in the northwest corner and the **Green Herb** against the south wall. Going for the herb, another Iron Maiden should spot Leon. Stand beside the red exploding barrel and blast the parasites off the Iron Maiden's body as it advances. As it closes in, turn and run to the northwest corner and then shoot the barrel to hurt the creature. Continue shooting the monster after that until it explodes. The Iron Maidens in this room each drop **20,000 Pesetas**.

Whistle for Ashley and make her help you push the next red container out of the doorway. Continue to the next room.

INCINERATOR

ITEMS FOUND

Item	Occurrence	Remark
Handgun Ammo	1	
Shotgun Shells	1	
Red Herb	1	
Green Herb	1	

Walking into an Ambush

Command Ashley to wait near the entrance, and charge forward to take on the enemies in the corridor.

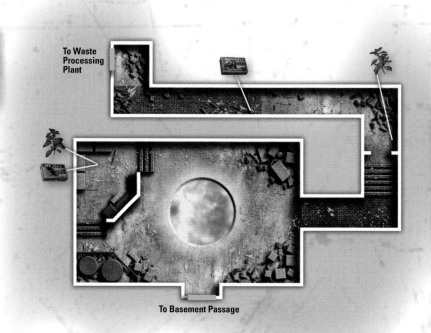

To Waste Processing Plant

To Basement Passage

hen the area is clear, open the double doors and head through the
ylindrical chamber into the next room. When Leon and Ashley drop off the
dge, enemies barge into the enclosure through the door on the right. Blast
em down with the shotgun, and try to knock a few in the central pit.

The Wrecking Ball

ake a mad dash for the control room in the northwest corner. Examine
e switch on the wall and choose for Ashley to pull the lever. Back into
e corner and blast enemies
ttempting to come through
oth doorways. Either continue
lasting enemies until none
nore show up, or escape
hrough the double doors as
oon as Ashley's cleared the
all remnants away with the
recking ball.

BASEMENT PASSAGE

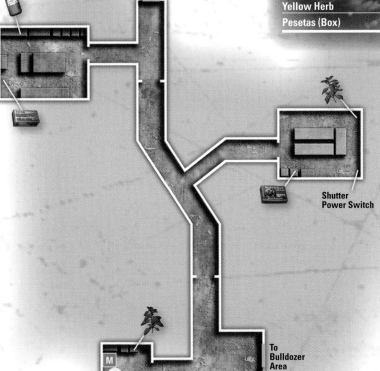

To Incinerator

Shutter
Power Switch

To
Bulldozer
Area

ITEMS FOUND

Item	Occurrence	Remark
Shotgun Shells	1	
Rifle Ammo	1	
Incendiary Grenade	1	
Red Herb	1	
Green Herb	1	
Yellow Herb	1	
Pesetas (Box)	2	5000 x2 - Enemies

Hide and Seek

Take a few steps toward the shutter door
and listen for the sounds of a monster on
just the other side. Open the shutter to
reveal the Regenerator, then quickly lead
Ashley into the west room.

Stand in the northwest corner of the room and aim through the bars on the door. Shoot the parasites on the monster with the infrared scope. The Regenerator drops **5000 Pesetas**. Open the cage and the refrigerator in the room to obtain a grenade and ammo.

Lead Ashley south in the passage until another Regenerator is spotted. Turn around and head north, then east into another side room. Stand at the back of the room and wait for the Regenerator to barge in. Blast the parasites on it to kill it and collect **5000 Pesetas**. Press the switch in the southeast corner of this room to unlock the shutter at the south end of the passage.

The Amazing Door Opening Duo!

The shutter opens only part way. Send Ashley under the shutter to open it from the other side, then continue to the intersection in the passage and collect the **Yellow Herb**. Enter the room to the southwest to find a merchant and a typewriter. Open the locker near the merchant to obtain a **Red Herb**. The merchant offers nothing new, so tune up existing weapons.

Lead Ashley back out to the passage. Guide her to one of the levers on either side of the door. Command her to wait near the lever, then move to the other lever

and operate it. The lights above the door gradually turn red, indicating a kind of countdown. Press ✖ when the center light comes on - not before and not after. Exit through the door.

ULLDOZER AREA

ULLDOZER AREA

EMS FOUND

Item	Occurrence	Remark
Shotgun Shells	4	
Rifle Ammo	1	
TMP Ammo	2	
Green Herb	1	
First Aid Spray	1	

low Ride

ck up with the items lined up on
her side of the room, then climb onto
flatbed of the bulldozer. Buckle your
tbelt, because Ashley is driving! As
hley pulls the bulldozer out of the garage,
emies pour out of the side area and
empt to jump onto the vehicle. Blasting
s before they jump onto the dozer may
m easier, but then you cannot collect
items they drop. Allow the enemies to
as close as your comfort level allows.

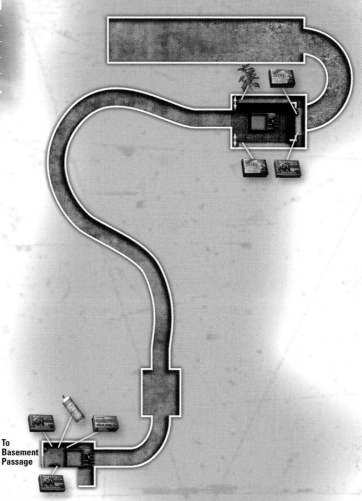

Collision Course

When the bulldozer starts going around a really long curve, a truck
approaches from behind, honking and threatening to ram the dozer. If the
truck hits the dozer, then you can
imagine the outcome. Shoot the
truck's engine to make it burst into
flames. After another wave of enemies
make a dash for the dozer's flatbed,
the truck starts up and tries again.
Shoot continuously to slow the truck.
If you reach the next room without
letting the truck collide, it will not
bother you again.

Activate the Lift

Ashley stays in the dozer, and Leon must climb to the upper level of the room to throw the switch to activate the elevator platform and raise the dozer. Climb up either ladder and blast through the enemies as fast as possible. Whichever side you climb up, the enemies run around the

other side, drop to the ground and try to attack Ashley. Additional foes drop from the levels high above. Snipe any enemies that get in the back of the dozer. Smash the crates and collect the items on the upper level. Pull the central lever and get back on the dozer.

The Last Haul

When the dozer reaches the top level, equip the TMP and try to snipe enemies on overhead platforms before they drop into the flatbed. Additional groups attempt to board the rig from behind. Use flash grenades to eliminate multiple exposed parasites when needed. When the shrill sound of a truck horn blares, face the front of the truck and fire at the grill of the oncoming truck to sidetrack it. Ashley crashes into the building to the side, ending the bulldozing fun.

MESS HALL

Nothing to Eat

Collect the **Handgun Ammo** near the bulldozer wreckage and proceed into the next room. Open the cabinet around the room to find ammo and **Gold Bars**. The duralumin case on the north wall contains the **Green Stone of Judgement** that fits into the lynx statue. Tune up at the merchant, and collect the **Pesetas** on the shelf by the exit.

ITEMS FOUND

Item	Occurrence	Remark
Handgun Ammo	1	
Shotgun Shells	1	
Hand Grenade	1	
Pesetas (Box)	1	
Gold Bars	1	5000
Green Stone of Judgement	1	

To Boiler Room

Gold Bars

ead into the next room for a confrontation with
addler. Ashley is kidnapped again. Will Leon ever
op losing the First Daughter?

CHAPTER 5-3

BOILER ROOM

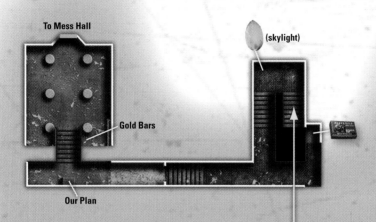

To Mess Hall

(skylight)

Gold Bars

Our Plan

ITEMS FOUND

Item	Occurrence	Remark
Shotgun Shells	2	
Flash Grenade	1	
Green Herb	1	
Pesetas (Box)	2	Locker
Gold Bars	1	5000
Emerald	1	Skylight over Stairs

To Machine Room

Man on Fire

void rushing out of the room after Saddler and Ashley, because they
e already gone. Search the east niche next to the stairs to find **Gold
ars** worth 5000 pesetas. Ascend the stairs and read the document on
e altar titled "**Our Plan**."

Introduction
Characters
Enemies
Weapons and
Ammunition
Key Items
and Treasures
Game System
and Strategies
Walkthrough
Secrets and
Bonuses

Proceed into the next room. Continue east and shoot through the boards covering the supervisor's room nearby to kill an enemy inside. This activity should alert other foes on the ground, who try to meet Leon on the stairs. Take out the enemies, and shoot out the skylights over the stairs meanwhile to obtain an **Emerald**.

Take out the archers positioned on the stairs and in the corridor in front of the boilers. Collect items upstairs in the superintendent's office, then return to the lower level and head west behind the boilers to the storage room. Collect the **Flash Grenade** and the random amount of **Pesetas** appearing in the storeroom, then head to the southeast door.

MACHINE ROOM

ITEMS FOUND

Item	Occurrence	Remark
Shotgun Shells	1	

Meeting of Rivals

Go through the corridor into the next room. Collect the **Shotgun Shells** on the floor and board the lift. Cross the room until Leon encounters his old training comrade, Krauser.

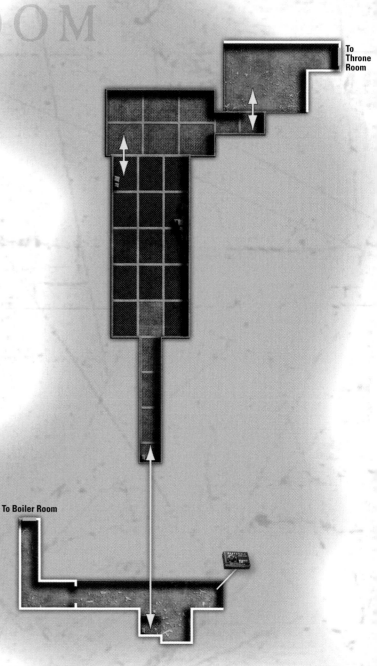

To Throne Room

To Boiler Room

though the characters start
lking, do not let your guard down
r a minute. During the scene, be
epared to press two randomly
etermined buttons to survive
ch of Krauser's deathblow knife
tacks, or Leon dies.

When Krauser throws Leon to the ground, prepare to tap one button rapidly. When
he threatens to press his dagger into Leon's chest, rapidly press the button shown
and then switch to the other button when indicated to hold off Krauser's knife.

After surviving the scene, head east, drop off the platform and exit via the
northeast door.

THRONE ROOM

ΞMS FOUND

Item	Occurrence	Remark
Emerald	1	Throne
Elegant Headdress	1	Wall

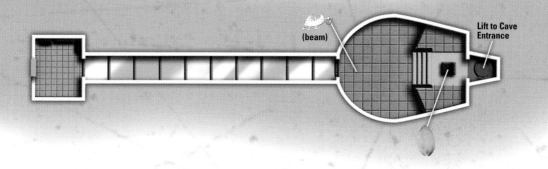

(beam)

Lift to Cave
Entrance

Momma Told You Not to Play with Lasers...

curity outside Saddler's sitting chamber is understandably tight.
ter the corridor and walk forward until three laser beams appear.
lk through the beams when the horizontal one is rising and the two
rticals are spreading apart. Continue down the corridor until five
ams appear in front of Leon. Two of the beams form a triangle and
en spread apart, and this is when you should run through the array.

An impassable number of laser beams appear in the corridor, and the entire array slides toward Leon. Press **L1** and **R1** the instant they appear onscreen to dive through the beams.

Take a few steps forward until a dozen beam emitters appear on either side of the room. Keep moving forward and press **L1** and **R1** to dodge when the emitters activate, and again when they slide toward Leon.

The final test comes when the switch to the right of the door is pressed. A large number of beams come at Leon from behind. Move several steps away from the exit toward the beams, so that the lasers are not traveling at too high a velocity when they arrive at Leon's position. Then press **L1** and **R1** to dodge the lasers for the final time. The door finally unlocks and you may enter the familiar-looking room.

Sit Where Evil Sits

Standing at Saddler's throne, turn around and look at the wall above the door. Shoot the glimmering object off the wall to obtain an **Elegant Headdress**. Examine the throne from the front to obtain an **Emerald**. When the "?" action appears, press ✕ to see Leon act weird for a moment. Go through the door behind the throne and ride the lift down into the caves.

CAVE ENTRANCE

ITEMS FOUND

Item	Occurrence	Remark
Magnum Ammo	1	
Red Herb	1	
Green Herb	1	
Emerald	1	

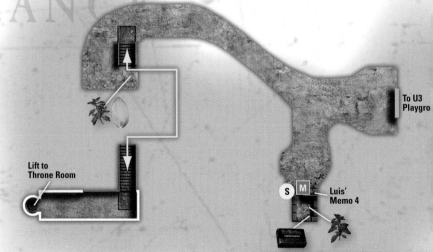

Lift to Throne Room

To U3 Playgro

S M Luis' Memo 4

Heading for Danger

Descend the stairs, and then search the area beneath the steps to find a **Green Herb** and an **Emerald**. Follow the passage east until reaching an open area where a merchant stands. Examine the ammo boxes to the left of the merchant to find **Luis' Memo 4**. The merchant offers new tune-ups for the Broken Butterfly and the Killer7. You may now maximize the levels and capacity of the Killer7. Enter the small room behind the merchant to obtain a **Red Herb** and **Magnum Ammo**.

U3 PLAYGROUND

Introduction

Characters

Enemies

Weapons and Ammunition

Key Items and Treasures

Game System and Strategies

Walkthrough

Secrets and Bonuses

ITEMS FOUND

Item	Occurrence	Remark
Handgun Ammo	1	
Shotgun Shells	2	
TMP Ammo	1	
Hand Grenade	1	
Green Herb	4	
Yellow Herb	1	
Pesetas (Box)	1	
Gold Bars	1	50,000 - U3

Cave Entrance

Lift to Campground

Playing With "It"

Move toward the edge of the abyss and head left of the bridge into a torn-open cage to obtain a **Yellow Herb**. Cross the bridge and collect **TMP Ammo** near the bonfire in the tunnel.

Equip a shotgun and continue into the next large area to get your first look at Saddler's sadistic little playground. As you try to head around the thing, an experimental monster attacks. Leon is flung into the playground and the monster follows.

The First Jettison Rig

Blast the monster with the shotgun until it leaps out of sight. Collect the **Shotgun Shells** near the opening. Head north and then west to a shutter door. Blast the green light to the right of the shutter to open it, and operate the console beyond.

Return to the middle aisle and be ready to dodge if the monster attacks from above. At the south end, head west to find a **Green Herb**. Then go east and blast the green light to the right of the shutter door to open it. Follow the passage north to another console and press the button.

Leon has only 30 seconds to get out of the container before the whole thing drops into the chasm below. Naturally the monster attempts to interfere, so dodge its attacks and avoid counterattacking as you head to the eastern exit.

Compartment Number Two

In the second compartment head south to find **Pesetas**. Then head east only to be attacked by the monster again. Blast it out of your path, and then go south and then east to find a lock panel.

Press the button, then head back toward the middle aisle and examine the north shutter. Blast the green light above the shutter door and continue. Head first to the northeast corner to obtain a **Hand Grenade**, then spin around and go west to the lock console. Press the switch to activate the timer mechanism, and dash out of the compartment before it is jettisoned.

Final Jettison Compartment

Head to the right and press the first switch to open the red shutter door. The monster enters the compartment and mutates. Quickly press the button shown to cut Leon' leg loose of its grip. The monster's only weak spot now is its new head with pincers.

Move up the middle corridor to the other side of the container. Follow the path to the north side and shoot through the gate to hit the green light, opening the shutter door.

Return to the west side of the compartment and go through the open shutter door to find the lock console. Press the button and then run all the way back through the center corridor to the east side. Open the door and ignore the monster. Jump for the hook cable before the compartment is jettisoned, along with the monster.

Equip a magnum handgun or the mine thrower and move forward. The monster climbs right out of the pit for a confrontation.

U3

Introduction

Characters

Enemies

Weapons and
Ammunition

Key Items
and Treasures

Game System
and Strategies

Walkthrough

Secrets and
Bonuses

Chapter 1-1

Chapter 1-2

Chapter 1-3

Chapter 2-1

Chapter 2-2

Chapter 2-3

Chapter 3-1

Chapter 3-2

Chapter 3-3

Chapter 3-4

Chapter 4-1

Chapter 4-2

Chapter 4-3

Chapter 4-4

Chapter 5-1

Chapter 5-2

Chapter 5-3

Chapter 5-4

Final Chapter

ll damage inflicted on the monster previously does not count oward shortening this battle. Extend Leon's life by "gating" he monster away from Leon, much like you did with the Iron aidens in the Waste Disposal Plant. Run into the passage to eon's right. Pull the lever just inside the passage to bring down he bars. While the reature is trapped on he other side of them, ast its pincer head epeatedly with the hotgun or the magnum, plant a mine on it and n away.

hen the creature breaks through the bars, continue down the passage and shoot the exploding barrel damage it. Collect the Handgun Ammo and continue to the other end of the passage. Open the bars d head left around he corner. Throw he switch to trap the onster behind bars ce again, and blast repeatedly before it eaks free.

he following portion of the strategy may be unnecessary if you used a powerful enough weapon to kill it this point. When it breaks through the bars, run to the south corner and allow it to approach. Shoot the xploding barrel to damage it further. At half its health, it begins burrowing underground and trying to come beneath Leon to attack. Remain alert and press the two dodge buttons shown onscreen when it attacks. ter three or four such attempts, the monster surfaces. Use a flash grenade to blind it and then blast it while is stunned, or bomb it ruthlessly with hand grenades and incendiaries. Make good use of the Green Herb and Shotgun Shells provided in this area as well. The U3 drops Gold Bars worth 50,000 pesetas.

Exit the Cavern

When the battle is won, head north and go through the door on the right. Follow the passage to an open area, and search to the right side of the stairs to find a **Green Herb**. Board the trolley on the west side of the rise and ride back across the chasm to the point where Leon first encountered the U3. Collect the **Green Herb** on the trolley platform, and then ride back and climb the ladder.

CAMPGROUND

ITEMS FOUND

Item	Occurrence	Remark
Handgun Ammo	2	
Shotgun Shells	2	
TMP Ammo	2	
Hand Grenade	1	
Yellow Herb	1	
Pesetas (Box)	1	
Gold Bars	1	5000
Emerald	1	
Blue Stone of Treason	1	

Surprise! BOOM!

Climb the second ladder and collect the ammo and grenade in the room. There's a number of villagers camped outside, so it is important to move quietly. Open the door softly and use the knife to smash the barrel near the fence to obtain **Handgun Ammo**. Equip the sniper rifle and step to the edge. Search the campsite below and aim at an exploding barrel near the villagers standing around the fire. Shoot the barrel to set off a chain reaction that blows up most of the camp. Contend with the one or two villagers left behind.

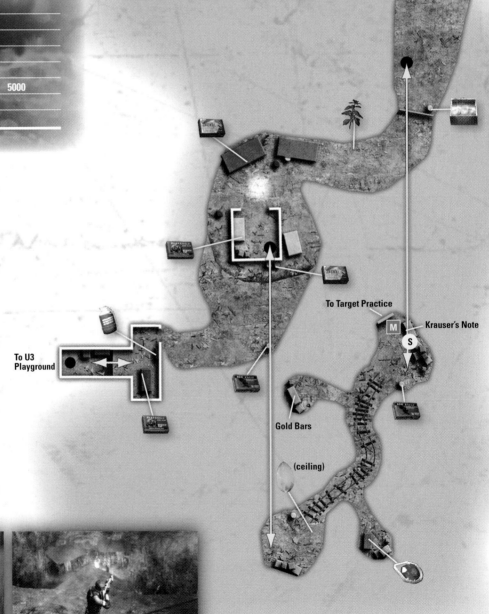

To Fortress Ruins

To Target Practice

Krauser's Note

M

S

To U3 Playground

Gold Bars

(ceiling)

Tent Hole

Search all over the camp to find items. The path to the north is fenced off. If you cannot go over, then go under. Enter the tent drop down the circular hole into a tunnel.

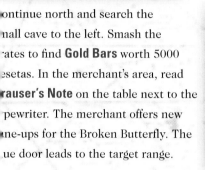

Shoot the shiny thing in the ceiling near the ladder to obtain an **Emerald**. Head down the tunnel and enter the first passage on the right to find the **Blue Stone of Treason**. The Golden Lynx statue can now be completely upgraded and sold to the nearby merchant for 35,000 pesetas.

Continue north and search the small cave to the left. Smash the crates to find **Gold Bars** worth 5000 pesetas. In the merchant's area, read **Krauser's Note** on the table next to the typewriter. The merchant offers new tune-ups for the Broken Butterfly. The blue door leads to the target range.

Climb the ladder and smash the barrel in the corner to obtain **Pesetas**. Enter the double doors.

ITEMS FOUND

Item	Occurrence	Remark
Handgun Ammo	2	
Shotgun Shells	2	
TMP Ammo	3	
Magnum Ammo	2	
Flash Grenade	1	
Red Herb	1	
Green Herb	4	
Yellow Herb	1	
First Aid Spray	1	
Piece of the Holy Beast, Panther	1	
Piece of the Holy Beast, Eagle	1	
Piece of the Holy Beast, Serpent	1	

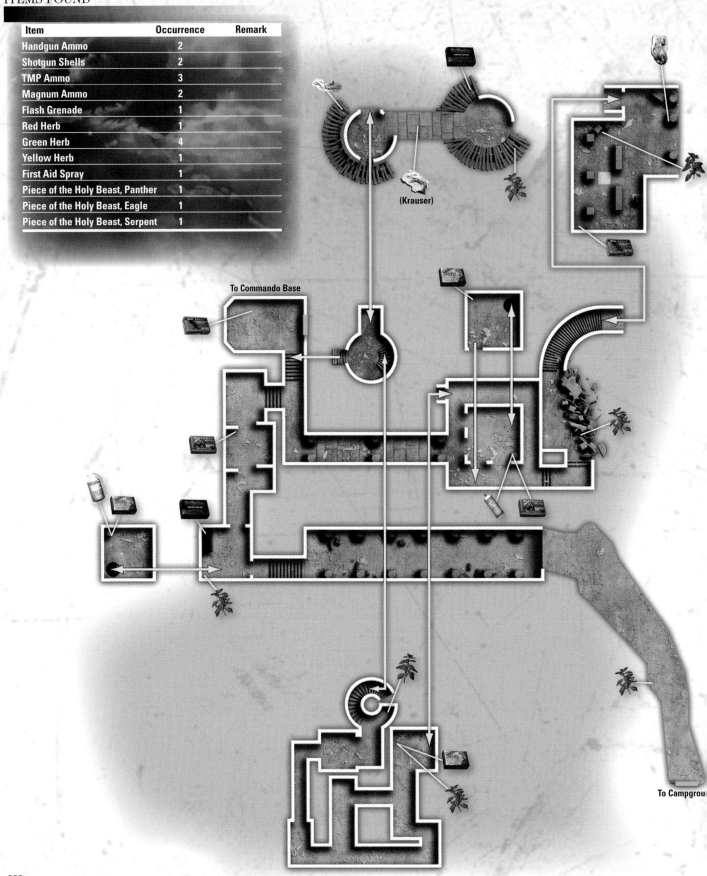

(Krauser)

To Commando Base

To Campgrou

Conflict of Interest

Drop over the cliff's edge and proceed through the area until Krauser attacks. Continue up the stairs, kick open the door and enter the building. The door on the right has a timer lock, and it will not open until the timer goes off. Krauser soon smashes through the door and enters building, so move quickly. Collect the **Green Herb** and smash the crate for **Magnum Ammo**. Climb the ladder and fight it out with Krauser on the roof. Shoot him with the TMP to inflict damage, and keep trying to shoot him until he throws a flash bomb and disappears.

Fighting Krauser

Even though the official boss fight against Krauser has not started yet, a solid strategy is required to drive off the crazed commando each time he attacks Leon. As soon as Krauser appears, shoot him with the TMP, a shotgun or a handgun with a really high firing speed. If all else fails, toss a frag and back up. Krauser initiates each confrontation by trying to fire back. If he is prevented from shooting enough times, he begins sliding from side to side so fast he cannot be targeted. When he starts this, raise the knife and cut him when he moves right up to Leon. Do this once or twice more, and Krauser should throw a flash bomb and disappear.

Fighting for Every Inch

When Krauser is driven off the first time, the timer lock on the gate soon opens. Kick through the door and walk north cautiously. Krauser hides behind one of the broken walls in this passage. By walking slowly through the area, you can spot him in time to shoot him.

Collect the **Shotgun Shells** on the left side of the walkway and continue down the stairs. Examine the door to the north to see where the three pieces of the Holy Beast need to go. Collect the **Handgun Ammo** on the left and head south past the stairs.

A Quick Bit of Sniping

Krauser is on the building at the other end of the central bridge. Take cover behind one of the pillars to the left and use the sniper rifle to hit him. Continue sniping him after he jumps down and tries to run your direction.

Jump inside the building. Collect the **Shotgun Shells** and smash the barrel for a **First Aid Spray**. Climb up to the roof and collect some **TMP Ammo**. Drop down the side of the building and head east

First Piece of the Beast

Collect the **Green Herb** in the passage and ascend the stairs to obtain the **Piece of the Holy Beast, Panther**. Then prepare for a showdown against Krauser. Press the dodge buttons to avoid a grenade he throws. Drive him off in the usual manner, and then collect the **Red Herb** and **Handgun Ammo** in the area.

To raise the gate barring the exit, push the statue out beyond the corner. Then push it south and work it onto the pressure pad. Pull the lever near the gate to raise it. This is a continue point, in case you die or want to retry after this

Krauser's Toys

Move around the north side of the house, and you'll spot Krauser's shadow on the ground. Toss a grenade to drive him out, then fight him in the usual way. Throw the lever next to the gate to open the lower area, and drop down.

Krauser has installed nasty little robots in the lower area. Once they spot Leon, they dash forward and start beeping. When the beeping stops, they explode. There are also floating machineguns in the area. One shot to the camera mounted on top of either type of device causes it to malfunction and explode. One shot to the exposed body detonates it instantly. Use a handgun to get through this area.

Shoot the two robot bombs south of the landing point. Collect the **Green Herb** and **TMP Ammo** across from the ladder, and head south. At the corner, shoot the camera bomb burrowed in the ground. Then wait for a machinegun robot to float in from the right, and shoot its camera.

Head for the High Ground

Head to the southeast corner, look north and shoot the two camera bombs in the passage. Proceed into the open. When Krauser addresses Leon, press ✖ to respond. If you do not respond in time, an additional scene between the rivals is missed. Two robots come after Leon following the event.

Enter the circular tower and collect the **Yellow Herb**. Ascend the stairs and climb the ladder. Head east across the roof and collect the **Magnum Ammo** and **Green Herb**. Then return to the west side of the platform and collect the **Piece of the Holy Beast, Eagle**. Just one puzzle piece remains, and you must get it from Krauser himself!

KRAUSER

At the start of the fight, press the dodge buttons to leap over the side of the platform to avoid Krauser's initial attack. Tap ✖ rapidly to climb back onto the platform. Avoid getting knocked over the side again by staying away from Krauser and staying away from the edges.

Not even a rocket launcher missile will kill this guy, though it damages him severely. Because Krauser has planted timer bombs outside the tower you currently stand upon, there is a time limit in which the madman must be defeated. Therefore, use a magnum handgun. As Krauser approaches, shoot him in the knees. When he drops to the ground and his head is exposed, shoot him in the head. When he gets too close for comfort, relocate and repeat this strategy of attack.

If Krauser manages to get close enough to attack, press the dodge buttons to escape his blows. Raise the knife and slash him to defend yourself. Keep shooting him in the knee, then in the head, until he perishes.

Introduction

Characters

Enemies

Weapons and Ammunition

Key Items and Treasures

Game System and Strategies

Walkthrough

Secrets and Bonuses

Resurrect the Holy Beast

When Krauser chokes his last traitorous breath, search his body for the **Piece of the Holy Beast, Serpent**. Drop down through the ladder hole to the level below. Exit through the doorway at the base of the ladder. Hurry, because you could still be caught inside the building when the bombs go off. Speaking of bombs, the demolition is worth sticking around to see. Assemble the Holy Beast on the door, and continue to the next area.

CHAPTER 5-4
COMMANDO BASE

ITEMS FOUND

Item	Occurrence	Remark
Handgun Ammo	1	
Shotgun Shells	3	
Rifle Ammo	1	
TMP Ammo	2	
Magnum Ammo	1	
Hand Grenade	2	
Flash Grenade	1	
Red Herb	1	
Green Herb	6	
Yellow Herb	1	
Pesetas (Box)	3	
Pesetas	1	15,000 - Enemy
Gold Bars	1	5000

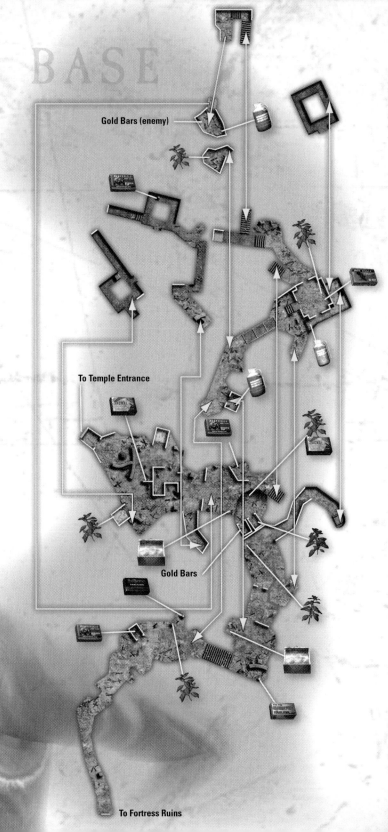

Gold Bars (enemy)

To Temple Entrance

Gold Bars

To Fortress Ruins

Call to Arms

Collect the **Green Herb** near the entrance, use the typewriter if desired, and continue up the hill. Leon faces an army of commandos in this area. Fortunately, an attack helicopter covers him from the air. This is starting to become a small war!

After the chopper takes out the enemies near the entrance, run forward until a ghoul mounts the machinegun turret on the nearby tower. Take cover behind a post on the right, and then dash into the nearby tent between machinegun bursts.

Then the helicopter levels the tower with a missile, continue east. Jump over the sandbags into the destroyed building. Enemies begin emanating from the nearby tower. Stay in the destroyed building and keep pushing the ladder down until the chopper swings around to provide cover fire, wiping out the enemies. Then jump down to the area below. Collect the items in the area, then decide how to get through the upper and lower gates to the next section of the base.

Working with Helicopter Support

The helicopter pilot passes back and forth, strafing the ground to pick off clusters of enemies. Leon may still have to deal with a few single enemies. But when the commandos have Leon pinned down and unable to move, the helicopter usually moves in and strafes the area. The pilot targets certain towers around the area, mainly where machinegun turrets are placed. Stay away from these areas until the chopper pilot gets around to firing a missile and taking out the building. He usually shouts "Take Cover!" or "What are you doing? Get out of the way!" when he's about to bomb a structure. Listen for these important radio cues as you proceed. The way to get through this area with the least damage is to proceed cautiously, assess the situation from a position of cover, and move in after the chopper clears a path for you.

Two Paths of Approach

There are two ways to get into the next sector of the base. One method is to break the large padlock off the gate in the lower level and proceed through the next area. In this case you must deal with several enemies on your own without supporting chopper fire. The other path in is to return to the upper level and head toward the gate to trigger the appearance of enemies. There are scores of enemies that may get out of control, but the chopper can provide covering fire the whole way. Decide, then move your butt agent!

Path One: Crossing the Bridge

When taking the upper area route, move toward the large wooden gate until enemies appear on the platform above. Hide behind the metal wall on the right. Dynamite-throwers should take out any enemies that drop to the ground for you, and then all you have to do is wait for the chopper to blow the gate.

When the blast debris settles, climb up the ladder on the left to find a **Green Herb**. Because the gate in the lower area was broken down in the blast, enemies may start climbing up after Leon from the level below. Stay at the top of the ladder and pick them off as they try to climb up. Then drop to the level below and cross the bridge.

Attempting to cross the bridge triggers the appearance of an enemy on the turret atop the next tower. Retreat and seek cover behind the metal wall again. Let the enemies hop out of the tower and cross the bridge, then blast them as they come around the corner of your wall. Wait until the chopper obliterates the tower, then cross the bridge.

Path Two: Tunnel under the Tower

In the lower area, blast the enemies out of your way and smash the barrel in the corner near the fence to obtain a **Yellow Herb**. Head through the tunnel. Climb the ladder at the back of the tower.

Head around the side of the building and shoot the barrel to obtain a **Flash Grenade**. Shoot the exploding barrel beyond the fence to eliminate enemies congregating in front of the building. Go through the side door.

The Shutter Door Lever

Collect the **Green Herb** and **Handgun Ammo** inside the north tower. Press the red button to open the northwest door, and proceed a few steps through it. A Gatling gun commando appears on the ridge across the area.

quickly run across the midlevel and seek shelter from the Gatling gun commando in the small wooden structure. Stay within this hollow and blast the few enemies that come after Leon.

When the enemies stop coming and the Gatling gun is not firing, dash up the steps to the top level. Use the sniper rifle to hit the Gatling gun commando in the head repeatedly until he dies, then grab the pulley and slide down to his perch. Collect the **15,000 pesetas** the gunner drops as well as the **Hand Grenade** in the corner.

Drop from the gunner's ledge and pull the lever to open the shutter door. Drop to the ground and collect **Pesetas** from the barrel at the edge of the pit. Before proceeding through the shutter door opening, search all levels of the area for ammo, herbs and money. Then head through the shutter door.

Trapped Between Mounted Machineguns

After the shutter door closes behind Leon, quickly run forward and press ✖ to crouch behind the sandbags while the gun turrets tear up the area.

Between volleys of machinegun fire, stand up and run to the left into a tunnel. Climb the ladder, stay in the tunnel a few minutes and blast enemies that try to climb up the ladder behind you. Drop back to the lower level to collect any pesetas they drop, then climb back to the upper level.

Between turret bursts, run out to the open area and stay behind the tall metal wall to hide from turret fire. You can crouch behind the low metal wall to the left. Stay under cover here until the chopper fires missiles into at least two of the towers in this area.

The Shutter Door Locks

When the towers to the north and south are gone, wait for the last machinegun turret on the ground to fire and stop. Then quickly run around the upper level walkways to the square area where the north tower previously stood. Collect **Shotgun Shells** from a smashed barrel at the back of the square platform.

Stay behind the metal wall and shoot any enemies coming up behind Leon from the east. As they walk near the edge of the square hole, shoot them to make them totter and fall to the level below. Wait until the chopper destroys the tower at the west end of the area, then continue west.

The shutter door at the exit closes. Kick down the gate barring the path and flip the red switch to remove one lock from the shutter door covering the exit.

Opening the Shutter Door over the Exit

Now return to the square area and drop through the hole to the ground level. Head straight south to collect **TMP Ammo** behind a broken wall. Kill the gunner behind the central turret if needed by waiting under cover until he shoots, then run behind him and blast him.

Kill the last dozen or so enemies remaining in the area on your own, and climb the ladder for the southwest platform. Move toward the shutter door and throw the second switch to open the exit. Drop back to the ground and continue through the double doors to the next exit.

TEMPLE ENTRANCE

ITEMS FOUND

Item	Occurrence	Remark
Shotgun Shells	1	
TMP Ammo	1	
Green Herb	1	
First Aid Spray	1	
Pesetas (Box)	1	
Emerald	2	Pillar Tops

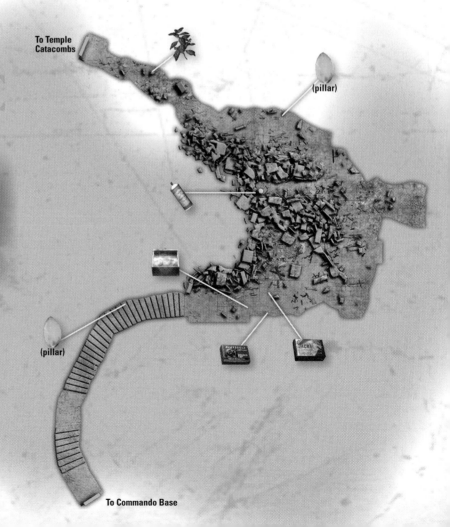

To Temple Catacombs

(pillar)

(pillar)

To Commando Base

Mike's Farewell Fire

Head up the stone stairs. After the helicopter kills all the enemies, collect the items dropped. Turn back toward the entrance and shoot the shining object at the top of the column, an **Emerald**. Smash the barrel in the narrow area under the archway to obtain a **First Aid Spray**. Shoot another **Emerald** off of the column on the north edge of the area. Head toward the northwest door, collecting a **Green Herb** on the right edge of the path.

TEMPLE CATACOMBS

ITEMS FOUND

Item	Occurrence	Remark
Handgun Ammo	1	
Pearl Pendant	1	

Give Your Girlfriend Pearls, not Bruises...

Head forward and drop down the ladder hole. Check the stone behind the ladder hole to obtain a **Pearl Pendant**. Head into the next room and collect the **Handgun Ammo** in the crate. Continue through the next passage and enter the double doors.

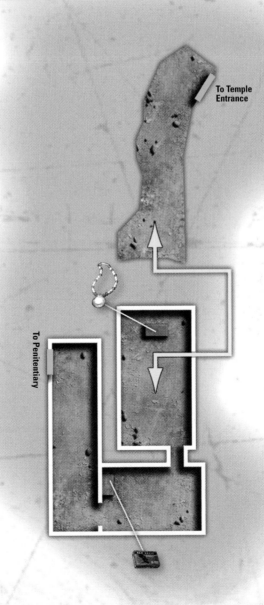

To Temple Entrance

To Penitentiary

PENITENTIARY

IARY

ITEMS FOUND

Item	Occurrence	Remark
Shotgun Shells	1	
Rifle Ammo	1	
Magnum Ammo	1	
Flash Grenade	1	
Red Herb	1	
Yellow Herb	1	
Gold Bars	1	5000 - Enemy

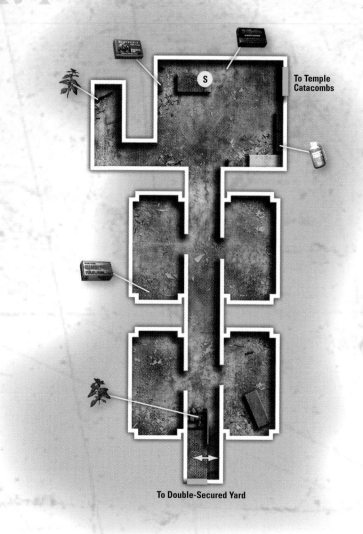

Creepy Confinement

Use the typewriter on the desk if desired, and open the drawer behind the desk to obtain **Magnum Ammo**. Collect the other items in the room near the entrance before proceeding farther into the prison.

Open the red bin to the left of the south doorway to find a squirming sack of flesh. Shoot the flesh bag. Keep an eye on the long corridor, as a Regenerator may start moving towards you from the last cell on the left. This one is especially tough, with the stamina of an Iron Maiden though none of the abilities. Use the infrared scope and sniper rifle to blast the parasites off it, then blast it with a shotgun or other weapon until it destabilizes and explodes. Collect the **5000 Pesetas** it drops.

Head down the center aisle. Kick down the first cell door on the right and collect the **Rifle Ammo** in the cell. Collect the **Red Herb** at the base of the broken stairs below the exit. Move to the left of the stairs and climb up onto the platform to reach the exit.

DOUBLE-SECURED YARD

ITEMS FOUND

Item	Occurrence	Remark
Handgun Ammo	2	
Shotgun Shells	2	
Rifle Ammo	1	
TMP Ammo	1	
Incendiary Grenade	1	
Flash Grenade	1	
Red Herb	1	
Green Herb	2	
Yellow Herb	1	
Pesetas (Box)	2	
Gold Bars	2	15,000 - Gatling Enemy, 5000 - Duralumin Case
Emergency Lock Card Key	1	Carried by Enemy

The Final Army

Collect the **Green Herb** below the stairs, and smash the crate for a random item or money. Reload all your weapons, then head around the corner and take out the crossbow snipers behind the sandbags. Snipe the enemy through the window in the upper room too. Continue shooting everyone until another Gatling gun-toting enemy emerges. Get atop the center platform and snipe him in the head until he dies. He drops **15,000 Pesetas,** so move to his position inside the midlevel warehouse as quickly as possible before the cash disappears.

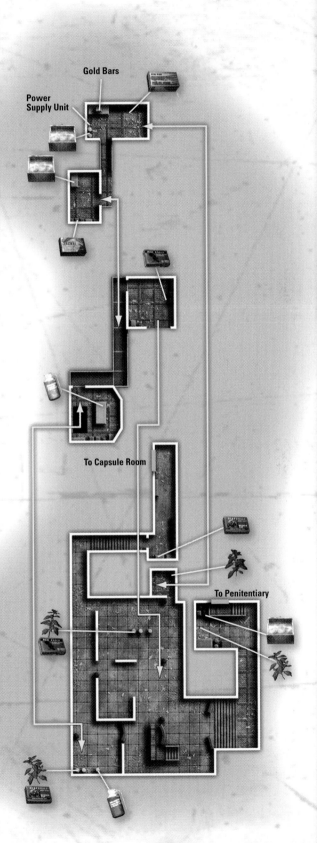

Gold Bars

Power Supply Unit

To Capsule Room

To Penitentiary

Two Locks and a Card Key

Examine either of the green-lit consoles on the midlevel or the exit door to the north to trigger an event where an enemy withdraws a card key from the lock system. Then take out the enemies in the area, using the exploding barrels on the ground level to your advantage.

One of the enemies drops the **Emergency Lock Card Key**. Reinsert the card key into the security system in the northern room on the uppermost level. Then press the green buttons on two consoles in two rooms on the midlevel to open the north door.

Head through the north door and down the stairs. In the bottom corridor, shoot the two guys holding shields, and use a flash grenade to eliminate resulting Las Plagas. Open the cage on the south wall to obtain **Shotgun Shells** and proceed to the next area.

CAPSULE ROOM

ITEMS FOUND

Item	Occurrence	Remark
Shotgun Shells	1	
TMP Ammo	1	
Magnum Ammo	1	
Red Herb	1	
Green Herb	1	
Gold Bars	2	5000 x2

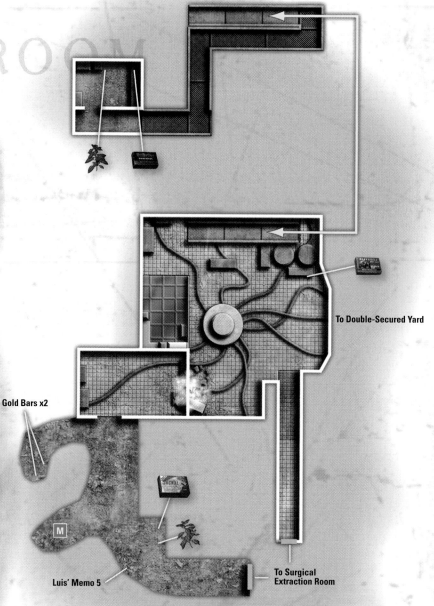

To Double-Secured Yard

Gold Bars x2

Luis' Memo 5

To Surgical Extraction Room

Ashley's Moment of Fate

Leon finally rescues Ashley, and the two find themselves trapped in a back corridor. Proceed through the double doors to find a merchant. Follow the path to the immediate right into a small niche and shoot the two barrels to find **Gold Bars** two times, equaling 10,000 pesetas total. Collect the **TMP Ammo** and **Green Herb** near the wall, and pick up the **Luis' Memo 5** from the rocks to the right of the exit.

Bit of Advice for Ya, Stranger

The merchant offers nothing new. Still, take the opportunity to sell off extra ammunition and weapons lacking ammo that are not very useful anymore. Then proceed through the southeast door.

SURGICAL EXTRACTION ROOM

ROOM

ITEMS FOUND

Item	Occurrence	Remark
Shotgun Shells	1	
Yellow Herb	1	

Parasite Removal Machine

Take out the enemies in the corridor with grenades and shotgun blasts. The west leads back to the capsule room previously seen during the cinema where Leon just rescued Ashley. Returning to this room is worthwhile in order to collect the **Shotgun Shells, Magnum Ammo** and **Red Herb** marked on our maps for those areas.

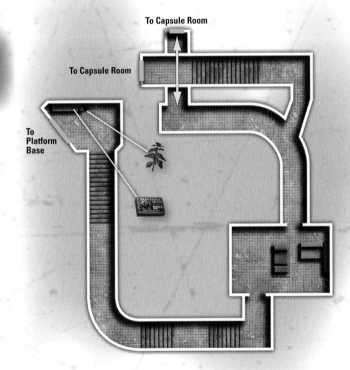

To Capsule Room

To Capsule Room

To Platform Base

Return to the lower corridor and open the double doors at the south end. Leon and Ashley finally extract the Plagas in their bodies. After the chapter ends, head through the south doorway and ascend the stairs. Collect the **Yellow Herb, Shotgun Shells** and the file titled **Our Mission** to learn what Saddler intends.

PLATFORM BASE

ITEMS FOUND

Item	Occurrence	Remark
TMP Ammo	1	
Green Herb	1	
Pesetas (Box)	1	

Last Visit with the Merchant

Grab the **Green Herb** in the corner to the left of the entrance, and smash the crates near the merchant for other items. Confer with the merchant and sell off all treasures and unneeded weapons. Keep a shotgun for sure, and a rocket launcher if you want to end the game quickly. Tune up the

shotgun as much as possible in power and magazine capacity. Then head down the stairs toward the elevator.

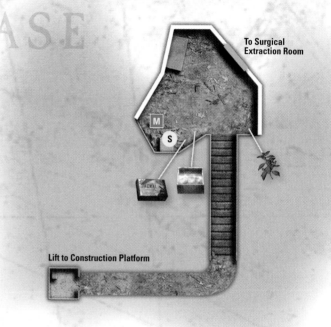

To Surgical Extraction Room

Lift to Construction Platform

CONSTRUCTION PLATFORM

ITEMS FOUND

Item	Occurrence	Remark
Handgun Ammo	1	
Shotgun Shells	1	
Green Herb	1	
Magnum Ammo	1	
Hand Grenade	1	
Rocket Launcher (Special Rocket)	1	Event
Jet-ski Key	1	Event

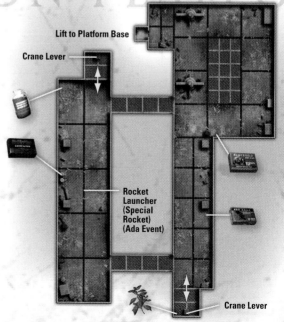

Lift to Platform Base

Crane Lever

Rocket Launcher (Special Rocket) (Ada Event)

Crane Lever

SADDLER

This great battle is easy to enjoy. Damage the monster Saddler
becomes by aiming for one of the smaller eyes on his legs. Shoot
the small leg eye to
make the entire monster
collapse in pain. The
eyeball is easier to hit
with a shotgun.

Once the monster's head falls to the floor and it exposes the
large eye in its mouth, run up to the head and press ⊗ to
climb it. Watch Leon try to rip out Saddler's main eyeball with
his knife. Once the attack is done, Leon leaps off the creature.
Turn and run away as the monster regains itself, and prepare
to do the same again.

Each of the front leg eyeballs can be shot twice and each
of the back ones can be shot once to cripple Saddler. When
shot once or twice, each eye closes permanently, becoming
unusable. The monster has enough stamina to withstand this many attacks, and more. Once all the leg eyes
have been permanently shut, your only target is the large eye on the central head. Or, you can use exploding
barrels and swinging cranes to damage him. Move to the southeast end or northwest end of the area and climb
onto the raised platform. Press ⊗ to grab the switch and look behind. When Saddler comes within ten feet of

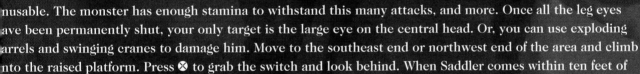

the platform, pull the lever
to swing a stack of girders
into the monster. This
causes Saddler to collapse
and tremble, so that another
climb and stab attack can be
performed.

The area consists of the
square area near the elevator, and then two strips. Between the strips are bridges that continuously collapse
and raise in timed cycles. If a bridge is collapsed, then Leon cannot cross from one strip to the other. A kind
of traffic light on each side of the bridges indicates when the
bridge will fall. If Leon is crossing the bridge when the light
starts to blink, be ready to press the two dodge buttons shown
onscreen to leap across to grab the opposite ledge. If Leon is
close enough to the other strip, he just might make it. Rapidly
press ⊗ to climb back up onto the platform.

Saddler attacks by seizing Leon in his eye mouth and slamming him to the ground. The tail section of the creature is made up of hundreds of tentacles that can slash Leon up pretty well. Stay back from the creature at all times to avoid these attacks.

When Leon is on a different strip of the platform than Saddler, the monster attacks by hurling a beam across the chasm. Press L1 and R1 to dodge the flying beam when needed.

Roughly halfway through the battle, Ada tosses a Rocket Launcher (Special Rocket) onto the western strip of the platform. After closing all of Saddler's leg eyes and striking him with one stack of girders, pick up this weapon, equip it, and lead Saddler towards the last stack of girders Leon can swing. After the monster's head eye is revealed, fire the red rocket at the target spot to end the battle. The amount of pesetas Saddler drops depends on how many leg eyes were damaged during the battle.

LAST ESCAPE

Timer explosives set all over the island are triggered during the events following Saddler's very fortunate death. Race back to the elevator quickly and reunite with the President's daughter. Lead Ashley through the escape tunnel to a small cave where a jet-ski is parked. Use the **Jet-ski Key** obtained during previous scenes to start up the jet-ski.

Only a short amount of time remains before the island goes kablooey, and you must pilot the jet-ski down an extremely long tunnel. Push the thumbstick up to accelerate, and tilt it left or right to dodge obstacles appearing in the path. Swerve to one side or another to shoot through open tunnels and avoid stalagmites jutting above the water's surface from the cave floor. As explosive start going off to the left or right, watch out for large rocks to start falling into the water and avoid them. When you see light at the end of the tunnel, gun it. You've got to get the President's daughter out in time!

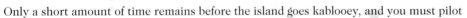

Showing Off

Hold down the L1 and R1 buttons to make Leon do a fancy spin during jet-ski jumps.

secrets and bonuses

Introduction
Characters
Enemies
Weapons and Ammunition
Key Items and Treasures
Game System and Strategies
Walkthrough

Secrets and Bonuses

Extras Menu

Professional

Round Two

Options

Assignment Ada

Separate Ways

The Mercenaries

The exciting extras unlocked by completing *Resident Evil 4* are detailed in this chapter. The information is provided in ase you have completed the game several times and still cannot seem to unlock something cool. To keep from spoiling the rprises, avoid reading this chapter until you have completed the game at least once!

EXTRAS MENU

omplete the game one time to unlock an all-new menu with an teractive background. Move the left thumbstick left or right to ntrol the scrolling panorama in the background, hold **R1** to zoom and **L1** to zoom out. When starting a new game, you may choose e new "Professional" mode. New mini-games available include ssignment Ada" and "The Mercenaries." You may also select lovie Browser" to watch all the Resident Evil 4 movies.

PROFESSIONAL

ay an all-new game at a harder difficulty setting. The scenario and em placements are the same, but enemies have greater resistance damage.

ROUND TWO

ter clearing the game, record a clear game save to a memory rd inserted in Slot-A of the console. Then load this save to play nother game, with all of the items, treasures and pesetas that were ill in your possession when you ended the previous play through. he merchant's menu opens, and you may buy or sell items before arting. Free new bonus weapons have been added to the shop list, collect your prizes before continuing.

Bonus Weapons

hen starting a Round Two game, the player has an opportunity to use the merchant's menu before starting. New weapons e available in the list as a reward for completing the game.

Handcannon

his free .50 caliber magnum is not compatible with the .45 Magnum Ammo und throughout the game, so do not make the mistake of selling the merchant ur magnums. The Handcannon is something of a paperweight at first, but after rchasing several expensive tune-ups an Exclusive upgrade becomes available for e Handcannon that enables infinite ammo! Save up your pesetas.

unlock the Handcannon, clear The Mercenaries mini-game with all five characters, oring 60,000 points or more to achieve an S Rank with each.

Matilda

This expensive new weapon fires Handgun Ammo in three-round bursts. While it consumes ammo quickly, enemies can be eliminated much faster. Can be upgraded to become an extremely powerful weapon with a 100 bullet capacity!

Infinite Launcher

Imagine getting a rocket launcher that fires an unlimited number of rockets—nice, huh? Although the price is high, you can decimate entire villages with a single shot!

P.R.L. 412

This sci-fi looking weapon has incredible power, but also is very practical – it prevents the ugly Plaga from popping out of alien heads. Very handy!

SPECIAL COSTUMES

When starting a new game or playing a Round Two game, a new option appears before the game starts. Chose the Special Costumes options to change the way the main characters look. Leon kicks it old school in his original Raccoon Police Department uniform from **Resident Evil 2** and a mafia outfit. Ashley wears pop sensation clothes that enhance her ballistics, as Luis would say. She also has a medieval getup in armor. Ada wears her black outfit from her mini-game, "Assignment Ada."

ASSIGNMENT ADA

In this short mission, Ada Wong must infiltrate the Island base and recover five Plaga Samples. The samples must fit into her small attache case along with her Punisher, TMP and semi-auto Rifle, so heavy item management is a must. Ada has no knife with which to break crates and barrels, so you must fire bullets to obtain items. Do not worry about killing every single enemy, and proceed to the next area as soon as possible.

Introduction

Characters

Enemies

Weapons and
Ammunition

Key Items
and Treasures

Game System
and Strategies

Walkthrough

Secrets and
Bonuses

Extras

Menu

Professional

Event Clue

Special

Costumes

Assignment
Ada

Separate
Ways

The
Mercenaries

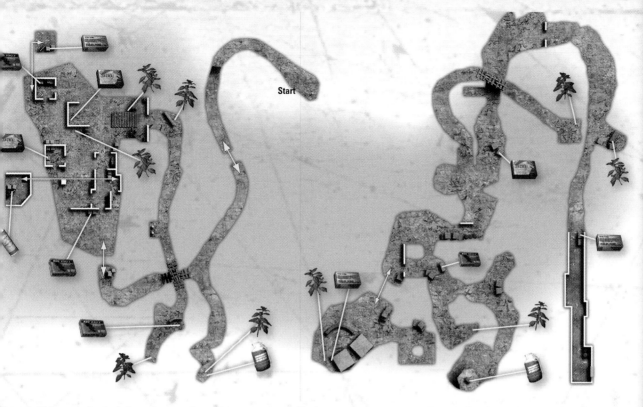

Start

hen infiltrating the beach area, avoid toppling enemies off edges into the water. Otherwise, Ada may run short on ammo.
limb the ladder at the rear entrance and crawl through the vent duct to get inside the building.

Once inside, check your in-game map. The locations of the five
Plaga Samples are marked with treasure icons on Ada's map. Obtain
the five samples and kill the enemies guarding them.

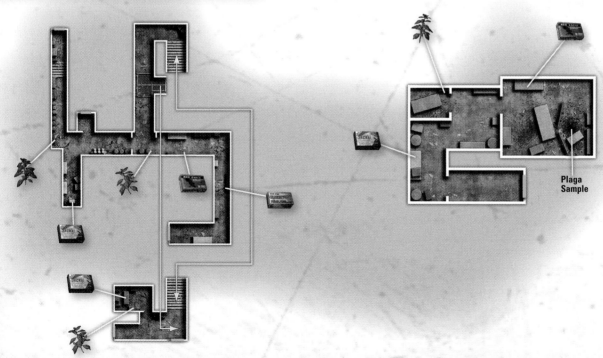

Plaga
Sample

219

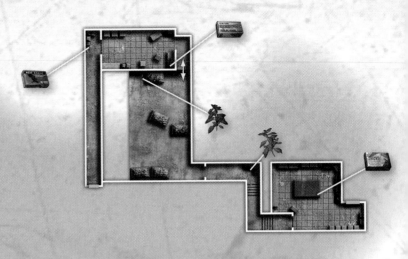

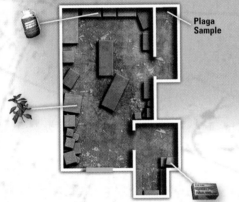

In the Research Lab, collect the Plaga Sample and then defend yourself from enemies that lock down the room. To get out, operate the security console to unlock the doors.

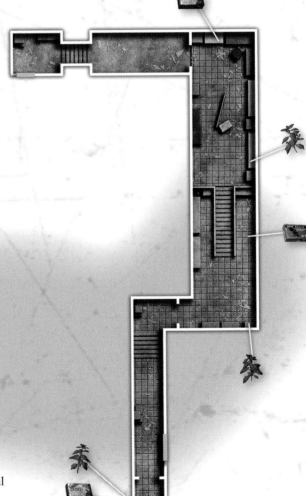

At the Communications Tower, use the remaining Hand Grenades and the TMP to defeat Krauser. He drops the final Plaga Sample. Ride the lift to the top of the tower and call the extraction chopper to pick up Ada.

Completing Assignment Ada adds the Chicago Typewriter to the merchant's list in Leon's game. This insanely powerful .45 caliber Thompson machinegun allows you to mow down enemies with infinite ammo!

Plaga Sample

Plaga Sample

x2

x2

x2

x2

Introduction

Characters

Enemies

Weapons and Ammunition

Key Items and Treasures

Game System and Strategies

Walkthrough

Secrets and Bonuses

Extras

Menu

Professional

Special Costumes

Assignment Ada

Separate Ways

The Mercenaries

separate ways

The PlayStation 2 version of *Resident Evil 4* also includes the game "Separate Ways." This stylish addition allows you to play portions of the original game from the perspective of sultry spy Ada. She's controlled the same way as in the "Mercenaries" mini-game.

For the most part, you're exploring the same environments as you did with Leon in the normal game, but now, as Ada, your goal is to help (or hinder) Leon. It only takes a few hours to complete, but it does give more insight into why Ada and other characters act the way they do.

Unlike the other mini-games, you may actually save your progress in Separate Ways, often at the same typewriter locations as the original game.

Level 1
PUEBLO

ITEMS FOUND

Item	Occurrence	Remark
Handgun Ammo	5	
Hand Grenade	1	
Flash Grenade	1	
Shotgun Ammo	2	
Chicken Egg	1	
Yellow Herb	1	
Red Herb	1	
Pesetas (Box)	1	
Random	5	
Spinel	2	

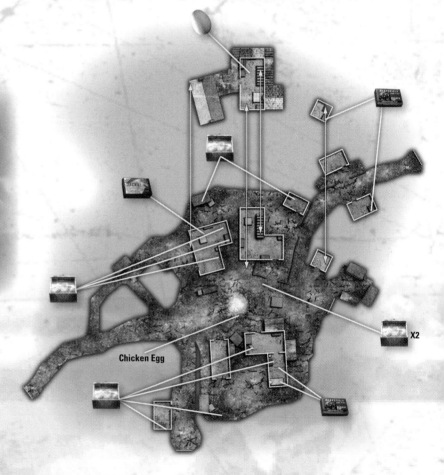

Chicken Egg

X2

Ringing the Church Bell

Under the orders of mastermind Albert Wesker, Ada drops into the Pueblo area searching for Plaga Samples as Leon is getting jumped by hungry villagers. Your mission is to ring the church bell to call off the enemies.

- CHAPTER 1 -
- Ring the Church Bell -

Parallel Lives

This scenario matches Chapter 1-1 in the regular game. Remember when the church bell mysteriously rang in the village?

...stant Battle

...he game starts you in the far east corner of the map. A half ...zen villagers immediately come after you. Take them out ...d head to the two-story home on the right. Inside you'll find ...andgun Ammo and, upstairs, more ammo and 1000 Pesetas. ...o out the top window onto the roof to grab a **Spinel**. Grab ...e **Red Herb** behind the northern houses and run over to the ...utheast entryway.

...ere you'll find a ...pinel and **Shotgun** ...mo. A woman ...ay follow you. ...oot her to get more ...andgun Ammo.

...oming back toward the bonfire triggers the appearance of ...ore villagers. Take your first right and run south towards the ...all house. Inside you'll find a box with a **Flash Grenade**. ...ke out the enemies once you get inside the house.

...ead up to the tower in the east and climb it for **Shotgun** ...mmo. This triggers Leon's entrapment in the two-story ...ouse with a chainsaw maniac. Come down and take out the ...llagers. Don't hesitate too long, or they'll start throwing ...enades at the tower.

...UNNEL

...Meet the Merchant

... merchant is waiting for you inside. You can't ...pgrade Ada's weapons, but you can buy weapons such as the ...MP and **Rifle**. Put your money toward the powerful **TMP**.

...side the room you'll find **Handgun Ammo**. Watch out ...r the Snake in the box. Save your game if you like and ...oceed down the hatch in the following room.

Moments later, a bird flies from the roof of the two-story house laying what appears to be a key. Run to the front area of the house and the option Grapple Gun will appear. Now you can use the ⊗ button to make Ada jump on the roof. Do this before the infinite posse of enemies shuffle onto the town center. On the roof you'll find the Insignia Key, which opens the door just south of the tower.

Jump off the roof and head for the door. Or you can stick around and mow down the unlimited number of villagers. They'll drop Pesetas, **Handgun Ammo** and other goodies.

If you have the energy, stop in the building just south of the two-story house and grab the **Elegant Mask** in the bedroom.

Snake

X2

S

ITEMS FOUND

Item	Occurrence	Remark
Handgun Ammo	3	
TMP Ammo	1	
Shotgun Ammo	1	
Green Herb	1	
Green Gem	1	

Introduction

Characters

Enemies

Weapons and Ammunition

Key Items and Treasures

Game System and Strategies

Walkthrough

Secrets and Bonuses

Extras

Menu

Professional

Round Two

Special Costumes

Assignment Ada

Separate Ways

The Mercenaries

Tight Quarters

Run down the passageway to the main open area and turn around – a couple of villagers are running up behind you. Take them out; the woman drops 1000 Pesetas. Walk back up the passage you came down to grab **Shotgun Ammo** and **Handgun Ammo** by the two lit candles

Get the goodies in the center area and run to the end of the passage. A howl announces five more enemies – three from the exit door and two more behind you. Knock down the ones behind you, run past them, and then take out all enemies in the tight passageway. Kick in the metal door and head up the ladder.

GRAVEYARD

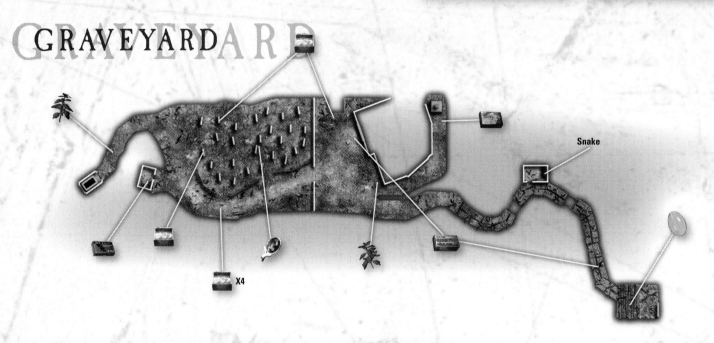

Snake

X4

ITEMS FOUND

Item	Occurrence	Remark
Shotgun Shells	1	
Handgun Ammo	1	
Green Herb	1	
Yellow Herb	1	
Rifle Ammo	2	
TMP Ammo	1	
Pesetas (Box)	7	
Green Catseye	1	

In the middle of the graves you'll find the **Red Gem**. Recheck the three twin graves for the church door puzzle if you forgot the symbols from the original game. Head up to the church and take out the two enemies. Aim upwards in the tree to knock down **Green Herb**. Head toward the back, but, unlike the original game you'll want to head to the bridge at the far right.

Night Shift

An ornery woman is waiting for you at the entrance. Take her out for **Shotgun Ammo**. Slowly proceed up toward the Graveyard to trigger the posse of enemies. Run back down the passage to shoot them one at a time. Then sneak up on the crows and collect Pesetas. In the western house you'll find **Yellow Herb** and **Handgun Ammo**.

Pop the enemies off the bridge as they appear. Watch out! Inside the small building you'll find a snake in the box. At the end of the bridge there's a chainsaw maniac; kill her and the two women with her with shotgun blasts. There's a **Green Catseye** at the end. Turn around and head to the area behind the church to find the same symbol on the Dial puzzle in Chapter 1-3 of the original game.

ompleting the puzzle triggers the exit to close and two
...emies to appear. Beat them down for some **TMP Ammo**.
...eturn to the puzzle and insert the **Green Catseye**. The door
...pens. Go toward the castle front and about a half dozen
...emies come your way. Shoot them to get **Rifle Ammo** and
...0 Pesetas, then head for the castle door.

You inserted the "Green Catseye".

CHURCH

...ivin' on a Prayer

...hoot the three enemies behind the altar. Watch out for the
...e that sneaks up behind you. Here you'll get **Handgun
...mmo**, **TMP Ammo** and Pesetas. Grab the **Purple Gem** and
...ash Grenade** in the eastern corridor and then climb the
...dder in the western corridor.

...un along the
...lcony and get the
...ree men. You'll
...d TMP Ammo
...d Rifle Ammo.
...me back to the
...ntrol panel you
...ssed and match
...e colors like
...Uniting the Colors"
...Chapter 2-2.
...st turn the Blue
...ns once. Mission
...mplete!

X OPERATE

...EMS FOUND

Item	Occurrence	Remark
Flash Grenade	1	
TMP Ammo	1	
Pesetas (Box)	3	
Purple Gem	1	

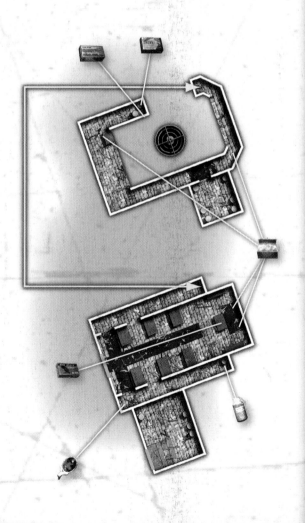

Level 2
VILLAGE CHIEF'S HOUSE

ITEMS FOUND

Item	Occurrence	Remark
Rifle Ammo	1	
Handgun Ammo	1	
Pesetas (Box)	7	
Red Herb	1	
Chicken Eye	1	
Green Eye	1	

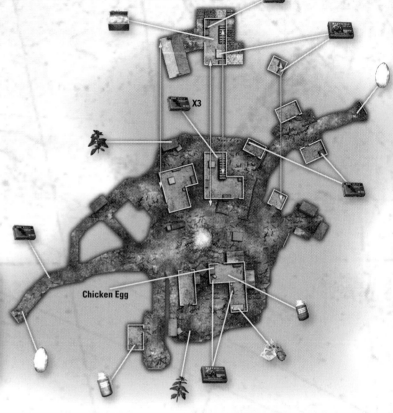

X3

Chicken Egg

Rescuing Luis

Come to find out, Luis is connected to Ada. Now he's been captured, along with Leon, by the enemy. Your job is to save him. After all, he may have the sample you need.

House Party

You start in the Village Chief's bedroom. Talk with the merchant and, if you like, sell your **Elegant Mask** with the three gems for a tidy profit.

Check the room for Pesetas, **Handgun Ammo** and **Chicken Egg**, and 2000 Pesetas in the hallway. Sweep downstairs for the Golden Chicken Egg, Hand Grenade and 250 Pesetas. Watch out for the guy in the kitchen. Head outside when you're done.

A chainsaw maniac and two cohorts will be waiting for you. Take them out with the **TMP**. He'll drop a **Ruby**. A few more enemies appea from the far end. Grab the Red Herb in the small shack and trigger a handful of enemies. They'll drop Pesetas.

PUEBLO

ITEMS FOUND

Item	Occurrence	Remark
Handgun Ammo	2	
Shotgun Ammo	4	
Chicken Egg	1	
Brown Chicken Egg	1	
Pesetas (Box)	13	

The Return

You're back to the Pueblo. It's a little less populated and new items are available. Head to the bonfire to take out the enemies, then take your time to explore the area. You can continue to take out enemies to collect randomly dropped Pesetas. Otherwise, head out the northeast exit when you're ready.

FARM

ITEMS FOUND

Item	Occurrence	Remark
Rifle Ammo	1	
Hand Grenade	1	
Pesetas (Box)	8	
Random	5	
Spinel	1	

Mowing Down the Farmers

See the twinkling **Spinel** on the right? To the left you'll find a small building with a **Typewriter** to save your game. Coming out, you'll be met by more than a handful of enemies. Hold your position and mow them down with the TMP. They'll drop 3000 Pesetas.

That's it for the enemies. Grab the Spinel from the vat behind you and head to the barn. There you'll find plenty of Pesetas downstairs and Rifle Ammo upstairs. Walk out of the upstairs window and jump off the side. Below you'll find the valuable **Gold Bangle** (in the location of the **Beerstein** in the original game). Push the bookcase aside, exit the barn and head out of the wide door. Watch out for the bear traps on the ground!

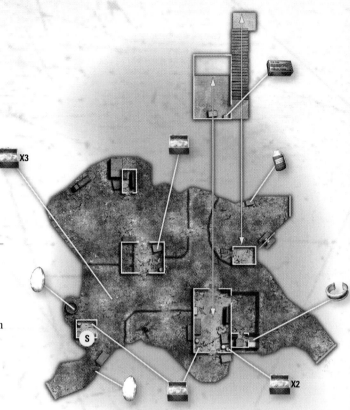

HOMESTEAD RUINS

ITEMS FOUND

Item	Occurrence	Remark
Handgun Ammo	1	
Rifle Ammo	1	
Pesetas (Box)	12	
Spinel	1	Nest

Introduction
Characters
Enemies
Weapons and Ammunition
Key Items and Treasures
Game System and Strategies
Walkthrough
Secrets and Bonuses
Extras Menu
Professional
Round Two
Special Costumes
Assignment Ada
Separate Ways
The Mercenaries

Around the Bend

Alls quiet this time around – this is where Leon had to outrun a boulder initially. Just run down through the tunnel. When you get to the tunnel, keep your eye peeled for TNT-tossing villagers. Use the TMP to blast back and focus on taking over the center building.

Fun with Guns

If you've got a Rifle, look up as you enter the Homestead Ruins level – you'll see a couple villagers on the bridge above. There's no reward (that you can get to) for taking them out, but the fun is undeniable.

After securing the house, a sequence shows villagers taking the drugged Leon and Luis to another location. Collect all the scattered items and head to the far east building. There you'll find a Typewriter, **1000 Pesetas**, various ammo and an angry farmer. Take him out as soon as you enter the building. Continue towards the back to find another angry farmer that'll drop **900 Pesetas**. There's an Incendiary Grenade next to him.

Now work your way back through the tunnel to where you came from. You'll find two guys – one drops **900 Pesetas** for you. Closer to the exit four more villagers fall from the trees. Mow them down to get various Pesetas amounts. Finally, two guys are guarding the exit. Make quick work of them to get **2000 Pesetas**.

Head back through the Farm and then to Pueblo, where they're planning to jump you. There are about two dozen villagers aggressively roaming the city – just run for the southwest exit.

Back at the Village Chief's House you'll catch the big guy about to kill Leon. You save Leon, but end up getting captured yourself. Oh well.

GONDOLA

ITEMS FOUND

Item	Occurrence	Remark
TMP Ammo	1	
Hand Grenade	1	Crow
Yellow Herb	1	
Iron Key	1	
Pesetas (Box)	6	
Spinel	1	

Sacrifice

Ada wakes up right before she ends up being sacrificed to the gods – press the flashing Dodge buttons to save her. Take out the surrounding goons and drop down to the hole ahead. Stop the two enemies below for Pesetas. Grab the Green Herb on the left and head towards the gondola. You'll find one guy standing guard by the stairs. Watch out – he may be harboring a Las Plagas in his head.

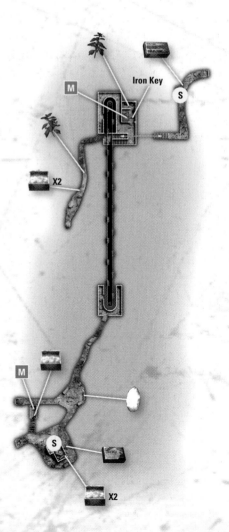

...ead upstairs, enter the gondola room and grab the **Iron Key** on the table. Talk to the ...erchant if you need more equipment. Sell your **Gold Bangle**, **Spinels** and **Ruby** if you've ...t one. Get the **Yellow Herb** from the locker and head downstairs. On that path you'll find ... **Typewriter** and **Rifle Ammo**. Use the key to open the door at the end.

Introduction

Characters

Enemies

Weapons and Ammunition

Key Items and Treasures

Game System and Strategies

Walkthrough

Secrets and Bonuses

Extras

Menu

Professional

Round Two

Special Costumes

Assignment Ada

Separate Ways

The Mercenaries

229

You got the Iron Key.

TORTURE SHEDSHED

ITEMS FOUND

Item	Occurrence	Remark
Handgun Ammo	1	
Shotgun Ammo	1	
TMP Ammo	1	
Yellow Herb	1	
Red Catseye	1	
Lift Key	1	

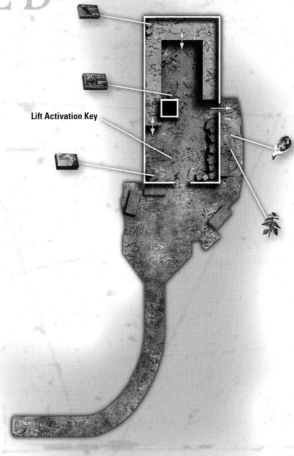

Lift Activation Key

Barnstorming

...o around the right side of the shed to grab the **Yellow** ...erb and **Red Catseye**. Enter the shed with shotgun armed ... a chainsaw maniac and two cohorts will be waiting for ...ou. The chainsaw wielder and her friend are right in front ...f you, but watch out for the third enemy, as he'll appear ...o your left when you enter. The chainsaw woman gives ...ou the **Lift Activation Key** necessary to start the gondola. ...utside, a few more villagers will be waiting for you. Walk ...ack to the gondola control room after you're done, taking ...ut a handful of enemies on the stairs. Insert the key in the ...ontrol panel and hop on the gondola.

...et off the gondola and go straight ahead, stopping to grab the twinkling **Spinel** by ...e big door on the left. At the bottom of the stairs you'll find a **Typewriter** to save as ...ell as Pesetas and **TMP** and **Shotgun Ammo**. Head upstairs to the Merchant, then ...o to the nearby big door. Getting close activates your grapple gun. Use it.

OTHER PASSAGE

ITEMS FOUND

Item	Occurrence	Remark
Shotgun Ammo	1	
First Aid Spray	1	
Green Herb	1	
Red Herb	1	
Yellow Catseye	1	
Spinel	1	

Grappling Along

Continue until you see the sparkling **Spinel** on the left-hand side. About there your grappling hook will be available. Use it to climb up and grab some **Rifle Ammo**. Jump down, go to the same area and turn around. Your grappling hook is available again. Use it to get **First Aid Spray** and **Yellow Catseye**.

Get the **Red Herb** right before the turn and before you face El Gigante. Ada's agility comes in handy here. Wait until he comes towards you and run between his legs. Don't forget to grab the **Green Herb** on the way out.

You finally find Luis just as he's leaving the cabin ambush. After a little flirting, you restate your orders for him to find the sample.

Level 3
COURTYARD

ITEMS FOUND

Item	Occurrence	Remark
Rifle Ammo	1	
TMP Ammo	1	
Bowgun Blasts	1	
Red Herb	1	
Pesetas (Box)	7	
Gold Bangle	1	

Bowgun Blasts

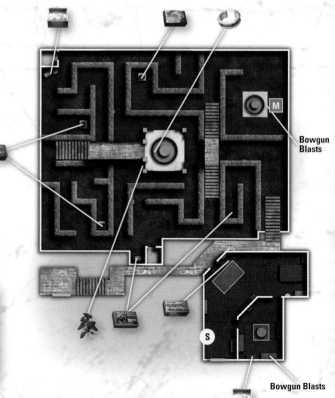

Bowgun Blasts

Bowgun Blasts

Retrieve the Sample

Ada and Leon have an intense confrontation in the courtyard bedroom. After this, Wesker orders Ada to kill him as soon as possible. Ada pretends to agree, but her priorities are on keeping track of Luis and the sample.

- CHAPTER 3 -

- Retrieve the Sample -

230

he level starts you in the courtyard. Buy the cool **Bowgun** om the Merchant, then pick up the **Bowgun Bolts** in the untain. The Bowgun operates like a crossbow with an frared beam. Go up the stairs, take out the two men and en continue around the bend until you reach the red aped enemy next to the treasure chest. Inside you'll find hotgun Ammo. Get back on the stairs and use the rifle to ipe the arrow-flinging enemy on the southern staircase.

ontinue going down the northern stairs and take a left to reach a red-caped enemy and a treasure chest with **TMP Ammo**. illing him triggers five more enemies to enter the maze. You can meet them on the stairs. Follow the stairs south, take a ght, another right and finally a left so that you're under the stairs you just crossed. A final red-caped enemy is there in ont of a fence. Shoot him to open the gate.

The remaining treasure boxes are filled with ammunition – not really worth your time. However, it is worthwhile to get to the center fountain. Inside there's a Gold Bangle with Pearls. Jump down, head through the gate, go up the southern stairs and into the bedroom when you're done. Inside the bedroom you'll find some ammo and **700 Pesetas**. Use the **Typewriter** if you need to save. Leave the bedroom and follow the outer balcony to the exit.

XTERNAL HALL HALL

TEMS FOUND

Item	Occurrence	Remark
Handgun Ammo	1	
Shotgun Ammo	1	
Rifle Ammo	1	
Hand Grenade	1	
Green Herb	1	
Yellow Herb	1	
Pesetas (Box)	5	
Hourglass	1	

Getting the Goods

he enemies start coming at you immediately. Shoot the hielded enemies down with the TMP. It also helps block the rchery foes. Turn the corner quickly to eliminate the archers aiting around the fountain. Continue south and take out ll the remaining foes. Then head back north and use your rappling gun to enter the locked room. Inside you'll find an nemy as well as a **Hand Grenade**, **Yellow Herb**, **Shotgun** mmo and, most importantly, a **Golden Hourglass**.

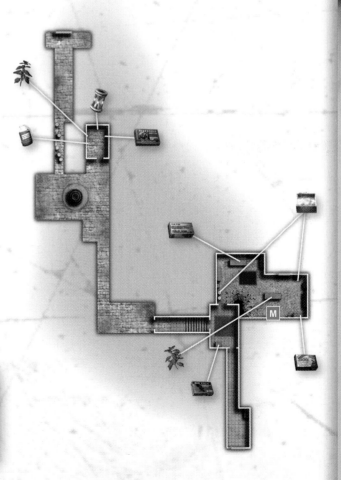

Introduction

Characters

Enemies

Weapons and Ammunition

Key Items and Treasures

Game System and Strategies

Walkthrough

Secrets and Bonuses

Extras

Menu

Professional

Round Two

Special Costumes

Assignment Ada

Separate Ways

The Mercenaries

Leave the room, go south and exit the area, and then turn left to find the Merchant. There's nothing new to buy if you bought a lot last visit. Head out the north door into the Last Supper area.

You got the Hourglass w/ gold decor .

LAST SUPPER

ITEMS FOUND

Item	Occurrence	Remark
Handgun Ammo	1	
Rifle Ammo	1	
Shotgun Ammo	1	
Green Herb	1	
Flash Grenade	1	
Pesetas (Box)	6	
Ruby	1	Man

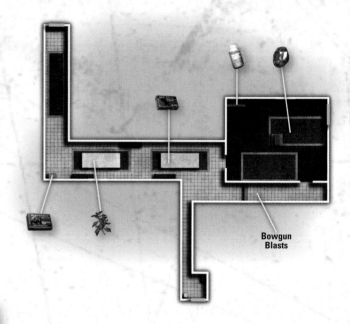

Bowgun Blasts

Feast

Four guys immediately come your way, but the TMP makes quick work of them. Head to the second door on the right. Remember this scene? You're stuck in a cage with cultists just like Leon was in the original game.

Concentrate on getting out of there as soon as possible. A door is on either side, so use multiple shots on the locks when you get near one. You can then run around the cage and pop off enemies easily.

Come back to the treasure chest after you eliminate the enemies. Place the Hourglass inside the chest to open the exit.

There is an indentation at the bottom.

Leon will be in a tight spot in the next room, but you can't blow your cover. Run across the balcony and fend off the foes coming from both sides. Enter the door, turn the corner and, unfortunately, watch a gruesome scene.

Level 4
METAL AREA

ITEMS FOUND

Item	Occurrence	Remark
Handgun Ammo	1	
Shotgun Ammo	1	
Rifle Ammo	3	
Hand Grenade	1	
Green Herb	1	
Yellow Herb	1	
Pesetas (Box)	6	
Golden Lynx	1	
Violet Blue	1	

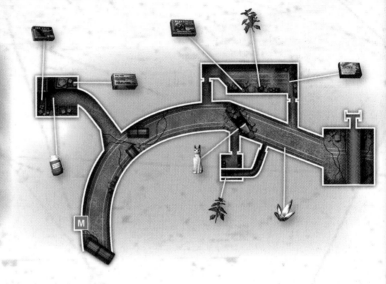

Stop Leon's Assassination

Wesker is tired of having Leon around, so he orders Krauser, Leon's old adversary, to kill him. Ada, perhaps out of feelings for Leon, goes out to stop this from happening.

Talk with the Merchant who, again, isn't selling anything spectacular. However, this is a good time to stock up on **First Aid Spray** and to sell off your big ticket treasures. It's a tough level ahead. Follow the parade of enemies into the side room on the left. Inside you'll find a **Hand Grenade** and, using your grappling gun, **Handgun Ammo** and **Rifle Ammo** on the left and right sides respectively. Take a left outside and sneak up on the group of enemies. Pop the nearby explosive barrel for nice results.

Enter the door on the left and be prepared to get jumped by five or so aggressive enemies. Lean against the back wall and don't let them get close. Outside you'll find a few more enemies, but be most wary of the archer perched high to your left as you enter. Hide in the entryway while you eliminate the grounded enemies, then jump out and knock the sniper down. You'll find a sparkling **Velvet Blue** on the floor.

Before you grapple to where the sniper was, go west, the direction that you came, and go towards the fire. As you get closer the grapple option will appear. Grapple up and climb through the ventilation system, taking care to kill the giant in the shaft. Landing on the other side gets you the **Golden Lynx**. Climb up the pile of boxes and grapple to where the sniper was killed.

Introduction
Characters
Enemies
Weapons and Ammunition
Key Items and Treasures
Game System and Strategies
Walkthrough
Secrets and Bonuses
Extras
Menu
Professional
Round Two
Special Costumes
Assignment Ada
Separate Ways
The Mercenaries

BATTLESHIP

ITEMS FOUND

Item	Occurrence	Remark
Shotgun Ammo	1	
Rifle Ammo	1	
TMP Ammo	1	
Hand Grenade	1	
Red Herb	1	
Bowgun Blasts	1	
Pesetas (Box)	11	

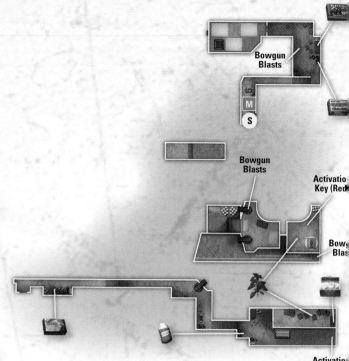

Top Gun

Ada finds herself on a parked battleship. The whole goal of this round is to sink it using the cannons placed around the military station. The first gun you encounter requires **Activation Key (Blue)**. The second requires **Activation Key (Red)**.

It's a Trap

After you reach the end of the pier, enemies crawl out of the woodwork and three guns on the ship start firing. Stay still and concentrate on getting rid of the posse of enemies first. Then listen to the gun fire and wait for a break before moving. The **Activation Key (Blue)** is just past where you are located.

Run between shot bursts and work your way back to the gun turret. Now it's your turn to have fun! Move the Left Analog Stick to aim the turret and ⊗ Button to fire. Take out the three guns and the elevator between the ship and the pier will activate. Run back towards the area where the key was located. Climb the ladder and hop on the elevator. Pop sniper enemies as you cross, but do save some ammo – a dozen or so enemies are waiting for you when you get to the ship. Climb up the ladder at the end of the ship when possible.

You got the Activation Key (blue).

Go up the stairs and head east until you reach the exit door. Just before you can enter five more gun turrets appear – including one right in your face. Stand still as it fires to the right of you, and then run right until you can grapple up. Above you'll find **Activation Key (Red)**. Use your grapple gun to zoom to the next platform and use the gun turret to finish this ship. You then have minutes to escape the area.

You got the Activation Key (red).

Walk out the short strip to find ammunition, a Merchant and a **Typewriter**. Stock up on First Aid Spray if you can.

UNDERGROUND AREA

ND AREA

ITEMS FOUND

Item	Occurrence	Remark
Shotgun Ammo	1	
Rifle Ammo	1	
Green Stone of Judgement	1	
Pesetas (Box)	5	
Violet Blue	1	

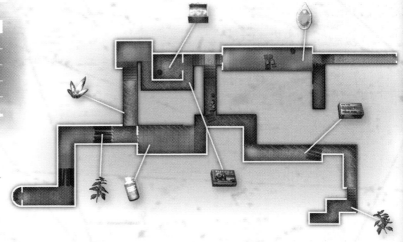

Underground

Work your way down until you reach the ground floor. Many enemies are there to greet you. Use the explosive barrel to take them out. Snipers are stationed on the bridge, so use your rifle to pick them off. Find a **Velvet Blue** under the bridge. Climb up and head right to find the **Green Stone of Judgment**. Go the other direction until you hit a second bridge, and continue on to finish the area.

OLD CHURCH

RCH

ITEMS FOUND

Item	Occurrence	Remark
Rifle Ammo	1	
Bowgun Blasts	2	
Hand Grenade	1	
Green Herb	1	
Yellow Herb	1	
Red Stone of Faith	1	
Pesetas (Box)	1	

Ruins

Go north and enter the door to get the **Red Stone of Faith**. Next door is **Yellow Herb**. Come back to the original room and head up the stairs. Continue left and stop at the **Typewriter** to save.

Enter the door and work your way down the stairs. Be careful – the three enemies charge up the stairs pretty quickly. Grab the **Green Herb** at the bottom and go out the door. Keep running until you hit the stairs, follow the steps to find **1000 Pesetas** in the locker, and go back downstairs and to the right to the exit.

Bowgun Blasts

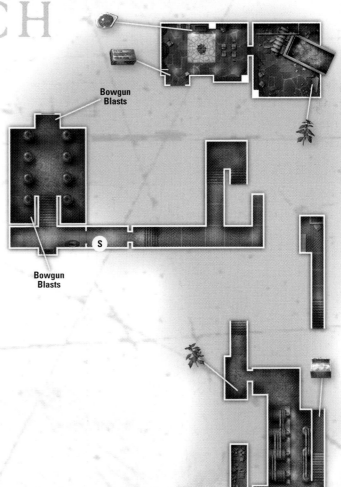

Bowgun Blasts

S

Continue through the next area, out the door, and you'll here the grunts of Krauser and Leon fighting. Grab the Velvet Blue in front of you and grapple above. Here you must fire in time to save Leon's life.

Level 5

COMMANDO BASE

BASE

ITEMS FOUND

Item	Occurrence	Remark
Rifle Ammo	1	
Shotgun Ammo	1	
TMP Ammo	3	
Hand Grenade	1	
Bowgun Blasts	2	
Green Herb	1	
Yellow Herb	1	
Pesetas (Box)	6	

Obtain the Sample

The final showdown! Krauser is presumed dead, so now Wesker is counting on Leon and Saddler to duke it out to the death – leaving the sample to him. Ada doesn't want Leon to die, but she does want the sample, so she goes after Leon.

Talk with the Merchant if you like. Walk around the corner and you'll see an ugly gunner excited to see you. He'll jump down off his ledge and start firing. Shots to the head are the best way to take him out. He'll drop **First Aid Spray**. Near his perch you'll find **Velvet Blue**. Grappling onto his perch will net you a **Blue Eye**.

After you're done, continue until you reach a ladder on the left. Climb up there to get a **Yellow Herb** and **Green Herb**.

Explosive Situation

Come down and cross the bridge. Enter the building ahead and an enemy throws an explosive barrel at the exit, engulfing the outside with flames. Now you must contend with enemies dropping from the ceiling. About a dozen come from the sky, all average enemies. Use a **Flash Grenade** when they get too close.

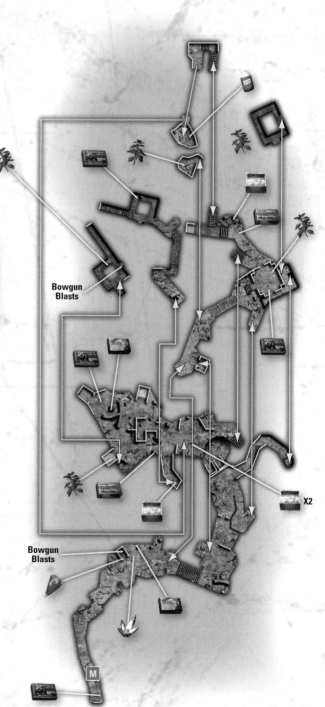

Bowgun Blasts

Bowgun Blasts

X2

he door opens when they are all eliminated. Immediately
hoot the explosive barrel outside to get the foes at the end
f the pier. Ascend the staircase until you reach the pulley.
lide down, grab the **Hand Grenade**, and then start shooting
he very dangerous sniper below you. Jump down to his level
nd hit the switch to open the exit.

The exit leads you to a heavily-protected area where guerrillas
are hiding behind sandbags. The fortified exit can only be
opened by hitting two switches – one on the right side, one on
the left. Take out the visible enemies, then go up the ladder
down the south passage. Shoot the snipers, using the metal as
cover, and then work your way across the right balcony. Both
the left and right sides are
guided by big gunners, but
working from right to left
seems easier. Hit the switches
to move to the next level.

TEMPLE ENTRANCE

EMPLE ENTRANCE RANCE

TEMS FOUND

Item	Occurrence	Remark
Handgun Ammo	1	
Green Herb	1	
Yellow Herb	1	
Pesetas (Box)	2	
Bowgun Blasts	2	

After the Wreckage

Run up the stairs, but watch out for the accurate
niper at base. At the top you'll see the "man" who
hot down the U.S. helicopter. You can shoot him in
he back to get some extra **Bowgun Blasts**. Exit out of
he northwest side after you get the **Yellow Herb** in
he passage across from the crash site.

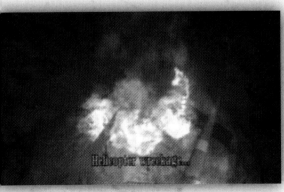

Helicopter wreckage...

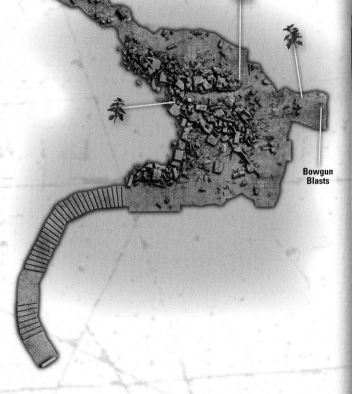

Bowgun
Blasts

Introduction

Characters

Enemies

Weapons and
Ammunition

Key Items
and Treasures

Game System
and Strategies

Walkthrough

Secrets and
Bonuses

Extras
Menu

Professional

Round Two

Special
Costumes

Assignment
Ada

Separate
Ways

The
Mercenaries

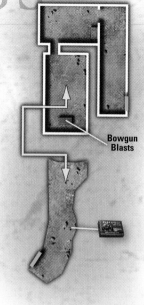

ITEMS FOUND

Item	Occurrence	Remark
Shotgun Ammo	1	
Bowgun Blasts	1	

Enter the Temple

Follow the path down into the temple and you'll
have another ugly confrontation with Leon
– except this time, neither one of you is in control.
His attempt to kill Ada shows how much power
the Las Plagas have. Still Leon goes to save Ashley.
Ada continues on her own.

PENITENTIARY

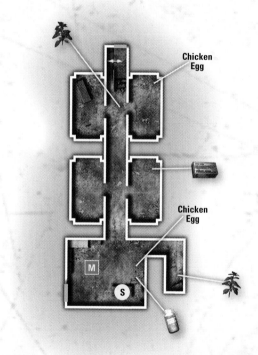

ITEMS FOUND

Item	Occurrence	Remark
Rifle Ammo	2	
Flash Grenade	1	
Yellow Herb	1	
Red Herb	1	
Chicken Egg	1	
Golden Egg	1	

Old Memories

Ada comes to the old jail that has creepy, unidentifiable living objects. It's
less intense as far as enemies, but still just as scary. A Merchant is there to
purchase any last-minute items before the final fight begins.

Comrade

After coming down the stairs you find Krauser, beaten but unbowed.
This truly final Krauser is actually very straightforward. He shields
his body with his large arm, but his legs are exposed – aim low
with the TMP. Do this over the course of three rounds and Krauser
is toast. You sometimes have to dodge by pressing the highlighted
buttons, but this rarely happens if you keep him far away.

After killing Krauser, Ada will grapple to a nearby ledge. Turn around the corner behind you to find the Butterfly Lamp. You can sell it to
the Merchant at the other side of the ledge. The area ends just past the Merchant.

CAPSULE

ITEMS FOUND

Item	Occurrence	Remark
Handgun Ammo	1	
Shotgun Ammo	1	
Rifle Ammo	2	
First Aid Spray	1	
Green Herb	1	
Red Herb	1	
Bowgun Blasts	1	

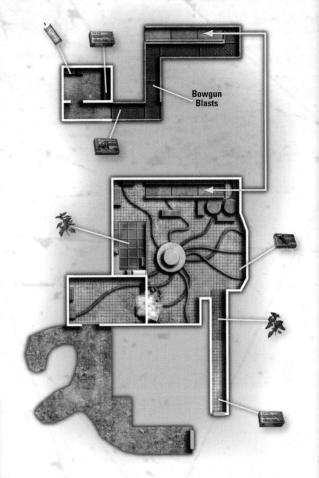

Bowgun Blasts

Showdown

Leon comes to Ashley's rescue just in time, but not quick enough to avoid Saddler's deadly grip. Ada distracts him by unloading a full TMP clip and Leon and Ashley are able to escape. Unfortunately, Ada gets trapped in the capsule room with the man himself.

You'll be on the second floor – just stand your ground for now. Blast him with at least 100 shots from the TMP, using the dodge buttons as necessary. He will then transform into a deadlier Saddler with the ability to turn his right hand into a Gatling gun. His only weakness is to suffer blasts from the Bowgun.

Revenge

Unfortunately, Ada still ends up captured, parallel to the end of the original game. Leon sets her free and, with the island rigged to blow in two minutes, Ada must help Leon by retrieving the **Rocket Launcher**.

Run as fast as you can along the scaffolding while avoiding enemies. It's better not to fight, especially since you will lose if you don't clear things in time.

The trouble is well worth it – not only do you get a cool ending from Ada's perspective, but now you can purchase the powerful Chicago Typewriter and the Matilda automatic handgun. The Typewriter will mow down Plaga in two shots!

Introduction
Characters
Enemies
Weapons and Ammunition
Key Items and Treasures
Game System and Strategies
Walkthrough
Secrets and Bonuses
Extras
Menu
Professional
Round Two
Special Costumes
Assignment Ada
Separate Ways
The Mercenaries

the mercenaries

Beating *Resident Evil 4* the first time unlocks several mini-games, though the most intense one arguably is "The Mercenaries". Here's a special guide to this adventure.

Five Characters, Four Levels

A frenetic mini-game becomes available after clearing the main game once. The Mercenaries is a high-pressure game with a time limit. Kill enemies to score points. By eliminating foes in quick succession, the combo rate increases. The higher the combo rate, the more points are scored for each kill.

Only two minutes remain until the chopper arrives. To delay the chopper, pick up hourglasses to increase the time remaining. The longer you stay in the game, the higher you are likely to score and receive a better ranking. Score 30,000 points or more to achieve a four-star ranking and unlock a secret character. Score 60,000 points or more to achieve a five-star rank.

By scoring a four-star ranking or better in each map, new playable characters can be unlocked. Unlockable characters include Ada Wong in her *Resident Evil 2* costume, the irrepressible Krauser, infamous Umbrella mercenary HUNK and the sinister Albert Wesker. Each character begins the game with a bevy of weapons and items, some of which are unique.

Score a five-star ranking with all five characters to unlock the Handcannon in the main game!

During each game you can select from one of four missions: Pueblo, Castle, Island Commando Base and Waterworld. With the exception of Waterworld, all areas will be levels you became familiar with during your first play through the regular game. However, the terrain has been modified in cool ways. For instance, the prominent, yet inaccessible barn to the left of you when you first enter Pueblo becomes a key strategy point for winning. Explore the areas thoroughly, as you never know what you may find!

PLAYABLE CHARACTERS

Leon Scott Kennedy

Unlock: Available from start

Inventory: Blacktail, Riot Gun, Handgun Ammo x30, Shotgun Shells x10, First Aid Spray

Leon is a familiar character by now, and it should be fairly simple to unlock most, if not all, of the other characters with his load out weapon set.

Ada Wong

(Resident Evil 2 Costume)

Unlock: Score a four-star ranking in the Pueblo map.

Inventory: Punisher, TMP, Semi-auto Rifle, Semi-auto Rifle Scope, Handgun Ammo x30, TMP Ammo x100, Rifle Ammo x5, Incendiary Grenade x3, First Aid Spray

Ada has no knife to defend herself with at close range, but she has looks and that goes a long way!

Jack Krauser

Unlock: Score a four-star ranking in the Castle Map.

Inventory: Krauser's Bow, Arrows x30, Flash Grenade x4, First Aid Spray

Krauser actually transforms his arm by pressing R2! After killing several enemies in a row, his arm begins to glow red. Press ✕ to transform his arm and then press ✚ to perform a power attack that instantly kills all enemies in a straight line directly in front of Krauser. Krauser also uses a knife like Leon, but with greater

lethality, and he kicks so hard he takes most enemies' heads right off. Krauser's bow weapon is a lethal one-shot killer, but ammo for the weapon tends to run dry quickly. Unless a major enemy - such as a chainsaw maniac or gattling gunner - is around, back up into a corner and take out enemies with Krauser's knife and arm attacks!

HUNK

Unlock: Score a four-star ranking in the Island Commando Base.

Inventory: Custom TMP, TMP Ammo x75, Hand Grenade x3, First Aid Spray

HUNK is the infamous Umbrella agent that bravely extracted the G-virus from Raccoon City. Now he faces an even greater challenge! HUNK has the very cool ability to grab staggering enemies and snap their necks in half. Use this to rack up a high combo and save ammo!

Albert Wesker

Unlock: Score a four-star ranking in the Waterworld map.

Inventory: Handgun, Handgun Silencer, Killer7, Semi-auto Rifle, Hand Grenade x4, Flash Grenade x3, Incendiary Grenade x1, First Aid Spray

The notorious Wesker is the most loaded of all the characters, weapon-wise. The handgun silencer allows him to kill enemies without alerting others nearby, if stealth kills are your forté. His amazing thrust punch attack should be familiar to fans of *Resident Evil CODE: Veronica X*.

ITEMS

Ammunition and life are extremely limited in this mini-game, so you'll want to take any items you can get your hands on. Here is a listing.

Herbs

Green, Red and Yellow Herbs are available in "The Mercenaries", too, and have the same properties. Green heals, Red, combined with Green, increases your healing, and Yellow with Green increases your overall stamina.

Ammo

Ammunition is available from dead zombies as well as the traditional barrels and such. The type of ammunition given is based on your character's arsenal.

irst Aid Spray
First Aid Spray

ne use totally refills your energy bar.

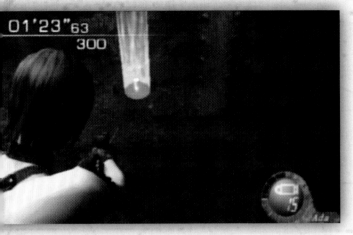

Extra Seconds

ssential to getting high scores. These glowing clocks give you 30
90 more seconds to play. Significant considering that the game
nly gives you 120 seconds with which to begin.

Bonus Time

tashed in big treasure boxes, Bonus Time gives you 30 seconds
here each hit is worth 1000 points. These are most important
you'd like to get up your ranking, as you're likely not going to
each the higher scores on tenacity alone.

Bonus Time! You have 30sec. from now in which
you will receive bonus points for each kill. Let's go!

Introduction
Characters
Enemies
Weapons and Ammunition
Key Items and Treasures
Game System Strategies

PUEBLO

Easy Start

This is the village where you first saw what the evil parasitic zombies are capable of. The enemies are tough, but more in number than in skill. Most of your time here will be spent managing crowd control.

Initially, townsfolk such as the knife-wielding mom or the graying local butcher attack you one at a time. It is a solid, steady pace of enemies, and hiding in a room and letting enemies stream in works fine at first.

Don't get lulled into safety. Depending on how quickly you mow down your opponents, but usually after about a dozen kills, twin chainsaw women come out of nowhere to get you.

Starting Points

Pueblo begins you at three random starting points: In the southwest corner of the map, behind the tower in the northeast, or on the roof of the row of houses at the north. All are relatively free of zombies, though from the roof position you can see the monsters mulling about.

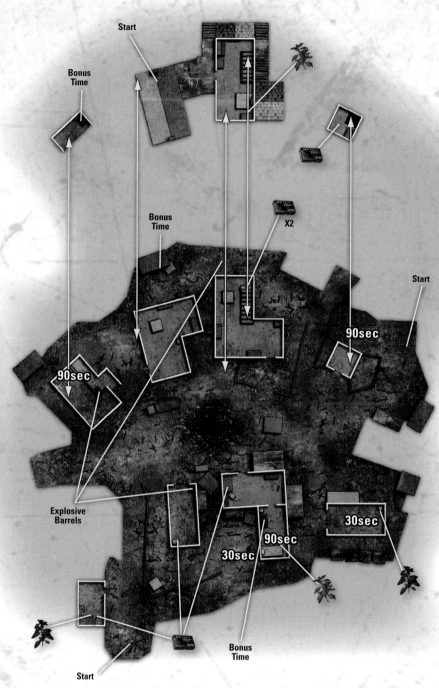

Room with A View

good temporary position is in the large southern house
hich stores Ammo, Bonus Time, a Green Herb, and 90
xtra Seconds. When the enemy load gets a bit heavier,
ter through the east window, grab the Bonus Time and
art blasting them away as they try to crawl through the
ening. Keep an eye on the northern door, as the smarter
mbies may try and attack you from your blind spot. If
u've got time, run to the northern room and push the
esser to block the front door before you position yourself
the east window.

wo Stories of Fun

e two-story house to the north is a great place to be
sitioned if you are a quick enough draw. The first floor
s two barrels of Ammo to grab, but not much else.
owever, the second floor has Ammo, a Green Herb and,
ost importantly, several entryways that can be covered
once. This allows many zombies to stream inside in a
anageable fashion. Put your back at the northern wall, by
e stairs, and blast away, running to get any dropped items
hen your ammunition gets low.

you need a break from the enemy stream, kick down the
dder at the southern window.

arnstorming

xcellent killing is to be had in the barn located in the
orthwest corner (it's the house with the colorful doors).
side you'll find an Explosive Barrel, 90 Extra Seconds and
onus Time. It is set up like a loft with a movable ladder.

ait until you get a nice crowd of zombies before you head
the barn. Then grab the 90 Extra Seconds on the first
or and run up the ladder to grab the Bonus Time. Pick
ombies off from this high position, knocking down the
dder if it gets too heavy. When the crowd gets thick, blast
e Explosive Barrel, preferably when Bonus Time is active.

owever, remember that you aren't completely safe. Lucky
throwers and Plaga can reach you at your high position.

Introduction

Characters

Enemies

Weapons and
Ammunition

Key Items
and Treasures

Game System
and Strategies

Walkthrough

Secrets and
Bonuses

Extras
Menu

Professional

Round Two

Special
Costumes

Assignment
Ada

Separate
Ways

The
Mercenaries

CASTLE

Macing Monks

"The Mercenaries" difficulty level picks up a little here at the castle balcony. The evil monks are both numerous and strong, brandishing maces and other weapons. Enemies also have a tendency to walk around you and grab you from behind.

This area also puts the shielded zombies into play, making stronger weapons, such as Leon's shotgun, a valuable commodity.

Less spacious than Pueblo, Castle really tests your ability to combat multiple enemies in close quarters.

Starting Points

Because of its size, Castle only has one starting point: the cannon room in the southeast corner - unfortunately the cannon isn't there to use! On the positive side, there are two barrels with a Green Herb and Ammo for you to grab before the section starts.

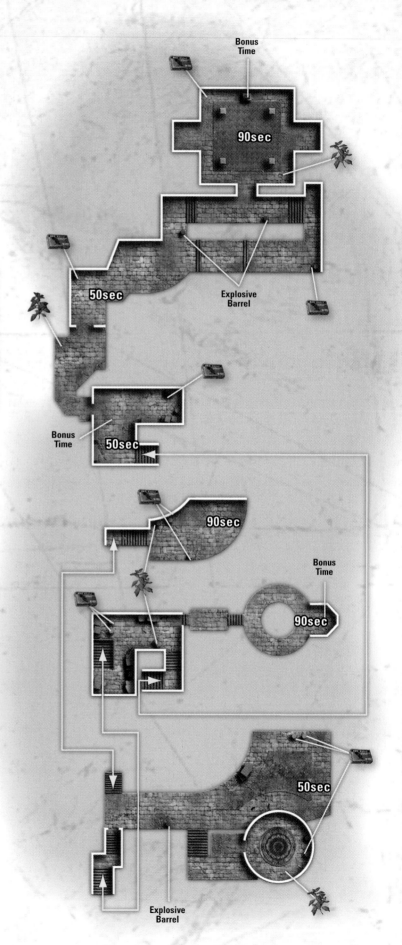

Get Out of the First Room

After you get the barrels, leave immediately and run up the stairs. A mob of monks, usually led by a shielded zombie, will start pushing their way down the steps a few seconds after the level starts. You don't want to be stuck in the cannon room without an exit plan, especially since there a so small.

Climb the Southwest Tower

Unlike the original Castle, there is a three-story tower that winds its way up. After you climb the first stairs, run to the east to the court area to pick up the surrounding goodies. (In fact, this area isn't a bad place to set up camp initially.) When you're ready to go, run straight ahead, going west, and – surprise – there is a door on your left at the end of the corridor.

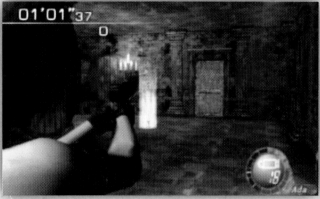

Climb the stairs inside just inside the door to reach the second landing where you'll find two packets of Ammo and bridge to the second cannon room. Continue to climb to the next room, an L-shaped wine "cellar". Here you'll find a Green Herb, 50 Extra Seconds, Ammo and Bonus Time.

Grab your Bonus Time and position yourself against the southern wall of the room with the window to your right. From here you've got a clear shot at the northern door as well as at zombies sneaking around the corner.

Barbarians at the Gate

Beyond the tower door is a small landing with a Red Herb and large double doors. Opening the double doors leads to the castle top. An evil priest appears and orders his armed guards to come after you.

There are plenty of goodies to be had on this high level, but not enough to compensate for the various directions enemies can attack you, especially considering there isn't any Bonus Time available here. There is nothing of note for killing the big guy, but he does take about twice as many hits.

If you do decide to stay on the top floor, gather as many enemies as you can around the two Explosive Barrels.

Introduction
Characters
Enemies
Weapons and Ammunition
Key Items and Treasures
Game System and Strategies
Walkthrough
Secrets and Bonuses
Extras
Menu
Professional
Round Two
Special Costumes
Assignment Ada
Separate Ways
The Mercenaries

COMMANDO ISLAND

No Vacation

The enemies and layout of Commando Island make the Castle look like a piece of cake. The elite soldiers you fight seem to come out of nowhere, and even taking one one-on-one can be a handful.

The level design is very complex, filled with high-rise girders, hidden tunnels and jumpable cliffs.

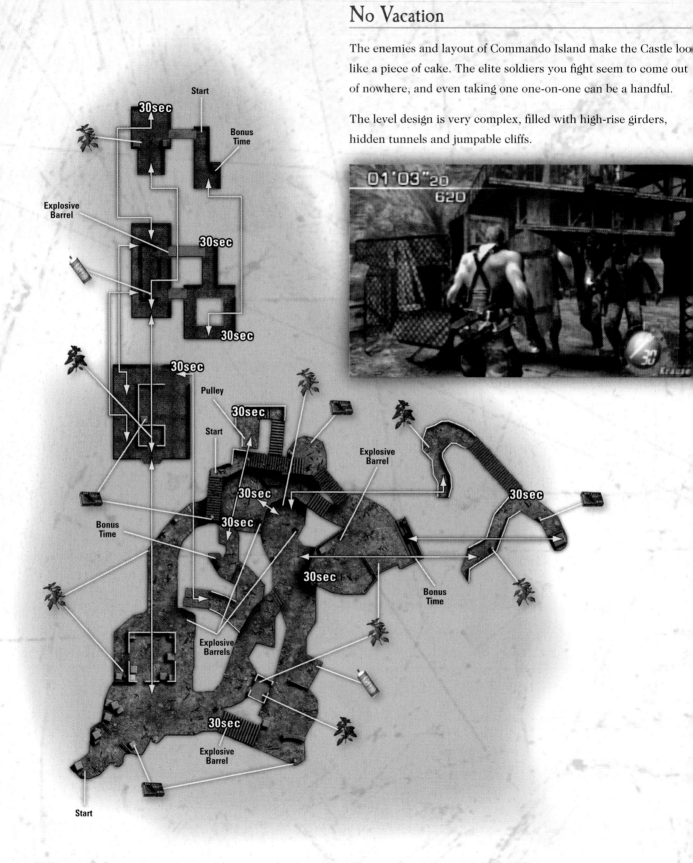

Introduction

Characters

Enemies

Weapons and
Ammunition

Key Items
and Treasures

Game System
and Strategies

Walkthrough

Secrets and
Bonuses

Extras
Menu

Professional

Round Two

Special
Costumes

Assignment
Ada

Separate
Ways

The
Mercenaries

tarting Points

ommando Island has two starting points: at the entryway in the southwest corner or atop the construction girders in
e center of the stage. The entryway is a safer start, though you'll waste a little time finding someone to kill initially. The
rders are much more chaotic, as enemies can attack quickly from three ladders.

On the Ground Floor

rom the first starting point, you'll be able to slowly build
our fight into a heated battle. You'll occasionally have a
y or two running toward you, but usually the coast is
ear. Grab the Ammo on the right just past the entryway.

un forward and grab the Extra 30 Seconds by the ladder.
en back up slightly, turn to the left and run into the
nnel. In the corner you'll find an Explosive Barrel and
ound the next corner, Extra 30 Seconds. Finally, turn the
ext corner and find a Green Herb. Fight your way back to
e barrel and use it on the cluster of enemies.

ollowing the next tunnel by the Explosive Barrel grants you a Green Herb and an Extra 30 Seconds. Continue to follow the
th and you'll find a short perch with a Green Herb and Bonus Time. It has a few entry points, but this area is generally a
od place to pick off foes. Don't forget to use the Explosive Barrel visible when your back is to the perch.

rom the Second Starting Point

mentioned earlier, enemies will immediately go after you
the girders. Take advantage of this. Turn to your right
d, straight ahead, there's a box with Bonus Time. Start
king out zombies and racking up points.

n back to where you started from, cross the small bridge
d grab the Green Herb and Extra 30 Seconds. Stay atop
til the wave of enemies slows down. Go to the southern
dder closest to you and jump down.

ght below the ladder you'll find First Aid Spray in a
rrel. The enemies should be swarming now. If you can
ke the heat, stick around and take them out.

Watch out for the Gatling

e gatling carrying commandos that showed up in the
ter levels of *Resident Evil 4*'s main game pop up when you
ock out about two dozen foes. They usually land on a
gh perch.

you're playing someone who has sniper capabilities
ch as Ada, just pop them a few times in the head. Other
aracters should sneak their way up to the high ground
take him out. He's not worth dodging while you're being
tacked.

WATERWORLD

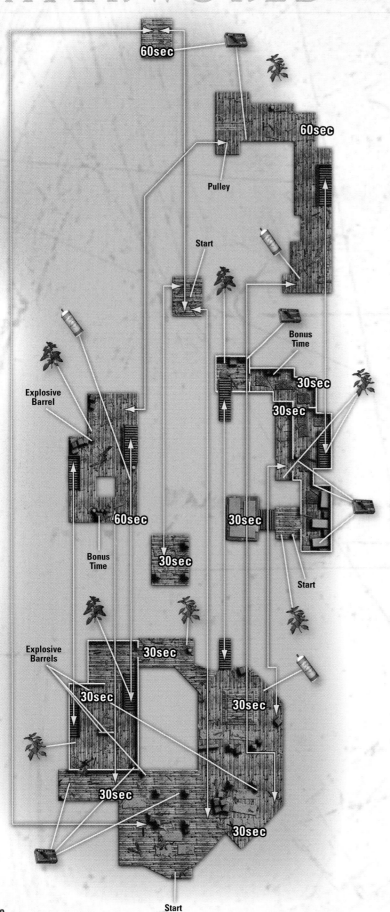

60sec

60sec

Pulley

Start

Bonus
Time

30sec

30sec

Explosive
Barrel

60sec

Bonus
Time

30sec

30sec

Start

30sec

30sec

Explosive
Barrels

30sec

30sec

30sec

30sec

Start

No Vacation

Don't let their seaside locale fool you. Waterworld is as layered and dense as Commando Island, and its enemies are even more aggressive. Men will live several seconds after "dying", so guys can still successfully grab and choke you after their heads ha[ve] been blown off.

The level is half tight rooms, half tight bridges, and all are teaming with commando enemies in low-rent pirate clothing. It also includes our favorite device, the pulley.

Starting Points

Waterworld has two starting points: on the southern perch or the small house in the southeast corner. Th[e] perch gives some room to move out of the way of the incoming crowd. There's no room to leave in the sma[ll] house – you'll have to fight your way out immediate[ly.]

Work Down from the Pulley

A good goal is to work your way up to the pulley at the north point of the map and then work your way down from there. Taking the pulley will drop you off next to an Explosive Barrel and, just a few steps to your left, First Aid Spray. Run for the First Aid Spray and more than likely a crowd will be behind you – the many folks you've gathered on the way up to the pulley. When the timing is right, let them have the Explosive Barrel.

Grab the Red Herb sitting on the crates right next to the barrel. Also grab the Extra 60 Seconds sitting across the ship hole behind you. Jump down in the hole to find a number of goodies, including a Red Herb below the northern stairs.

Put yourself against the southern wall. It provides an excellent vantage point as zombies stream in.

Watch Out for the Big Guy

One of the uglier adversaries is a big, towering chainsaw man. He violently swings a chainsaw that's about the size of Leon, killing you instantly with one hit. He tends to hang out on higher ground, but there is no general rule as to when he will appear. He could come when you've killed two people or 20.

He's physically tough to get around, so the only exit is several shotgun blasts to the head. His range is much wider than other chainsaw opponents, so keep a very wide distance. Luckily his appearance is relatively rare.

High Jinx

It may be tempting to head for the higher ground, but only do so on the well-connected northern platforms, not the southern. It's easy to get stuck in a rough situation up there.

For instance, if you do start on the southern perch, avoid the ladder to the left. It leads to a small platform that offers you more seconds and, more often than not, a battle with the humongous chainsaw man. Unless you're lucky enough to knock him off as he's climbing the ladder, you're as good as dead.

Aside from the cool pulley area, it's best to stay close to the ground. Even the underground battle areas are more desirable than the isolating high platforms.

Introduction
Characters
Enemies
Weapons and Ammunition
Key Items and Treasures
Game System and Strategies
Walkthrough
Secrets and Bonuses
Extras
Menu
Professional
Round Two
Special Costumes
Assignment Ada
Separate Ways
The Mercenaries

Exclusive Art

LEONN

ADA

resident evil OFFICIAL STRATEGY GUIDE

BRADYGAMES STAFF

Publisher	DAVID WAYBRIGHT
Licensing Manager	MIKE DEGLER
Director of Marketing	STEVE ESCALANTE
Editor-In-Chief	H. LEIGH DAVIS
Creative Director	ROBIN LASEK
Assistant Marketing Manager	SUSIE NIEMAN
Assistant Marketing Manager, Online	RACHEL WOLFE
Marketing Coordinator	AUTUMNE BRUCE
Team Coordinator	STACEY BEHELER

CREDITS

Sr. Development Editor	CHRISTIAN SUMNER
Screenshot Editor	MICHAEL OWEN
Lead Designers	KURT OWENS
	CAROL STAMILE
Production Designer	TRACY WEHMEYER

ACKNOWLEDGEMENTS

Dan Birlew wishes to greatly acknowledge the contributions of other individuals to the creation of this guidebook, without which project could not have been possible. Thanks to Leigh Davis for assigning me to another fantastic title, and to David Waybright for playing the game and geeking out with me over it. Thanks to Alex Garner for rendering dozens of high quality maps virtually overnight, and thanks to flawless translations as usual. Thanks to Phil Navidad, Takashi Kubozono, and Toshihiro Tokumaru for providing us with new builds instantly as well as documents containing much of the information found in this book. Special thanks to Christian Sumner for doing a first-rate management job, and a very special thanks to my very own dame in a red dress, my wife Laura, the most patient, loving and supportive woman in the entire wo

ABOUT THE AUTHOR

Dan Birlew is the author of more than 40 official strategy guides for video games published by BradyGames, covering many Capcom hits including *Onimusha 3: Demon Siege*, *Resident Evil Outbreak*, *Resident Evil CODE: Veronica* and every other *Resident Evil* game except for number two. He is a graduate of the University of Texas but will not be attending the Rose Bowl, much to his dismay.